Literature as Experience

Literature as Experience

WALLACE A. BACON

Professor of Interpretation and
Chairman, Department of Interpretation
Northwestern University

ROBERT S. BREEN

Associate Professor of Interpretation
Northwestern University

McGRAW-HILL BOOK COMPANY, INC.

1959   NEW YORK   TORONTO   LONDON

Preface

$\mathcal{L}$ ITERATURE AS EXPERIENCE is grounded in the conviction that the experience of literature is a *necessary* part of the experience of any educated man—or indeed of any man, regardless of the degree of his education, who cherishes awareness of life about him. It looks constantly at the relevance of literature to life, and of life to literature. While it recognizes and tries to define ways in which the art of the writer modifies or clarifies or extends life-experience, it takes the position that literature is not so sharply separated from life as students of the art at first imagine.

The value of any study of literature lies in the enrichment of the student's own life through his study of the particular mode of experience which literature provides through its imitation of life. Literature is no necessary key to happiness, to health of body, to success—but it is of the utmost value in the education of individuals who hope to be, as human beings, sympathetic, sensitive, and aware: in short, to be in the best sense *human* beings.

We have tried to take into account, in our description of the nature of literary art, the best of contemporary thinking in literary criticism, in aesthetics, in psychology and related sciences; we have also tried to include such traditional views as have resisted the changes of modern science. The volume is organized into three parts. The first part considers primarily the experience of both writer and reader apart from, or anterior to, or existing

v

side by side in the experience of the work of art itself; the second part describes the particular qualities of the work of art in relation to the experience especially of the *reader;* the third part considers certain problems in literature conceived of as expressive action. Part 3 will be of special interest to students concerned with the problems of oral reading of literature, though it is to be hoped that both Chapter 12 and Chapter 13 will also be of interest to the general reader.

Within this framework, much of the discussion proceeds deliberately on an associative basis. We have taken what seems to us a natural and easy way of getting from life to literature, and from details to whole works of literature. The organization by association seems to us to work for rather than against our notion of literary study. The student begins his study of a piece of literature wherever he *can,* and encompasses the whole as economically as possible, but not in a fixed and unchanging order of procedures. We hope that the order of association in our plan will not appear to be without its own logic.

If we have seemed to qualify and modify and caution a good deal, that is because we feel that talk about literature may suffer from too much generalization just as it may suffer from too little. We prompt and cajole the reader much as we would prompt and cajole ourselves in our own reading. We have tried to leave doors open to further discussion, to further illumination; we are aware that any good book must leave room for good teachers —for without good teachers, the teaching of literature will always fail.

We do not look upon the matters which we have covered in the volume as being *advanced* in difficulty. They are the *basic* matters, and we have avoided going beyond a moderate level of difficulty.

The book is intended for use in conjunction with a collection of works of literature. The market is filled with excellent anthologies, many of them in inexpensive, paper-back editions, and doubtless each teacher will wish to make his own choice from among them. For illustration and example within our own volume, we have chosen literature from a variety of periods, styles, and types, though we make no claim to being fully inclusive in our choices.

The exercises appended to most chapters are meant to open up "typical" problems for discussion, rather than to cover every significant point in the chapters. Teachers will find it easy and probably desirable to add exercises of their own; we should encourage that.

The bibliography at the end of the volume is suggestive rather than complete; we hope that we have not omitted any *essential* title from the list, however.

It is necessary to make a special point, finally, of a subject which both of us take to be of great importance: the interpretation of literature in oral performance. As an academic discipline usually embraced by departments of speech (though occasionally, we are happy to say, by departments of English), interpretation has today pretty much accepted literature as its "text" for performance. Almost all books in the interpretation of literature take as their basic problem the problem of communication to an audience; it is unnecessary, for this problem, to add another book to those already in existence; furthermore, as with all the performing arts, it is possible to feel that the instruction in the last analysis must be left to the good teacher in the classroom. We feel, however, that the *basic* problem is a problem of understanding—in short, the basic problem for the student of interpretation is the same as that for the student of literature under any system. The whole history of instruction in the creative and performing arts shows that it is always to their peril that students neglect the matter upon which their talent or skill is exercised. And surely it is absurd to center a whole curriculum in interpretation on the problem of performance before audiences when it is only the most exceptional student who is ever likely to spend his life in such performance. If, on the other hand, "performance" or "communication" is more narrowly regarded as submission of oneself to a literary text by way of a direct expression of the text, then any student may look forward to a long life of oral performance even though his critical self may be the sole auditor. It is the experience of submission orally to a literary text, rather than a too easy satisfaction with subvocal expression, which concerns us, whether we are talking about the student alone or the student reading in the presence of others. We should hold that in certain respects oral performance is one of the best ways of insuring *full* response of students to litera- ture, since it demands of the reader a considerably richer par- ticipation in the literary text than that ordinarily demanded by silent reading. Interpretation demands that literature really *be experienced*—not simply, in some paraphrasable sense, "under- stood." Without minimizing the values of historical, textual, linguistic, and other modes of literary study, we suggest that in- terpretation has an important contribution of its own to make to literary studies, and that the study of performance ought to be kept sharply relevant to the understanding of the work be- ing performed. When Thomas Sheridan sat, as a young boy, at the feet of his father's house guest, Jonathan Swift, and listened to that great genius reading aloud to him, he was listening, not to a man "speaking," but to a *man* speaking, and it was the senti- ments of the *man* which informed Sheridan's whole later life.

A thoroughly sensitive reading of a poem will give the poet more pleasure, on the whole, than a sensitive essay about his poem, though he will value understanding in whatever form it comes. A thoroughly sensitive reading of a poem will give a *reader* more pleasure and understanding, on the whole, than a sensitive essay about the poem, though he will value both contributions to his awareness. For the student performer, the reading of a fine piece of literature is an adventure in life, an adventure which always yields its own rich rewards.

While both authors assume responsibility for the point of view of the whole book, in carrying the project to completion R. S. Breen has been responsible primarily for Chapters 1 to 5 and Chapters 12 and 13 and W. A. Bacon for Chapters 6 to 11.

W. A. Bacon has also in the interests of uniformity reviewed the whole manuscript and has contributed the preface.

We should like to express our gratitude to Gertrude Breen for her patient assistance in the typing of the manuscript.

Wallace A. Bacon
Robert S. Breen

Contents

PART *1*

The Nature of Experience

$\mathcal{T}he$ $\mathcal{I}ndividual$ and $\mathcal{E}xperience$

$\mathcal{L}$ITERARY CRITICS have shown great interest in the questions "What is literature?" and "How is it written?" Comparatively few have shown interest in the question "How is it read?" The relationship between the writer and his manuscript has been explored extensively, while the relationship between the writer's manuscript and its reader has on the whole been neglected.

This neglect is all the more puzzling when we remember that, while few of us are actively engaged in the art of writing, most of us think of ourselves as actively engaged in the art of reading, and therefore interested in whatever may be said that will make us *better* readers. It is the intention of this book to talk about the art of reading from the point of view of the *reader's* experience.

Literature as Actual Experience

Reading literature is a common experience; it is by no means a simple experience. Literature may seem a simple matter of fact when one thinks of it as being black marks on white pages; but as soon as the reader recognizes the marks as words—and as phrases, and sentences, and paragraphs—he has begun to leave the realm of simple experience of the "real" object, the printed page, and has begun to move in the world of abstractions. The black marks are soon seen to be symbols of other things, to "stand for" objects, processes, and situations.

In spite of the abstract quality of language, there is a comforting familiarity about the printed page, for the words can be appreciated as common sounds and meanings remembered from conversation. Even when the words are unfamiliar, the dictionary will tell the reader the correct sound and meaning. It all seems real enough and simple enough, for language is second nature with the adult and he does not think much about it. Indeed, it is probably true that for most readers books are palliatives, something to fill the awkward pauses between periods of significant activity. Books pour from the presses and are read without being remembered—but "when literature is not memorable it is nothing." [1]

Literature as Imaginative Experience

Readers who believe that literature provides a memorable experience, who take the printed page seriously as an opportunity to enjoy a significant experience, are sometimes regarded with suspicion, as if they had lost their touch with reality and become escapists victimized by the unrealities of the imagined world of fiction. Such suspicions are groundless, for the very world of reality in which we all live our daily lives is filled with imagined experience. We look out the window at the street and we say, "It is wet out." This is an imagined experience, for wetness is a tactile sensation, not visual. We can judge the weight of a stone without lifting it because our visual response to the stone stimulates through our imagination (recollections of past experiences

[1] David Daiches, *A Study of Literature,* Cornell University Press, Ithaca, N.Y., 1948, pp. 6–7.

with stones) kinaesthetic sensations of muscular tensions. Much of thought proceeds by hypothesis—that is, by trial and error. Imagination, the representation of things not present, is essential to our lives.

Those who feel strongly the separation between literature and life, who are reluctant to suspend their disbelief, have in a great measure missed one of the most profoundly civilizing of processes —the education of the senses and the pleasurable acquisition of that knowledge which is necessary for our understanding of human experience.

Life and Literature

Yet life is not literature, nor is literature life; the two are distinct, but so much has been made of the distinction that they are often seen as alien to one another. It is the alienation that does so much damage, that allows the writer to grow careless in his art and the reader to become casual and uncritical. It is when the reality of life and the imagination of literature are brought together that the writer is honored for his skill and the reader is alerted to the importance of the art of reading. Marianne Moore asks that poets become "literalists of the imagination" and [2]

> present
> for inspection, 'imaginary gardens with
> real toads in them'....

A reader's experience with a book is no different in its nature than his experience with other objects in life. All experience is interactive; it is a traffic between the object and the subject. Actuality, the sense of living through an event with its emotional quality of enjoyment or suffering, characterizes the experience of reading as it does the experience of living.

In life, objects appear to us and we have sensations and impressions of them as they impinge on our sensory organs; we adjust

[2] Marianne Moore, "Poetry," *Collected Poems,* The Macmillan Company, New York, 1951, p. 41.

to the objects with every confidence that they are real. How often we are mistaken in our interpretation of the sensation, our judgment of the impression! Theseus, in *A Midsummer Night's Dream,* speaks of the errors we make in judging:

> in the night, imagining some fear,
> How easy is a bush supposed a bear!

The corrected impression may come in time or too late or it may never come at all.

Sometimes we are expected to adjust to objects which do not appear to our senses. Someone describes a pretty girl to us and we find ourselves wreathed in smiles and looking forward to meeting her. The response to the *image* of the girl may not be as vivid as the sensations surrounding the *actual* figure of the girl when we do meet her, but still the difference is only one of intensity. It does not always follow that the actual is more vivid than the imagined; anyone who has succumbed to the rhetoric of a real-estate salesman knows how plain and uninspired is the reality of the actual property as contrasted with its description. It is not that the salesman has lied, precisely, but his art of selection and his ability to cast a spell with his tone of voice or his emphasis is what fires the buyer's imagination.

In literature as in life the magic of the imagination creates vivid images that may develop in the reader a disposition to accept the images as physical reality, and what was at first imagined becomes at last directly sensed. John Keats went so far as to express a *preference* for the imagined when he said,

> Heard melodies are sweet, but those unheard
> Are sweeter....

Perhaps Keats was an uncommon reader, for most of us still cling to the notion that we enjoy direct, lively sensations in life, but only the pale, reflected image of those sensations in literature. Generally, however, we underestimate the power of literature to affect us directly. Indeed, we may not *want* it to move us deeply; in that case, when the images threaten to transcend their mirrorlike flatness and to become solidly real, we seek refuge in further abstractness: we become more "educated," and a consciousness of words *as* words replaces the images evoked by the words, and consequently we are at a further and safer remove from life.

Literature as Dramatic Experience

The common reader is "safe" with a story in a book, or with a poem, because when the story or the poem threatens to become too vivid, it can be regarded as "cold print," and kept comfortably suppressed and remote. Such a reader is proof against the full effect of literature because something is always reassuring him that after all it is only a story. But when literature is presented to this same reader, not on the page between the covers of a book, but on the stage before his very ears and eyes in the form of a play, he falls easy victim to the illusion of reality. The characters are living and breathing; the settings are real. A moment's reflection will dispel the illusion as effectively as the reflection that the novel is only a story or that the poem is just something made up by the poet; nevertheless, literature and life seem not so widely separated when the form of literature is dramatic.

But even nondramatic literature implies someone speaking and something spoken. In this sense, all literature is dramatic: there is always a conflict expressed or implied, and a prevailing emotional state. Such are the conditions of drama, and such are the conditions which give all literature the semblance of life.

Literature and the Writer

It is possible, of course, to press the similarities between life and literature too far. The experience of one will not always serve satisfactorily as a substitute for the experience of the other! However, it is more often the case that the separation of literature and life is insisted upon until each is regarded as autonomous. *For an understanding of what this book proposes as a means of improving the art of reading, it is important that correspondences between* actual *experience which life presents and* virtual *experience which literature presents be reinstated in all their primitive force.*

Consider the writer. He is man and artist. As a *man* his experience is both general and specific. The general and the specific may be related only accidentally. As an *artist,* however, he sees in the unique experience of his own life and that of others characteristics of general significance. The artist in man explores the motivations in man and the artist gives to his discoveries shape and meaning. Eliseo Vivas has stated the dual nature of the man-artist's relationship to experience and literature: [3]

To discover in its specificity the nature and structure of experience as lived, and to present it in terms that men can grasp, is the creative task of the artist. And it is an essential task. He is engaged in giving us a refurbished picture of our world in concrete terms. He teaches us to discern what we in our purblindness cannot see for ourselves; he tells us what is the dramatic pattern of human life and thus defines for us its sense .... without his aid our comprehension of our culture coarsens, we get confused, our sensibilities harden; and because, as a result, our imaginative grasp falters, our daily living insensibly relapses to the level of instinct, automatism and animal brutality.

It is true that the living world of reality is full of things that have weight, shape, texture, color to which literature can only point with words. But this is no weak or second-best thing, for words have the shape and force of our attitudes and actions. Sticks and stones may break our bones, but words have equal power to wound; the imagined slight will destroy the lover's appetite as effectively as the odor of strong meat. It is not so much the objects of the real world that have meaning for us; it is our attitudes toward them that make them significant. It is the special talent of a writer that he sees in himself and in others the psychological shape of experience; it is the function of literature through his genius to clarify, intensify, and extend the primary data of human experience so that our duller perceptions may be sharpened and our self-knowledge extended.

[3] Eliseo Vivas, *Creation and Discovery,* The Noonday Press, New York, 1955, p. 122. Quoted by permission of the publishers.

The Reader and the Writer

The reader may not share with the writer his uncommon talent for the creative management of language, but in his own way he is an artist. He contemplates the literary text with a disinterested interest; he recognizes the laws of its being and may even pass judgment on the quality of its internal articulation. If he behaves merely on the basis of attraction and repulsion by accepting what he likes and rejecting what he dislikes, he may remain simply an artist-reader. But if he reflects on the relationships between the text and life, if he entertains implicative speculations that branch out from the text, he will be a *human* reader. The argument underlying all that is said in this book is this: *A writer fashions a work of art which reveals his discoveries about life, and a reader tests the value of those discoveries by a kind of sympathetic and critical imitation of the actions and reactions found in the writer's work.*

The writer *realizes* his insights in concrete terms: he sets a world of people and things in motion. He knows that he cannot make words *embody*, literally; he accepts the limitations of his art and urges language *toward* embodiment. This is both the challenge and the virtue of his art. And the careful reader, while he never altogether forgets his own reality, will transform the writer's words into imagined experience: he will find the real frogs in the imaginary garden and he will weep over the fate of the paper-and-ink characters with as much sincerity of feeling as though they were flesh and blood.

Having said this much about the impulse that urges a writer to force his language toward embodiment, and a reader to accept this symbolic experience as "real," it must be said that it is not the true and essential function of language to present the reader with sensuous reality. Language is less interested in the direct translation of natural substance than in the transmission of its spiritual form. The significance of literature is best seen as the concrete sensory experience recedes, allowing the "form" and relations of consciousness to become clearer.

The antithetical pull between the concrete and the abstract, the sensuous and the spiritual, the actual and the ideal is part of the life force of literature. There is no real division here, but rather a synthesis. The spiritual life is based on a sensory contact with the concrete world. Ernst Cassirer concludes [4] that "the intuitive world of art, myth and language—constitutes, as Goethe said, a revelation sent outward from within, a 'synthesis of world and spirit,' which truly assures that the two are one."

Acts and Attitudes

While the reader responds sympathetically to the world of literature, he is never entirely forgetful of the real and immediate environment in which he himself exists, and his responses to the literature are conditioned by his realization that he is not *in fact* a part of the fictional scene. The author describes actions appropriate to the world of his story, and the reader develops attitudes, empathically induced, which bear a close resemblance to the actions described; indeed, it is the reader's capacity for assuming accurate attitudes that measures his success in understanding the work of literature. Nevertheless the attitudes of the reader are not *identical* with the acts of the literature.

For example, the character in the work of literature may be in real agony, but the reader gives evidence of his participation in that agony only, perhaps, by knitting his brows, drawing his lips back slightly over his teeth, and responding with a general muscular tension. The reader's proper reactions remain attitudes and do not become acts because he realizes that his own actual environment is different from the fictional environment of the fictional characters.

It is this capacity in the reader to respond through attitudes rather than through acts that makes possible his examination of the behavior of others. A fully active response to Othello might end in disaster for the reader! If we are to form judgments and make evaluations of the action of a story, we must see it in terms

[4] Ernst Cassirer, *The Philosophy of Symbolic Forms,* vol. I, *Language,* Yale University Press, New Haven, Conn., 1953, p. 111.

of the *potential reactions* that constitute the form of the experience. By watching Othello act, we as readers assume attitudes which let us feel how Othello feels without making us act as Othello acts. Hence we have the power of evaluating Othello's acts. We achieve this through *abstracting* from the sensuous content of the play's action, for language is by its very nature abstractive: it is an intermediary between the substantial actuality reflected in the images of the literary actions and the spiritual form manifested in the reader's attitudes.

The Silent Reader and the Oral Reader

It is often the case with silent readers and "eye" readers that their attitudes are formed in a static series, not dynamically related. Their attitudes are *substitutes* for acts and not *preparatory to action*. Because their behavioral participation is so far below the level of overt response, they find it easy to contemplate the fictional acts—but the results of such contemplation are likely to be dry and unspirited. The oral reader, on the other hand, is quick to anticipate the attitudes of others because his disposition to act (developed through his insistence on a physical expression of the literary text) is closer to the genuine act than are the substitutive attitudes of the silent reader. Hence social education proceeds at a faster rate for the oral reader than for the silent reader because the oral reader is likely to be in more active—and hence fuller—contact with the experience which constitutes the work of literature.[5]

Summary

This opening chapter has been concerned with certain fundamental relationships existing between the individual and experi-

---

[5] For a fuller discussion of the value of attitudes as preparatory social acts, see George H. Mead, *Mind, Self and Society,* University of Chicago Press, Chicago, 1934, pp. 135–226, and Kenneth Burke, *A Grammar of Motives,* Prentice-Hall, Inc., Englewood Cliffs, N.J., 1945, pp. 235–247.

ence. Specifically, it has discussed the relationship existing between the experience of an individual called the *writer* and the experience of another individual called the *reader* as these two are brought together through a third experience called the *work of art*. The medium by which the sharing of the third experience is made possible is *language*. There are ways in which the experience of literature and the experience of life are similar; there are ways in which they clearly differ—but it has been our argument that much is to be gained by pointing to the similarities before literature is cut too sharply off from life and made to seem unreal and ineffectual.

In the chapter which follows, we shall be concerned more specifically with the nature of the individual who experiences.

Exercises

1. If we are to make our way in the physical world without mishap, we must learn to interpret our sensory impressions accurately. However, we are sometimes deceived by our sensations, and we misinterpret them. For instance, the sound of a train can be used to judge its distance from us, but the conformation of the hills between us and the train may make the sound so loud as to convince us that the train is near when in truth it is still a long way off. Because the dummy's mouth is moving, we "hear" him speak when, for a fact, it is the ventriloquist who is speaking. We hear the *sound* of a bobwhite and we say, "Listen to that bird," but wiser listeners say that it is an Indian. Someone is mistaken in his interpretation of the sensation of that sound.

Can you discover in your own experience similar instances of misinterpretations of sensory impressions?

2. Elizabeth Barrett Browning wrote a sonnet which opens with a question: "How do I love thee?" The question implies not only a speaker but a listener—a listener who, perhaps, has asked the speaker a leading question.

Examine other sonnets for evidence of a speaker-listener situation. See whether you can characterize the speaker from what he says in the poem, or from the way he says it, or from the situation in which the speaker finds himself.

3. Read a short story, preferably aloud, and make an effort to distinguish what may be called *actual* experience from *virtual* experience. For instance, the words on the page will make an actual impression on your eyes; the sounds you make with your voice will be actual. On the other hand, the actions of the characters will be virtual; the moonlight or rain in the story will be virtual. There may be moments when the actual and the virtual come close together; for instance, a character may rush upstairs and say to his mother, "Oh, mother, John's here," and you will recognize these actions as virtual; but as you read the passage aloud with full response to the emotional excitement of the character you may find yourself speaking in a breathless fashion which is actual though the running up stairs was virtual. The excitement in the character was virtual, and the excitement in you, the reader, was actual. In such fashion are literature and life brought together in the reader.

4. Since objects in the world of concrete reality have meaning for us largely because of the attitude we take toward them, it is interesting to see whether or not our valuation of an object changes with our attitudes. Try taking an attitude toward an object, say, a brush. See it first as having harsh bristles that make your skin burn and turn red as, in your imagination, you rub it vigorously over your body. Notice whether or not you have any peripheral reactions—tensions in your muscles, tensions in your jaw as you describe the brush, facial expressions, changes in breathing, etc. Now change your attitude by changing the words with which you describe the brush and how it makes your skin glow with a pleasant sense of exhilaration. Notice now whether or not there is any change in the peripheral reactions.

Try the experiment with a variety of objects. Try the experiment in class with a single object, and compare the reactions of various members of the class.

5. Try to describe the effect of an object that is only verbally identified. The identification should be general—for example, *brush*. Now notice how the imagined appearance of the brush changes as you change the description of its effect on you. Notice, too, how different pupils will see different brushes even with the same description of effects.

6. Find examples from your own experience of the truth that words have the power to affect us with the same force that concrete objects have. Look for instances where words have more power, or less power, or no power at all, compared with the physical objects or situations which the words identify.

2

The Physical Nature
of the Individual

$\mathscr{J}$ F A CASE is to be made for regarding literature as an analogue of human life, it will be necessary to take a close look at the creature who is capable of creating life *and* literature. The means man has to meet the exigencies of his daily living are the very means wherewith he writes poetry. If we are to understand the nature of man's literature, we must first understand some things about the nature of man himself. His physical nature will tell us something about his physical needs, and they will give us some insights into his behavior. The process by which man as a biological and social creature makes use of his environment to satisfy his needs must inevitably throw light on his literature.

The Biological Organization of Man

Every man is an individual, biologically organized into a functioning unit. He performs the fundamental acts that perpetuate life, the common and continuous acts that have for him very little biological interest when he is normal and healthy. But when there is some interruption of the natural continuity, he becomes aware of his body and its surprising—and frequently irritating!—resemblance to a mechanism. If he cuts himself deeply, he will note that the blood spurts with rhythmic pulsation; he will be reminded of the otherwise neglected fact that his blood flows in the arterial system of his body with a pulsing rhythm. If he runs unusually far or fast, he will feel very strongly the pounding of his heart in his chest cavity and he will be forced to notice that his heart is a powerful muscle operating with strongly rhythmic alternations of contraction and relaxation.

Constitutionally men are much alike. It is a great comfort for us to have this commonality on a biological level, for we have no fully satisfactory way of sharing with one another the thoughts and feelings that play so subtly over our consciousness. As men mature, their constitutional qualities and their environmental opportunities together make for increased individualism and perhaps for sharper separateness. It may be the function of literature in particular, and of art in general, to close the gap between men by showing to them the common source from which ambition, pride, honor, and a thousand other vices and virtues stem. Literature can reassure us that the infinitely varied means lead ultimately to common ends.

The physiological ends for which man seems to have been so elaborately organized are (1) to take in food and air and to transform them or metabolize them into energy and tissue and (2) to reproduce other individuals of the species. These are the goals served by the directive activities of the human organism; these are the facts which seem to give meaning to the organic activity of the human individual.

Perception as Physical Experience

To satisfy his fundamental needs, man has learned to use his environment. To make the best use of it, man has developed his sensory processes for the purpose of making contact with the external world. He has, in addition to his customary five senses, those of pain, warmth, cold, pressure, and perhaps others. In addition to these senses which relate man to the *outer* environment, there are receptors which allow man to perceive changes in his *inner* environment—changes in movement, position, tension. These latter receptors have to do with man's kinaesthetic responses.[1]

Perception as Psychological Experience

We know from experience that what a man knows of the world depends less on the efficiency of his sensory organs than on his interpretation of their data. What one *senses* and what one *perceives* are not necessarily the same. Two men undergoing the same sensory experience will have different perceptions of that experience because they have different pasts. They bring to the present experience different dispositions and values. They have different motivations, or, at the very least, they are motivated in different degrees. The process by which a man organizes his environment so that he can make the best use of it is called *perception*. Each of us sees or perceives the world from the point of view of his own unique position in time and space, and out of his own background of needs and experiences. For better or for worse we tend to project what we have learned of the world into each fresh sensation and so attribute certain aspects of our own experience to the external world, though we persist in the feeling that the external world exists independently of our experiences. So the question that underlies a study of perception is the one that concerns the correspondence between how the world *appears* and what in fact it *is*. In other words, perception deals with the relationship between how big an object *looks* and how big it *measures*. Misinterpretations at this level are called *illusions*. If a person

[1] For further information on the mechanics of perception see a standard work on physiology such as L. L. Langley and E. Cheraskin, *The Physiology of Man,* 2d ed., McGraw-Hill Book Company, Inc., New York, 1958, chap. 4.

sees heat waves on the desert and because of his extreme thirst sees them as water, he is suffering an illusion; but if in fact there are no heat waves—that is, if a normal person at this time and place sees no mirage, but the thirsty man does—then the latter is suffering a hallucination.

We can learn to bring our perceptions and objective reality closer together through training. Wine tasters have developed a high degree of discriminating perception. Objectivity is an essential part of training perception. The emotional state of a witness will often distort the evidence he offers. Perhaps no parent ever sees his child as he really is, or as others see him.

Definition of Perception

In its simplest terms perception can be defined as *"knowledge through the senses of the existence and properties of matter and the external world."* [2] Since knowledge is for use—that is, for the satisfaction of needs, whether they be hunger or pleasure—we can expect man to see the external situation in terms of his internal situation. Perception, then, involves "the organization of external and internal stimuli into a meaningful pattern." [3] How men act when they are moved to satisfy their needs will depend a great deal on their powers of perception, on the interpretation they place on the data gathered from their environment through their senses. The meaning of any particular perception pattern depends on what attributes from his past experience the perceiver decides, consciously or unconsciously, to attach to the immediate environment.

Perception and Literature

When we read literature, we respond on the lowest level of perception to the visual aspects of the words on the page; then we perceive the words on a symbolic level, for we recognize that they

[2] *Ibid.,* p. 59.
[3] Bert R. Sappenfield, *Personality Dynamics: An Integrative Psychology of Adjustment,* Alfred A. Knopf, Inc., New York, 1954, p. 8.

are but symbols, that they "stand for" some object or process in nature. As long as our perceptual reactions to the symbol can be distinguished from those elicited by the object or event to which the symbol refers, we are innocent of "perceptual identification." Whenever we interpret the symbol and the object as having identical value, we are guilty of perceptual identification.[4] But who would ever mistake the word *horse* for the animal itself? Yet those "four-letter" words which stand for certain sexual and excretory functions can produce stronge reactions—strong enough to convince us that we are often capable of identifying symbols with the things symbolized.

The writer identifies with his characters, though they may only be imaginary, and the reader, too, identifies with them as though they were real and not simply "verbal constructs." Actors strive to "be" the characters they portray and pride themselves on a high degree of identification. Ethel Waters, in her biography,[5] tells of her experiences playing the part of Hagar in *Mamba's Daughters*. So many women identified Miss Waters with the role of Hagar and wished to tell her of their own troubles with men that she found it necessary to stay in her stage clothes after a performance so that those who came backstage to see Hagar would not be disillusioned.

If we accept *no* identification of symbol and object, we cannot profitably read literature, and yet, if we cannot distinguish them *in some degree,* we are maladjusted indeed. It is part of the intention of this book to help the reader find his way between these two alternatives and make the most of both worlds.

The Value of Literature as Vicarious Experience

The pattern of our daily lives is simple, and the stimulation level of our routine experiences is generally low; were it not for

---

[4] See *ibid.,* chap. X, for a full discussion of the function and value of perceptual identification.

[5] Ethel Waters and Charles Samuels, *His Eye Is On the Sparrow,* Doubleday & Company, Inc., New York, 1951, pp. 239-250.

the vicarious life of literature, many of us would lose the fine edge of awareness and succumb to spiritual atrophy. Literature, like the other arts, provides us with a set of assumptions which, together with those provided by ordinary experience, serve as the bases for future action. That literature is imaginal and life is real in no way invalidates the former's capacity for providing the human intelligence with assumptions that will effectively condition future perceptions of the real and external world. By means of these assumptions we produce the world we know—the world of experience which is in the mind.

To understand a literary text requires some modification of our assumptive world. These modifications affect future perceptions, and so the external world changes for us, thanks to the literary reconditioning of our present perceptions.

Perception and Motor Activity

Since all impressions depend upon actions, there must be a close relation between perception and motor activity. The responses we make to sensory impressions which the nervous system has first interpreted, and respecting which it has issued orders, are generally *motor* in character. In the presence of a pleasant odor, for example, deep breathing may replace shallow breathing and the eyes may close slightly or completely in order to shut out distracting visual impressions. A pleasant taste may lead one to smack one's lips as part of the more important action of clapping one's tongue against the roof of the mouth in order to get the widest distribution of the tasted substance over the taste buds. In seeing, the eyes are often widened or narrowed to adjust the field of vision to the occasion; in hearing, the head is often cocked or turned.

Some physiologists and psychologists suggest that the reaction patterns of the human being to environmental stimuli are basically motor. Even the sedentary practice of reading literature involves neuromotor responses of widespread intensity. The reader responds kinaesthetically to the image of the daffodils dancing in the breeze; attitudinally he repeats the action described in the words, and the feelings of the poet and the poem are manifested in the reader's own minimal actions.

Kinaesthesis

In a motor theory of perception it is assumed that the special sensation known as *kinaesthesis,* which gives the organism a sense of bodily movement, position, and tension, will be of primary importance. Such a theory recognizes that a person adopts an attitude toward a situation or an object and that the kinaesthetic sensations deriving from that attitude provide the person with his interpretation of the object or situation. At least this is the condition described by psychologists for the early stages of a person's responses to a novel experience. When we hear symphonic music in the concert hall, we are impressed with the auditory rhythms which provide the *core* of the musical experience. At the same time we may be impressed with certain sensations derived from the accentual beats of the conductor's baton, which is providing a *context* for the auditory rhythms. In other words, the conductor's energetic movements excite kinaesthetic sensations in us, the listeners, and thus contribute to the final meaning of the music. Later we may hear a recording of the same music and be impressed again with the auditory rhythms, but we will, of course, have no direct sensation of the conductor's movements. We may, however, have kinaesthetic *images* of the original bodily sensations which continue to provide a context of meaning for the core experience.

Further hearings of the music will almost certainly mean a reduction in the vividness of the contextual imagery. That is to say, the kinaesthetic images of the original bodily sensations of muscular response to the conductor's baton will fade. This does not mean that meaning will fade—it only indicates that the imagery has fallen below the level of consciousness and can be restored in a moment by an act of will.

Sometimes verbal responses, like the kinaesthetic images, will provide a context that gives meaning to a perception. Since continued stimulation tends to weaken contextual imagery and the responses slip below the level of awareness, literature may fulfill a valuable function in restoring our sensitivity through the presentation of fresh insights into the ordinary or customary. Literature may give us again the innocent eyes with which to see the world new-minted.[6]

Since we take little pleasure in that to which we have become accustomed, we assume that much of the pleasure we get from our aesthetic experiences is due to the freshness or novelty of the new sensations. Our attitudes are enlivened and our deeply embedded kinaesthetic impulses are triggered. Our perceptions are activated along with our proprioceptors (more numerous than all the other receptors), and so we get the strong impression that perception is based in muscular activity.[7]

Empathy

The sensation of movement which we feel in our muscles permits us to feel ourselves into the apparent behavior of the objects in our environment. This *feeling into* describes in a general way what is called *empathy*. Empathy is a kind of identification, a personification of the object by the perceiver. The weight of objects, their shape or contour, their distance from us, etc., are all functions of our muscular disposition toward them.

There are two main forms of motor attitude that may be assumed in regard to an object, one of which particularly concerns aesthetics, the other not. The one is an adjustment *toward,* the other an adjustment *in* the object. When one sees a tree swaying in the sunshine, one can either have the motor impulse to put out one's hand to stop the

---

[6] For a more extensive discussion of the core-context theory of perception and its contribution to a motor theory of perception see Floyd H. Allport, *Theories of Perception and the Concept of Structure,* John Wiley & Sons, Inc., New York, 1955, pp. 77–81.

[7] E. J. Kempf, "The Autonomic Functions and the Personality," *Nervous and Mental Disease Monographs,* ser. 28, p. 23, 1918.

motion, which is in a sense a defensory attitude, or one may have the impulse to sway with the moving tree and thus to realize the true nature of its motion.[8]

It is the adjustment *in* the object which is particularly relevant to the reading of literature, because we must first stand in the shoes of the characters before we can judge them aright. We must rage with Lear before we can understand his rage, and we must stretch with Robin Hood's bow if we are fully to enjoy his adventures. Adjustments *toward* an object or situation are apt to show too much consideration of self or indicate a practical response, whereas the adjustments *in* an object or situation suggest the aesthetic attitude, the identification *with* and the feeling *into*. There would appear to be an exception to Langfeld's notion that the adjustment *in* is customarily aesthetic when we consider that comedies frequently ask us to laugh at the misfortunes of others. This seems to be an adjustment *toward*. We shall consider this apparent contradiction in Chapter 3 (pages 36 to 37).

Empathy and Projection

A writer depends upon the empathic responses of his readers for the success of his work because the responses show the extent to which the reader has modified his own responses to meet the demands of the text. But there is another kind of reaction among readers that tends to modify the objects and events in the literature to suit the predispositions of those readers. This kind of reaction is called *projection*. In empathy the observer transforms himself to correspond to the object or event; in projection the object or event is transformed to correspond to the observer. The mother who identifies the child in the story with her *own* child, disregarding the evidence that would distinguish the fictional child from the real, is guilty of projection.

[8] Herbert S. Langfeld, *The Aesthetic Attitude,* Harcourt, Brace and Company, Inc., New York, 1920, p. 112. The italics are the authors'. Quoted by permission of the publishers.

It is important that the reader's responses to the literature be characterized by an *interrelationship* between the remembered experiences of the reader and the novel adjustments demanded by the unique conditions of the text. It is difficult to maintain this balance. When empathy becomes sympathy, that is, when we feel as another person feels, our critical judgment may be somewhat impaired. Aristotle very wisely saw pity, rather than sympathy, as the hallmark of tragedy because in pity there is a just sufficient degree of alienation and avoidance of perceptual identification to allow the one who feels pity to see himself as being in some degree *different* from the pitied object. Again and again the critics have advised the reader to maintain an ambivalent relationship to literature that will allow him at once to give and to receive.

Empathy and the Misinterpretation of Social Action

In symbolic experience, the reader gains knowledge vicariously at a minimal cost in consequences. When an author manifests the inner state of his characters through their external behavior, he makes it possible for readers by their empathic identification with that behavior to reinstate within themselves the inner conditions of the characters. If it were as simple as that always, men would quickly come to an understanding of each other; but we have long since learned the social grace of concealing our inner feelings by adopting an external behavior at variance with them. With a little practice, we soon learn how to conceal our feelings: any adult who has been taken in by the external behavior of an "angel child" only to be awakened to his error in judgment by the sharp stab of a pin when his back is turned has had a lesson in the school of social hard knocks. Literature, too, makes use of such lessons.

Autistic Gestures

Not all external behavior is consciously controlled. Hence, no social action can be counted on to be completely successful in deceiving the alert observer. Men have a large vocabulary of overt gestures of which they are unaware. To the observer who can interpret them, certain aspects of character become an open book. Such gestures as pulling the lobe of the ear, fingering the upper lip near the nostrils, flicking imaginary particles from the clothing, hitching the trousers, etc., all have reference to attitudes on the part of the performer. Since they are unconscious, they are reliable indices of true inner states. Behavior of this sort is called *autistic* (literally, "of the self"), for it represents an automatic self-communication.[9] Such behavior is not intended for social consumption but is instead a communication of the self with the self. But since the gestures are external, they are subject to social interpretation, and for those who learn to read the signs they are an infallible index of true feelings.

An astute author will give his characters a number of these autistic gestures so that the observant reader will come to some appropriate conclusions about the characters without having to be *told* by the author. The reader enjoys the illusion of discovery. If he participates empathically in the behavior of the characters, he will through his "identity" with the characters at the autistic level come to a deeper understanding of them.

Literature captures the inner processes of human nature. It takes advantage of the motor basis of man's expressions of his thoughts and feelings, whether they have their origin in consciousness or unconsciousness. The printed words excite images, and the images, if they are sufficiently vivid, produce attitudes (dispositions to act) in the reader.

Thought as Motor Activity

Ordinarily one is not aware of a muscular disturbance during the process of thinking because, except for the learning period, there is little muscular activity. Muscular activity is reduced when thinking becomes routine; but when we are learning, during the

---

[9] See Maurice Haim Krout, *Autistic Gestures: An Experimental Study in Symbolic Movement,* Psychological Review Company, Princeton, N.J., 1935.

period of modification, the thought processes are motor indeed. Dr. Margaret Washburn has suggested [10] that in a great deal of our thinking "as the tentative movements ... become organized into systems some single slight movement may by association ... come to stand for, to act in place of, such an entire system. This is the whole process of symbolizing in thinking." There seems to be no reason, if Dr. Washburn is correct, why we should not draw from this relationship an important inference about the proper way to read literature: If the representation in words on the page is to be understood with the vividness and immediacy that characterized the author's impressions gained from the primary data of human experience, should not the symbolic movement of the reader, his motor activity as he responds to the text, assist the process of symbolic thinking which understanding of the literature necessitates? And is it not possible that the oral reader is at this point superior to the silent reader?

Summary

The physical nature of man and the symbolic nature of literature have much in common; the symbolizing processes in human thought are as natural to man as the circulation of his blood. It is man's nature to interpret and to evaluate experience through the use of symbols; man's action is often symbolic. Through kinaesthesis and empathy men come to appreciate the nature and function of other men and of objects.

One of the objects men enjoy through the exercise of these motor activities is the literary text. Through the exercise of imagination, the reader reinstates under the guidance of the text the virtual experiences reported in the literature.

In this chapter we have considered principally the motor aspects of man's nature and how they contribute to his understanding of literature. To a degree largely ignored by the general reader, liter-

[10] Margaret T. Washburn, "Emotion and Thought; A Motor Theory of Their Relations," in *Wittenberg Symposium of Feelings and Emotions,* Clark University Press, Worcester, Mass., 1928, p. 114.

ature points to the physical nature of men as a primary conditioner of our culture and tries to reveal to us the laws of this conditioning; men act as they do, think as they think, feel as they feel because they are physiologically what they are. The average reader too frequently makes the mistake of ignoring the conditioning agents for the sake of looking solely at the cultural results.

In the next chapter, there will be a fuller consideration of the emotional nature of the individual and its relation to the adaptive and conventional modes of human behavior.

Exercises

1. Examine an object, a painting or photograph, of sufficient complexity to insure a variety of reactions. First, decide whether the general perception of the object gives you a pleasant or unpleasant feeling. Then try to decide what it is, specifically, that accounts for the feeling. Are you distorting the object by projecting your own predispositions into the object? Are you aware of any interference with the intention of the object by your past experience with the object?

2. Select a passage from literature which stimulates a kinaesthetic response in you and try to describe as accurately as you can just what the response is. Is it appropriate to the author's intention? If you think your response is inadequate, try making the correct response consciously, even if you have to make it *overt*. When you think it is adequate, try reading the passage aloud and see if the kinaesthetic response appears in a *covert* fashion.

3. Examine the passage on pages 109 to 110 from *Hubert's Arthur*. To what extent are your responses empathic or projective? Does your sympathy for any party involved in the action distort the author's intention? Do you find your empathic reaction to the albino condition of Snowdie in "Shower of Gold" (pages 138ff.) a help or a hindrance to the symbolic value suggested by the author? Are you able to muster any satisfactory empathic response to the old man who is drunk in Hemingway's "A Clean, Well-Lighted Place" (pages 242 to 246)?

4. Though literature cannot serve directly the physiological ends for which man seems to have been organized (see page 16), it expresses indirectly the ends of being for men. Read Shakespeare's sonnets "Not marble nor the gilded monuments" and "That time of year

thou may'st in me behold"; try to relate their themes to the fundamental ambitions of the human organism. Do the same for other well-known works of literature.

5. Examine the behavior of the instructor for evidence of autistic expressions. Discuss them with the instructor in an effort to discover their relevance to his inner states. Do the same for the autistic behavior of your classmates. Examine the stories reprinted in this textbook for evidence of autistic behavior on the part of the characters.

3

$\mathcal{A}$daptive and $\mathcal{E}$motional $\mathcal{B}$ehavior

$\mathcal{I}$F MAN's adaptive behavior could always be relied upon to satisfy his needs, if he were never frustrated in his basic designs, there would be little or no emotional life for him and hence little use for literature. It is because men have no guarantee that flight will save them from a present or threatening danger that they suffer fear. Because society discourages direct attack on one's enemies, men become angered, contemptuous, petulant, annoyed, etc. The discipline that humanity undergoes in the process of becoming civilized requires continuous modification, restraint, and sublimation of primitive impulses and drives. The conflicts that arise out of this social process form the lifeblood of literature, for where there is conflict there is also, of course, emotion; and where there is emotion, literature may flourish.

In primitive man, adaptive behavior was very likely to be accomplished simply. His flight was instantaneous and precipitate; his attack was immediate and wholehearted. If his adaptive behavior was successful, a sense of satisfaction followed; if it failed, a sense of dissatisfaction developed. Beyond these simple emotions, he had little in the way of an affective life. But with

29

the development of civilization man had to learn the value of inhibition. His actions could not be as direct in communal society as they had been in the days of his primitive individualism. With the multiplication of personal frustrations, man grew emotionally complex. Glandular disturbances, characteristic of emotional conditions, either aided or balked his adaptive behavior: he might be paralyzed with fright or might find himself urged by his fear to perform superhuman feats of strength. Social emotions such as jealousy, envy, kindliness, etc., became refinements of the basic emotions of hate and love.

Emotions Integrate Adaptation

It is not surprising, then, that emotions are essential to our consciousness of the world. Such consciousness is highly adaptive in its most integrative phase and unadaptive in its disintegrative phase. For example, the man who accomplishes extraordinary feats under emotional conditions finds his coordination facilitated by the emotion; the man who suffers paralysis during an attack of fear finds his adaptive mechanism inhibited and his coordination impaired.

Dr. Washburn thinks that the visceral changes in mild emotional states supply the physical energy required by thought. It is her experience that the "flow of ideas is heightened by mild emotion." [1]

The stimulation that emotion in its integrative aspect offers to man seems to alert him to the nature of his environment and to the possibilities for adaptation. Even a mood of mild depression, for example, may alert a person to his physical debility, or to his thought patterns which are not satisfactorily adaptive, or to disruptive attitudes of which he is not conscious. An awareness of these states is the first step toward their alleviation; hence the adaptive nature of the mood that sharpens awareness.

[1] Margaret T. Washburn, "Emotion and Thought; A Motor Theory of Their Relations," in *Wittenberg Symposium of Feelings and Emotions,* Clark University Press, Worcester, Mass., 1928, p. 114.

Emotions Disintegrate Adaptation

Emotions may integrate human behavior by encouraging adaptive or purposive activity, but emotions may also disrupt human behavior if the physical disturbance affecting the viscera, heart, and glands is acute. In panic, people will sometimes destroy rather than save themselves, even when the latter course is open to them.

Some physiologists believe that the term *emotion* should be reserved for the violently disturbed or disintegrative condition of human beings. Yet it must be acknowledged that

in all human behavior, no matter how completely disorganized it may be, there is always to be found some element of organized activity—perhaps a reflexive response pattern such as crying, smiling, vomiting, or the startle pattern; perhaps some goal-oriented activity such as striking at an enemy, running from danger, calling the police, pouring water on a fire, stepping on the brakes. In other words, along with the emotional disorganization there is a back kick of organism against environment; the organism does something about the situation. This integrated component of emotional behavior must be kept constantly in view....[2]

Emotional responses to literature are not to be encouraged if they lead to disruptive behavior. Those impressionable young men who were believed to have taken their own lives in emulation of Goethe's hero Werther were not the best of readers. If the reader is despondent in sympathy with a despondent character, the mood or feeling can be justified aesthetically only when it leads to reflection or contemplation. If it leads to suicide, the reader is at fault and it must be concluded that his own character is unstable. Literature often deals with characters suffering disruptive emotions; but if it is to bring *understanding* to the reader, literature must excite *in* him integrative rather than disruptive responses.

In any case, integrative or disintegrative, adaptive or disruptive,

---

[2] Paul Thomas Young, *Emotion in Man and Animal,* John Wiley & Sons, Inc., New York, 1943, pp. 51–52. Reprinted with permission from the author and publishers.

emotions are nevertheless an active part of our consciousness of the world of objects and feelings, attitudes and motives. It is emotions that seem to give value to human experience.

Emotions as Expressive Behavior

Consider the expressive value of behavior that was once in our human history adaptive, but is no longer so except in a vestigial sense—for example, the baring of the teeth in the preparation for attack or defense. In primitive experience, the use of the teeth for tearing and rending an enemy was common enough, and a very effective means of adapting to an environmental necessity. Today, the use of teeth in this primitive fashion is rare, but the *baring* of the teeth is still very much with us. In an attitude of pugnacity, men will frequently clench their teeth and draw back their lips to expose their teeth. This action is a reinstatement of the primitive pattern of biting though there is no *real* intention of using the teeth in such a fashion. It remains a social gesture, an emotional expression indicative of hostility. The "tough guy" talks through his teeth because he is habituated to an attitude of aggressiveness. When he bares his teeth, it is a warning to all who see him that he is prepared to attack or to defend himself. His speech is characterized by a nasality because his oral cavity is closed and his breath escapes principally through his nose. Lip action in speech is curtailed because the jaw tensions infect the muscles of the face generally and the lower jaw is held so close to the upper jaw that there is little room between the lips for even their normal activity. Restriction of the lip action results in the tough guy's talking out of the corner of his mouth.

When we see a person bare his clenched teeth, curl his lip, narrow his eyes, deepen his breathing, etc., we conclude that he is angry. These are the *signs* of attack in our ancestors which have become for us *social symbols expressive of an emotional state* known as *anger*.[3]

[3] Charles Darwin, *The Expression of the Emotions in Man and Animals,* Philosophical Library, Inc., New York, 1955, chap. 1.

The rejection of food by vomiting is an adaptive pattern that men have modified for the social expression of disgust. Just as the child may reject certain foods, so the adult may reject certain elements in the environment. Vomiting is a violent reversal of the peristaltic action that normally aids in the swallowing of food, and to facilitate vomiting the muscles of the throat hold the opening as wide as possible. This means that the vocal folds are held apart, too. When one speaks while the muscles are holding the throat open, a special quality is lent to the sounds which we may describe as "superior," "condescending," "patronizing." The attitude of rejection is apparent in the quality of voice which is produced by the adaptive preparation for the rejection of distasteful or disgusting food. The corners of the mouth are frequently drawn down in an expression of superiority, and that, too, is part of the pattern of regurgitation.

Emotions and the Situation

In addition to the adaptive movement and the acute bodily disturbance, both of which characterize emotions, there is the *situation* to be considered, too. The psychological nature of the situation is important for the identification of emotions. Emotions are nondiscriminatory in character; that is, fire and flood both give rise to the emotion of fear. The adaptive behavior, however, is adjusted to the situation—not necessarily the objective situation, but the situation as the emotion interprets it.

While it is true that much of the disturbance of the body occasioned by emotions is internal, affecting the viscera, heart, lungs, etc., there is often external evidence of the emotional condition. Following a sudden fright, a woman may suddenly put her hand over her heart and at the same time utter some exclamation. The gesture is expressive of the emotional condition of fear because it is almost conventionally associated with the behavior of stilling the heart, which is beating inordinately as a result of the sudden release of adrenalin into the blood stream. There are a great many signs of this indirect sort by which we identify emotional states in others, emotional states of which we can have no direct evidence because they are confined principally to the viscera.

If emotions had to be judged solely from the external expressions, it would be difficult if not impossible for us to discriminate even such widely differing emotions as joy and sorrow. It is not uncommon for people to cry in joy *and* in sorrow. Discriminating subtler emotions would be even more difficult were it not for the fact that the psychological situation can be depended upon to identify the emotion.

The psychological situation is not merely the physical environment. It includes the total behavioral relationships between an organism and the external world. Subjectively considered, the psychological situation includes memories, thoughts and imaginations, as well as perceived events and objects.[4]

Investigations of fear, rage, and pain showed no distinguishing features among the bodily changes which would discriminate these three emotions. However, the situational responses of flight for fear, attack for rage, and aimless, uncoordinated movements for pain distinguish the emotions well enough.

Emotions in the Interpretation of Literature

It is a part of William James's theory of emotions that the conscious assumption by a person of the external signs of emotion—such as the clenching of the hands and teeth in anger along with narrowing the eyes and increasing the depth of breathing—may lead to the acquisition of symptoms beyond the conscious control of the subject—such as a flushed face and a dry mouth. The appearance of such unconscious responses indicates the development of a genuine emotion of anger. The critic William Archer questioned a number of actors on the point of whether or not they felt a genuine emotion in the course of acting a role; he found that some *did* suffer a genuine emotion, and some did not.[5]

[4] Young, *op. cit.,* p. 333.
[5] William James, *Psychology,* The World Publishing Company, Cleveland, 1948, p. 383.

For the reader of literature, the significance of Archer's findings with respect to actors is that there is always a risk in submitting to the emotions of a text. If too little is risked, nothing is gained; on the other hand, if the reader fails to realize that he is only symbolically related to the events of the story, he may suffer a serious loss of identity. For the successful reader, submission is never so complete that his identity is lost in identity with the characters. This is as true of the oral reader as it is of the silent reader.

The emotional tone of the empathic process of the reader is characterized by implicit or minimal gestures. If the reader is to understand the condition of the character, he must experience to a "just sufficient" degree the character's emotion. A physiologist might be offered the same evidence of human behavior and come to an understanding of its significance through a process of abstraction and generalization, without being emotionally engaged in *any* degree; that is the way of science. The way of literature, however, asks the reader to respond empathically to an individual's behavior by assuming the same behavior in a minimal fashion and so experience more or less directly the emotional condition itself.

A word of caution must be urged at this point. *Minimal action* refers to an economy of action. Only those tensions which are expressive of the original act need be induced for appropriate empathy. There is a style in reading as in writing. A writer with a sense of style accomplishes his ends with an economy of means, and a reader with a sense of style in the art of reading will develop just those dispositional sets or attitudes which are appropriate and to just that degree of intensity which will satisfy the law of economy of means. Minimal action is likely to be incipient and relates to overt or full action as an image relates to direct sensation. It is by no means true that minimal action is weak simply because it is generally restrained. Occasionally an accident will reveal how extensive the motor reactions are in what might seem to be the most passive of pastimes, reading. I. A. Richards recalled [6] just

[6] I. A. Richards, *Principles of Literary Criticism,* Harcourt, Brace and Company, Inc., New York, 1948, p. 107.

such an accident: "Reading Captain Slocum's account of the centipede which bit him on the head when alone in the middle of the Atlantic, the writer [Richards] has been caused to leap right out of his chair by a leaf which fell upon his face from a tree." But for the mischance of the leaf falling no one would have guessed, not even Richards, that the restrained minimal action incipient in his muscular disposition to act contained tensions sufficient to catapult him from his chair. Let no reader suppose that we mean by minimal action anything more or less than the appropriate motor disposition of the reader's attitudes during the process of perception.

A question arises: How is one to experience the emotions, say, of *two* characters, one of whom is angry, the other frightened? The answer is to be found in the experience of our daily lives. Who has not at some time in his life experienced the full agony of pinching his finger in a drawer and expressed his emotion by waving his hand or holding the pinched finger tightly in the other hand while he danced around? Then, when the pain subsided a little, that is, reached a minimal degree of intensity, and while tears were yet in the eyes and the voice choked with one emotion, it is likely that another emotion appeared. Who has not found himself laughing at the absurdity of his behavior, even while he was still crying over the pinched finger? It is important to notice, however, that the laughter cannot come until the pain has been somewhat reduced; on the other hand, the pain need not disappear altogether before laughter appears.

Recall that the reader's emotional identification is *minimal;* the sophisticated, experienced reader moves swiftly and readily from one emotional condition to another, so that he does, for all practical purposes, experience both fear and anger *at the same time.*

A further question presents itself for consideration: If the scene in which the characters express fear and anger is nevertheless a comic scene, how then is it possible for the reader to experience both these emotions and at the same time be amused? A full answer to this question would take us too far afield at this point in our discussion, for it would require an examination of the difficult question of how an author maintains a comic tone when his characters are expressing fear and anger. It can only be said here, in brief, that the reader will probably not find the scene amusing *until* he has learned to experience a degree of anger and fear. The reader of literature finds that his understanding of the scene depends first on his ability to experience simultaneously the emotions of fear and anger and ultimately on his being amused. For the physiologist's understanding of the emotional processes of the two characters, amusement is irrelevant.

True, the reader is interested in the experience of the emotion only as a means to understanding the emotion in terms of the character and the situation in the literature, and the author evokes emotional responses in his readers only that he may clarify their true understanding of such responses. A lesser writer sometimes evokes emotions as an end in themselves, it is true—he feels successful if he shocks you or makes you cry, perhaps; but this is confusing the means of art with the end of art, and no good reader will be taken in by such a writer, though he may be moved by him.

Remember that understanding is not entirely a rational matter, nor is it entirely a matter of the heart. Here as elsewhere, there must be a balance between sense and sensibility.

There is a conviction among some readers that *any* "demonstration" of adaptive and emotional behavior such as we have been discussing would be vulgar. (Some silent readers are pained by the notion of reading aloud.) But if such behavior is *appropriate* to the situation and the character in the piece of literature, it cannot in the nature of art be vulgar. If it somehow seems indecent to express such feelings and actions in the flesh and voice, remember that literature, and especially great literature, is not noted for being polite. It is possible that a great story, fully understood, is not even legal.

The charge that might be advanced with greater justice is that such "goings on" are not *necessary* to the understanding of literature. The argument that the author has skilfully *implied* the behavior of the characters through his management of symbolic language can be justified. As we grow more adept at abstraction and intellectualizing, we become more and more content with vicarious experience. In primitive peoples the inseparable unity of speech, gesture, and thought during emotional excitement produced an expressive range of considerable amplitude. Civilized peoples retain the same patterns, but the amplitude has been considerably reduced.

Werner Wolff says [7] that "the intensity of unified expression decreases with the development of personality, but the phenomenon itself seems not to vanish. If we could attach a magnifier to that decreased expression, we would get the same effect as in its primitive form." Art does attach a magnifier, by reinstating, clarifying, and intensifying the largely adaptive data of experience. If the reader would do as much for the text as the author has done for the raw experience which has supplied his subject matter, then, it is possible, the reader would no longer tolerate in himself the widening gap between literature and life. Let the reader become the *oral* reader, which means that he must use symbolic action. Let him increase the amplitude of his expression to the point where he achieves an active congruence between himself and the literature.

Carl Gustav Jung sees in the work of literature an effort on the part of the author to meet the spiritual needs of the society in which he lives. He insists that if we are to grasp the author's meaning we must allow the literature "to shape us as it once shaped him," [8] since only then will we understand the nature of his experience. He says that the author [9]

has drawn upon the healing and redeeming forces of the collective psyche that underlies consciousness with its isolation and painful

[7] Werner Wolff, *Diagrams of the Unconscious: Handwriting and Personality in Measurement, Experiment and Analysis,* Grune & Stratton, Inc., New York, 1948, p. 98.

[8] Carl Gustav Jung, "Psychology and Literature," *Modern Man in Search of a Soul,* Harcourt, Brace and Company, Inc., New York, 1933, p. 172. Quoted by permission of the publishers.

[9] *Ibid.,* pp. 198–199.

errors; that he has penetrated to that matrix of life in which all men are embedded, which imparts a common rhythm to all human existence, and allows the individual to communicate his feeling and his striving to mankind as a whole.

The secret of artistic creation and of the effectiveness of art is to be found in the return to the state of *participation mystique*—to that level of experience at which it is man who lives, and not the individual.... That is why every great work of art is objective and impersonal, but nonetheless profoundly moves us each and all.

Summary

Adaptive behavior seeks to accomplish the fundamental ends of human life. When it is frustrated, an emotional condition arises. The whole social process is a continuous modification and restraint of primitive impulses and drives in which man's emotional life becomes inextricably associated with his sense of values. Literature is concerned with man's emotional evaluation of human experience. The emotional responses excited in the reader must be of the integrative type if literature is to produce in him the fullest understanding of experience. Since emotions are often simply the expressive feature of those adaptive patterns which are no longer socially functional, our assumption of these emotions through empathic identification will amplify the usually obscured, but nevertheless fundamental patterns of human motives and impulses. Such amplification of normally suppressed behavior permits us to examine closely the most universal and basic elements of human experience. Literature reflects the interaction of primitive individualism and social altruism through its reinstatement of adaptive action and emotional conflict.

In the following chapter, there will be a consideration of the role played by emotion in the aesthetic experience of literature.

Exercises

1. Recall occasions in your own life when you experienced a strong emotion that produced either integrative or disintegrative action.

Search the literature in this text or outside it for instances of integrative or disintegrative action occasioned by strong emotion.

2. Perform certain gestures for the class that in your opinion express certain emotional states. Be sure there is no context for these gestures which would serve to identify the emotion they express. Ask the class, then, to identify the emotions expressed by the gestures.

Now provide a context for the gestures by using them in the course of an oral reading of a literary passage, say, from a play. Ask the class to appraise the expressive accuracy of the gestures.

3. Test William James's theory of emotions (see page 34) by assuming the characteristic expressive patterns of a specific emotion. Do you experience further symptoms of the emotion—especially those beyond your conscious control?

4. Examine scenes in literature which feature the emotional reactions of the characters. Discover for yourself whether the emotional responses under the specific circumstances are appropriate or inappropriate to the characters. If you decide that the emotional level is inappropriate, try to determine whether the emotions are overstated or understated. What are the cues in the text that lead to your proper evaluation of the emotional level?

5. Review pages 5 to 7 for an understanding of the relation of literature to life. Examine a specimen of literature when orally expressed in order to discover how and in what measure oral reading brings about an active congruence between the reader and the literature.

4

Emotions in Literature

EMOTIONS ARE important in our social lives; they are an index of our happiness or unhappiness. But they are not the whole of our lives. In literature, too, emotions are featured; but again, as in life, they do not constitute the whole of our interest. It is perhaps unfortunate that we cannot always see literature steadily and see it whole, but with patience we can examine it in each of its many aspects and come finally to some appreciation of its *full* value.

Care must be taken in any discussion of the place of emotions in reading literature to make clear *whose* emotions are being discussed. There are the emotions "suffered" by the *characters* in the story as they go about their fictive lives. There are the emotions evoked in the *reader* as he goes through the story with the characters. And finally, there may be expressed in the literature, quite apart from the emotions of the characters, the emotions of the *author*.

Emotions of the Author

In the drama there is, normally, no place for the author's emotions to find expression. We accept "the illusion of free will" for the characters in a play and believe only in their emotions with no thought for those of the author.

In the novel or the short story, the presence of the author may be felt as a kind of "central intelligence" describing the setting, selecting the action, and ultimately directing the destiny of the characters. In the very diction of the narration it may be that the reader can "hear" the voice of the author and sense his emotional attitudes. The dangers of an uncritical acceptance of narrative style as an expression of the author's emotional dispositions will be considered in Part 2.

We think of the lyric as the place in literature where the author speaks out most directly in his own person. But even here a warning must be issued—not all poets admit to a personal expression in their lyrics. Keats, for one, did not wish his readers to regard the "I" of his sonnets as *invariably* the poet himself. Nevertheless, the tradition is strong in literature that lyrics express the author's emotions.

Emotions and the Reader

All authors—dramatists, novelists, and poets alike—have hopes of moving their readers or audiences. Dramatists are so open in their avowed purpose of arousing emotions in the audience that they have been known to measure their success by the number of laughs clocked during a performance of their comedies. Novelists and poets have no such objective measure, but it is hard to imagine their being disappointed to hear a reader of their works confess that he was emotionally aroused. It is possible, of course, that an author would be disturbed to hear that his readers were moved to laughter at a work of his which he regarded as a tragedy! An author has failed no less for having moved his readers to an inappropriate emotion than for his having failed to move them at all.

In Chapter 3 there was some discussion of the process by which a reader makes an empathic identification with the characters in a story, poem, or play. The identifications are generally of an emotional nature. If the identifications are unpleasant and too intense, we may put the book down and never go back to it. If the identifications are too feeble, our interest flags, and we put the book down, never to return to it. Sometimes the emotions we share with the characters in the fiction are intense *and* unpleasant but nothing would induce us to abandon the book. Why do we deliberately submit to the unpleasantness, why do we say to our friends that some tragic story we have been reading is thrilling or exciting or wonderful? Why do we find a story stimulating when others find it depressing? Apparently there is some condition, perhaps an emotional condition, that prevails in the reading of literature that is apart from the direct, simple identification with the emotions expressed in the text.

It has been said that "there is no specifically aesthetic emotion":[1] that is, an emotion which is peculiar to the sort of disinterested contemplation of literature that is generally called "aesthetic." There are, however, artistic and inartistic emotions. The former are appropriate to the experience of a work of art, and the latter are not. Adolescents who giggle at Ophelia's mad scene are thought to entertain an inappropriate emotion. Perhaps they are suffering a personal embarrassment in being associated so intimately in public with a human being who has taken leave of her senses. In any case, the giggles are inadmissible to the aesthetic appreciation of *Hamlet*. There is something distinctive about the emotion which *is* admissible to the aesthetic experience: it is a fusion of emotion and analytical discrimination. If there is such a thing as an aesthetic emotion, it must be seen, not as different in nature from any natural or normal emotion, but only different in

[1] Stephen C. Pepper, *Aesthetic Quality, A Contextualistic Theory of Beauty*, Charles Scribner's Sons, New York, 1937, p. 105.

its origin or motivation. John Dewey, who *does* believe there is such a thing as an aesthetic emotion, issues a similar warning:[2] "Esthetic emotion is thus something distinctive and yet not cut off by a chasm from other and natural emotional experiences."

There must be a measure of serenity during the evocation of emotions, for art must lead to understanding even while it expresses and evokes emotions. Understanding will not come if the reader's emotions are overwhelming; but it is no less true that understanding will not come if his feelings are in *no* way engaged. The mechanism is not clearly seen, but somehow the reader who is moved without allowing his intelligence to be sentimentalized is in the best position to appreciate literature.

Some critics, like Wellek and Warren, insist that "for proper readers, literature does not and should not incite emotions."[3] Other critics, like Eliseo Vivas, are of the opinion "that the emotion is an accidental consequence of esthetic apprehension."[4] Despite the critics it is the expectation of the "common reader" that he will be moved in some degree by the literature he reads. Aristotle saw the purgation of pity and terror as the function of tragic drama. It could not be expected that the audience would come fully charged with these emotions, but Aristotle knew that the altruism of pity and the individualism of terror were deeply rooted in primitive instincts. It was the preliminary function of the tragic play to bring these strong emotions of pity and terror to the surface and make them fully potential. Then by some mysterious process which Aristotle called *catharsis* these emotions were to be encompassed with a tranquilizing understanding. Apparently the playwright had the gift of muting the painful elements of the emotions without nullifying them. By this special kind of emotional reduction the imagination of the audience was free to function.

[2] John Dewey, *Art as Experience,* Minton, Balch & Co., New York, 1934, p. 78.

[3] René Wellek and Austin Warren, *Theory of Literature,* 2d ed., Harcourt, Brace and Company, Inc., New York, 1956, p. 25.

[4] Eliseo Vivas, "A Definition of the Esthetic Experience," in Eliseo Vivas and Murray Kreiger (eds.), *The Problems of Aesthetics,* Rinehart & Company, Inc., New York, 1953, p. 406.

S. H. Butcher gives an excellent account of his understanding of why Aristotle insisted on the presence of fear in the tragic emotion: [5]

The tragic fear, though modified in passing under the conditions of art, is not any languid emotion. It differs, indeed, from the crushing apprehension of personal disaster. In reading or witnessing the *Oedipus Tyrannus* we are not possessed with a fear that we may be placed in circumstances similar to those of Oedipus, or be overtaken by the same calamities. Yet a thrill runs through us, a shudder of horror or of vague foreboding. The feeling is immediate and unreflective. The tension of mind, the agonised expectation with which we await the impending catastrophe, springs from our sympathy with the hero in whose existence we have for the time merged our own. The events as they pass before us seem almost as if we were directly concerned. We are brought into a mood in which we feel that we too are liable to suffering. Yet the object of dread is not a definite evil threatening us at close quarters. In the spectacle of another's errors or misfortunes, in the shocks and blows of circumstance, we read the "doubtful doom of human kind." The vividness with which the imagination pictures unrealized calamity produces the same intensity of impression as if the danger were at hand. The true tragic fear becomes an almost impersonal emotion, attaching itself not so much to this or that particular incident, as to the general course of action which is for us an image of human destiny. We are thrilled with awe at the greatness of the issues thus unfolded, and with the moral inevitableness of the result. In this sense of awe the emotions of fear and pity are blended.

Butcher is describing here two kinds of emotional involvement for the reader or witness of tragic drama: (1) the pity and fear associated with the reader's sympathetic identification with the hero's agonies, and (2) the exhilaration that accompanies the aesthetic contemplation of the hero's agonies. It is not reasonable to expect an audience to gather in the theater at their own expense of time and money simply to endure sympathetically and empathically the pain and agony of the tragic hero. Yet for more

[5] S. H. Butcher, *Aristotle's Theory of Poetry and Fine Art,* Dover Publications, New York, 1951, pp. 261–263. Quoted by permission of the publishers.

than two thousand years audiences have been doing just that—but not *simply* just that. There is another kind of emotion that the audience experiences even as it agonizes with the hero, an emotion of such quality and power that it makes the endurance of pity and fear in some way pleasurable—"We are thrilled." The "tragic emotion" is an experience to be enjoyed.

There is, apparently, an emotion that accompanies the reading of good or great literature that is other than the emotions experienced in the process of identification with the emotional states of the characters or author. The pleasure of a happy absorption in an aesthetic contemplation was recognized by Coleridge [6] when he said of the reader of poetry, "The reader should be carried forward, not merely or chiefly by the mechanical impulse of curiosity, not by a restless desire to arrive at the final solution, but by the *pleasurable* activity of the journey itself."

The pleasure one takes in an aesthetic experience derives from the recognition of experience made meaningful (so that it becomes *an* experience), from the realization of the significance of certain human events. The imagination of the author has so ordered the trials and triumphs of his characters that their unity and coherence can be apprehended. This peculiar pleasure that human beings take in the apprehension of well-ordered, meaningful relations, this generalized thrill that comes with the appreciation of the organic unity of a play or a poem or a novel has been called an *aesthetic emotion*. It differs from other emotions only in its source; it is a concomitant of a certain kind of contemplation, most often experienced in association with works of art. It has physical symptoms like any other emotion.

Some aestheticians prefer to speak of *aesthetic feelings* rather than aesthetic emotions. The substitution of *feeling* for *emotion* is a compromise. If emotions are essentially disruptive or personal, they are going to interfere with our understanding of literature as an aesthetic experience. If readers are not at all moved by literature, that is a fault, too. Perhaps there is a *feeling* we get when we make contact with a work of art that is something like an

[6] Quoted in Dewey, *op. cit.,* p. 5. The italics are ours.

emotion—not disruptive, but integrative, and so conducive to an aesthetic experience.

No very satisfactory distinctions have been made between feelings and emotions. Even the psychologists for whom these terms are working tools find the term *feeling* so generalized by use that it defies definition. The desirable thing to do here is not to *distinguish* feelings and emotions but to *relate* them. Feelings that are related to sensory experiences are for the normal human being immediate and multiple in the course of a given complex experience. A series of related feelings sometimes has sufficient unity and persistence to justify its being referred to as an emotion. Generally speaking such a unified process has greater intensity than an isolated feeling. Perhaps the best that can be said about any difference between emotions and feelings is that the former are more intense and more complex.

Some writers on aesthetics will allow emotion a place in the literary work, but under special conditions. The emotion must be "sincere," or "significant," or "impersonal," or "precise," but at no point is it ever made clear just what a sincere or significant or impersonal or precise emotion is.

Thought and Feeling

In any sensible definition of the aesthetic experience room is going to have to be made for both thought *and* feeling. The combination of thought and feeling, sense and sensibility was a consideration for Wordsworth in his view of poetry. He saw that poetry was intimately concerned with emotion, but he also found that if it was to be integrated with the expressive act which resulted in a poem, emotion or feeling had to be transformed through thought, "recollected in tranquillity." The notion of poetry as emotion recollected in tranquillity implies that emotion comes first and that thought is then brought to bear in the interest of evolving the poem out of the experience which was initially emotional. Is it not the common experience of imaginative people that thought and feeling are inextricably woven into the fabric of any significant experience? Wordsworth acknowledges the union of thought and feeling when he goes on to say [7] that "the emotion is contemplated till, by a species of reaction, the tranquillity gradually disappears, and an emotion, kindred to that which was before the subject of contemplation, is gradually produced, and does itself actually exist in the mind."

What Wordsworth saw as the conditions for the poetic process undergone by the *poet* describes in part the aesthetic activity of the *reader*. When the poet contemplates the emotion in tranquillity, he reinstates the symptoms of that emotion which are most under the control of the will (see Chapter 3) and finally experiences those symptoms which are *not* under the control of the will (blushing, sweating, palpitations of the heart, etc.). It is this process, no doubt, that Wordsworth refers to as a "species of reaction." By this same species of reaction the reader, too, induces in himself emotions kindred to those expressed in the text. That Wordsworth saw these emotions as existing in the *mind* is only another way of saying what William James has said about emotions being but the *awareness* of the bodily symptoms which finally register in the consciousness.[8]

When André Gide [9] said, "I have the gift of combining at the same moment two states of mind as different, as contradictory, as passion and lucidity; or as the fever, the delirium, the inward tremor of lyricism, and the chill of reason," he was describing a condition as essential to the reader as to the writer. If the general reader has a smaller capacity than the writer for controlling and ordering the issue of combined thought and feeling, that is not to say that he cannot, in the course of his aesthetic experiences, entertain thoughts in close company with feelings or emotions. Both the artist-writer and the artist-reader suffer the tensions of

---

[7] William Wordsworth, "Observations Prefixed to 'Lyrical Ballads' (1800)," in James Harry Smith and Edd Winfield Parks (eds.), *The Great Critics: An Anthology of Literary Criticism*, W. W. Norton & Company, Inc., New York, 1939, p. 514.

[8] See this chapter, p. 52.

[9] Roger Martin du Gard, *Recollections of André Gide*, The Viking Press, Inc., New York, 1953, p. 96.

being "half in life and half out of it." [10] They must be *in* life if they are to sense its texture, but only *half* in it if they are not to be absorbed. They must be at least half *out* of life if they are to see it and describe it, but only *half* out if they are not to lose its meaning.

Expression of Emotions in Literature

How does an author preserve in literature the affective tone of an original experience? Direct verbal references are rarely satisfactory. It does no good for the author to state bluntly, "He was sad," nor is it ever convincing to rely entirely on intensifying modifiers— "He suffered a great sorrow." The character must be seen in action, the words must carry associational values, and the rhythm of the language must underwrite the emotional condition of the character. In Part 2 there will be considerable elaboration of the writer's technique in managing emotional expression.

It is not possible to present emotions directly on the printed page, but it is possible through the formal elements of language to produce an emotive value. The formal aspects of literature are those which determine the order of the words on the page and hence the order of the references to objects and actions which produce images in the mind of the reader. There is infinite variety in this ordering of the imaginal experience and infinite subtlety in the literary means for evoking emotions. It is understood that the language forms are not the forms of the actual emotions or feelings—the latter are *inferred* from the former. In a sense the language forms are symbolic of the emotions, and so they become *expressive* of human feelings.

The Nonrational Basis of Literature

It is valuable now to consider the problem of the symbolic expression of emotions in literature from the standpoint of the actual

[10] A. L. Rowse, *The English Past,* The Macmillan Company, New York, 1952, p. 230.

experience of emotions. How does the writer know that certain forms of literary expression will express certain specific feelings? On the primal level physical behavior is highly rhythmic, as in the involuntary actions of breathing, the beating of the heart, peristalsis in swallowing, or the simple adaptive movements of walking, eating, etc., where muscular alternations of contraction and extension are involved. Under the influence of tribal joys and disasters the movements of members of the community are strongly affected by the natural periodicity of the human body (jumping up and down, beating the chest, shouting), and their physical action dominates their consciousness at the expense of the environment. One could say that behavior under these circumstances was instinctual, nonrational. The rhythmic ordering of the sounds and images of poetry and the rhythmic inflections of the speaking of poetry have their basis, too, in this original nonrational behavior.

The nonrational foundations of poetry in no way invalidate the uses of poetry to civilized man. Darwin has pointed to the value of instinct as a driving force in the struggle for survival and the vestigial remains of our primitive behavior in our cultural behavior.[11]

It is the poet's special sensitivity to the subterranean life of men that gives him his value to us. His formal control of language enables him to symbolize for us the power of our instinctual life, which is often frustrated by the demands of social conformity and conventional responses.

Even primitive man could not indulge his instincts. As he emerged into tribal and communal life and became an agrarian, he found that instincts told him nothing of how to plant and when to harvest, how to provide for the future. But the instinctual energies could be made to serve the social acts of preservation. By an act of will the "lower" levels of response could be made to

[11] Charles Darwin, *The Expression of the Emotions in Man and Animals*, Philosophical Library, Inc., New York, 1955, p. 356: "most of our expressive actions are innate or instinctive. . . ."

serve the "higher" levels.[12] His emotions could be collected and channeled toward useful and economic ends. Primitive man's language was rich in words that had acquired emotional associations. These words were chanted in unison and their effect was collective—work went more smoothly and hearts were lightened. These collective emotions pervade primitive societies, where social cohesion is strong. In modern society, which is highly differentiated, collective emotions are dissipated. Nevertheless modern man carries his collective emotions into solitude, and there he sings his songs, which are stirred by his collective images, his race memories. Collective emotions, because they are highly generalized and shared by all, can be given a degree of objectivity. They can be located objectively in phenomena like storms or sunsets. It is possible to say that the objects arouse the emotions. Modern man has separated himself from nature and has given primacy to his rational view of the world; he has individualized himself out of his earlier communal irrationality.

Poetry recreates the "I" not in the individual sense so much as in the social sense. The emotional world of poetry is everyman's world—the objects in that world are aesthetic because they are socialized, disinterested, and objective. It is the communal aspect of the emotions invoked by poetry that gives us the experience of an aesthetic emotion.[13]

The tensions between the universal and the individual characterize literature as do the tensions between the rational and the instinctive or intuitive. Emotions are sure to arise wherever tensions prevail in human experience. So long as the literature proves its greatness by its power to hold in balance the universal and the individual, the rational and the instinctive, the social and the personal, there will be an emotional aura of pleasurable ex-

---

[12] See Chap. 5, pp. 56–57.

[13] Christopher Caudwell, *Illusion and Reality: A Study of the Sources of Poetry*, The Macmillan Company, New York, 1937. For an extensive discussion of the characteristics of poetry as they derive from an economic-social interpretation of primitive life see chap. 7, pp. 133–148.

citement. That peculiar aura can be referred to as an aesthetic emotion or feeling.

Emotions regarded as expressions of inhibited primitive adaptive behavior are seen to have social value.[14] Civilized man has learned the value of taking the word for the deed, and likewise the emotion for the adaptive act. Certainly the reader who has an awareness of the social value of the expressive forms of emotions will quickly learn the aesthetic value of those forms in his appreciation of literature.

If the aesthetic contemplation of an emotion leads by a "species of reaction" to a gradual induction of the genuine or social emotion in the reader, there is a danger that the reader may find himself *more* than half *in* life and that his reading experience will become somewhat sentimentalized. If, however, the reader's imitation of emotional behavior which he undergoes in the aesthetic contemplation of the emotions in the text leaves him *more* than half *out* of life, he may find his reading experience somewhat mechanical and remote.

The notion that emotions can be induced even as one contemplates the emotions expressed in the literature may seem to be absurd—contemplation and emotion seem mutually exclusive. William James describes the genesis of emotions in such a way as to relate intimately the exercise of the conscious will with the seemingly spontaneous generation of an emotion or feeling. He says [15] "that *the bodily changes follow directly the perception of the exciting fact, and that our feeling of the same changes as they occur* is *the emotion.*"

In life the perception of the exciting fact *does* in some satisfactory way result in an emotional condition, if we are normally receptive or sympathetic. In literature very often we are considerably less disturbed than the characters in the text, and we feel that this is as it should be. We have no intention of being ruffled or upset, and even healthy laughter may, perhaps, be sup-

---

[14] Darwin, *op. cit.,* chap. 1, "General Principles of Expression."
[15] William James, *Psychology,* The World Publishing Company, Cleveland, 1948, p. 375.

pressed for the sake of those around us. We face, of course, the likelihood of being more *out* of life than is proper for a full aesthetic experience.

It is possible that we find it difficult to sympathize fully with the characters in the text (and it should never be *easy* if literature is to stretch us to the fullest realization of what we may be) when they differ from us in some marked fashion. Sympathy may, nevertheless, be gained if we are willing to *learn* the emotional ways of the characters. We learn by imitation; we copy the manifest behavior of the characters in a symbolic fashion, and that often gives us the emotion itself. William James confirms [16] this view: "any voluntary and cold-blooded arousal of the so-called manifestations of a special emotion should give us the emotion itself." You can verify the truth of James's statement by a few simple experiments. Hang your head, sigh and mope, speak in a sober voice with the corners of your mouth drawn down slightly, drag your feet and a melancholy mood will settle over you. On the other hand, refuse to express a passion and it dies. Whistling in the dark is more than a figure of speech.

Summary

If it is true that literature is interested in attitudes and motives in human experience, then the emotions that give force to those attitudes and motives are of special interest to the reader. When the reader is an *oral* reader, he finds in his gestures, postural sets, vocal intonations, and even his silence an activity that may speak louder than the words, an evaluative technique that may transcend the lexical meaning of the words. If the reader fears the charge of sentimentality, let him be no less afraid of emotional impotence.

The aesthetic experience of literature is the experience of an organized linguistic construct which both pleases and interests, and which is distanced from life to the degree that it does not raise questions of practicality. It both articulates and objectifies feeling by providing in the work of art an "objective correlative."

[16] *Ibid.,* p. 382.

The two *enemies* are (1) practicality and (2) habit, operative along lines once laid down by practicality.[17]

If the reader is to have a satisfactory aesthetic experience, one which is half in life and half in literature, he must, in addition to his intellectual realization, enjoy an emotional participation. Oral reading is the surest way to an affective experience of literature.

Exercises

1. On page 43 there is a discussion of the reader's emotional response to literature, its appropriateness or inappropriateness. You would not, of course, giggle at Ophelia's mad scene, but perhaps you do have emotional dispositions that are inappropriate to the literary experience. It would be understandable if you smiled at the wounded Scarus, who says to Antony in Shakespeare's *Antony and Cleopatra,* "I have yet / Room for six scotches more." It is not an appropriate moment for the reader to smile or laugh, but if he does, it is because the association of *scotch* with *whisky* is more immediate and stronger than his association of the word with *cut.* Be alert to instances of your own inappropriate responses to literature, and try to assign reasons for inappropriateness.

2. It is not likely that you are immune to sentimentality. We all have our particular susceptibility. With some it is the appearance in literature of a dog or a baby that triggers the sentimental response. Examine your own reactions to discover what it is in literature that leads you to a sentimental response. It is important to your critical development to be able to recognize your weakness for certain sentimentalities.

[17] For a fuller discussion of matters relating to the definition of the aesthetic experience treated in this paragraph see René Wellek and Austin Warren, *Theory of Literature,* 2d ed., Harcourt, Brace and Company, Inc., New York, 1956, p. 231. T. S. Eliot in his essay on *Hamlet* suggests that the only way to express emotion in literature is by finding an "objective correlative," that is, "a set of objects, a situation, a chain of events which shall be the formula of that particular emotion." In other words, the aesthetic experience of a feeling or emotion must be *indirect.* The emotion itself is evoked by the reader's apprehension of the circumstances (objects, situation, chain of events) which the literary text presents as the objective correlative.

3. If it is generally true that good literature establishes its emotional tone indirectly (see page 49), test the validity of the generalization by examining D. H. Lawrence's "Snake" (pages 229 to 231). How does the poet induce the proper emotional response without directly specifying the emotion by verbal references? Consider other poems with this question in mind.

4. Read a poem aloud. Do you find that your activity speaks louder than the words (see pages 301 to 305)? Does it interfere with the proper understanding of the poem? In what ways does it interfere? How could your activity be altered to sharpen your realization of the meaning of the poem?

5

Personality and Literature

*T*oo often literature is regarded as a form of social criticism, a prescription for moral betterment. Literature has its uses, to be sure, but it is dangerous to see those uses as active directives for improved behavior. Literature works best by indirection; it shows descriptively what men are by showing what men do. If the reader infers from the literature he reads that men had better mend their ways, that is an inference to which he is entitled, but it must be recognized as *ex*trinsic or derivative. Literature, by nature, is not didactic; it is not preceptive.

The discussion thus far has emphasized the primal nature of man's adaptive and emotional behavior. It has been shown that the primary data of man's biological nature are indeed the subject matter of literature as well as the roots of his spiritual and social evolution. *But such an emphasis is justified only if it is regarded as a corrective.* As social beings we are more conscious of the governing action of the higher cortical centers than of the demands of the lower visceral centers. We have too quickly forgotten that man is *still* a biological animal whose higher neural centers *serve* his lower visceral centers. This may not be a very flattering view of humanity, but it is necessary that we adopt it if we are to evaluate properly the increasing complexities of civilized life.

To speak of man as "merely biological" is no more accurate than to speak of him as "merely spiritual." Man *is* a biological animal, but he has been undergoing a spiritualizing process for thousands of years, a process that has encouraged the optimistic view of man as a perfectible being. Christianity has sought to rescue man from the tyranny of his biological nature. It is certainly clear that civilization is moving from a biological phase into a psychosocial phase. The biological phase (when hunting, fishing, fighting, and mating were more directly related to survival and the means of satisfaction were simply physical) is being replaced by a psychological (that is, repressive and expressive emotional interpretation of the fundamental realities) and a social or cooperative interpretation of human relationships. Malformed infants are no longer exposed on the hillside to die, they are no longer the victims of their fateful biological condition. Today, infant welfare and modern medicine *cooperate socially* to encompass the child's physical and individual disabilities. Today, human mating is *primarily* a psychosocial ritual and *secondarily* a biological reality. The natural ends are of smaller concern than the means. Courtship is a complication of the means; economic and social security are preparatory steps to the penultimate act of marriage, which has become a matter both religious and civil. Human behavior is relatively simple in the ultimate satisfaction of its basic needs but manifests infinite variety and ingenuity in the ways and means of bringing men and women to the final propinquity. The female runs the gamut of wiles from the clinging vine to the unapproachable, and the male from the cave man to the idolater.

The consequences of the shift from the biological phase to the psychosocial are far-reaching and cannot be fully examined here. The tensions created by the shift are seen most vividly, perhaps, in the nineteenth century, when the perfectibility of man was challenged by the findings of Darwin and Freud. They brought men back to a sharp awareness of the continuity of their biological natures; they opened the way for a more tragic view of life by emphasizing the *im*perfectibility of man. The Christian hope of salvation, redemption, and final grace was opposed by the inevitable and immutable biological nature of man. Survival and the gratification of instinctual drives were seen to be the laws of life by Darwin and Freud. Society and culture were organized to inhibit the aggressive and destructive passions of the biological individual.

Opposed to Freud's view is the notion sponsored by Rousseau—man is fundamentally good, moral, and even innocent, while society is the source of evil in him. In man's "natural" state he would be noble, benign, and perfect; in a social state man becomes corrupted and enslaved. Freud insists that man's trouble lies deep in himself and is not the consequence of adverse social conditions.[1] It may be that the human self can never be fully realized except socially; no more can the socialized self prosper without coming to terms with its biological nature.

If Freud showed us that human life was nasty, brutish, and short, and had always been, he was only holding the mirror up to our own faces, saying what the great philosophers and the great tragic writers have always said. If we are serious, our reaction to this bitter truth is neither to evade it with one or another anodyne, nor to kill ourselves, but to set out humbly through the great tragic rhythm of pride and fall, so curiously alike in psychoanalysis and literature. At the end of this hard road we can see faintly beckoning that self-knowledge without which, we are assured on good authority, we live as meanly as the ants.[2]

The pursuit of self-knowledge is dangerous and arduous, but it is a game well worth the candle. Nature sets the game in

---

[1] For a fuller discussion of these conflicting views see Will Herberg, "Freud, The Revisionists, and Social Reality," and Stanley Edgar Hyman, "Psychoanalysis and the Climate of Tragedy," in Benjamin Nelson (ed.), *Freud and the Twentieth Century*, Meridian Books, Inc., New York, 1957, pp. 143-163, 167-185.

[2] Hyman, *op. cit.*, p. 185. Quoted by permission of the publishers.

action and society makes the rules. Though winning and losing are important, man's interest in human behavior looks beyond the results and shows greater enthusiasm for the elaboration of the rules and the individual styles of the players. Literature takes the same interest; it takes great pains to imitate accurately the actions of men in social environments. While it remains true that literature looks *through* the surface of life into the depths of human motivation, where lie the hidden springs of natural impulse, it is no less true that literature makes a thorough examination of the refracting surface of social action. It is the *process* of achieving goals that interests human beings more than achievement itself. It is in the process of living that human personality is fashioned.

It is the individual differences among human beings as they are shaped by the dynamics of social experience that constitute *personality*. The term personality refers loosely to those qualities which distinguish one person from another. It is true that a man resembles *all* other men in some respects; that is, he shares with them a heart, a head, two legs, etc. He resembles *some* other men in that he is a father, an American, a plumber, etc. Finally, he resembles *no other* men in that his size, weight, name, address, occupation, etc., all add up to a unique individual with a perfectly distinguishable set of fingerprints.

The physical make-up or constitution of an individual plays an important part in the formation of his personality. Inheritance through the chromosomes accounts for a great many constitutional differences, ranging in importance from sex to eye color. Physical differences are no less important in the development of personality than psychological differences. The nervous system, for instance, is of immense importance in establishing patterns of personality.

Social conditioning is quick to modify the constitutional disposition of the individual, however. The rules of the game impose such restrictions on the free exercise of human nature that no individual can ever be said to act "naturally." It is at once the pain and the pride of human beings that they survive and even prosper under the conflicting laws of their biological nature and their civilized nurture. Every man has a second life in dreams, imagination, and the unconscious memories of prelife, perhaps— a vision of what he is but can never be.

Literature dramatizes for man the nature and destiny of his secret life by rendering its social surface in such a way as to *expose* the inner process. Literature uses selection, clarification, and intensification in the interest of making manifest the inner workings of the soul, the heart, and the mind of human beings. In Part 2 there will be a detailed examination of the literary devices that authors use to accomplish selection, clarification, and intensification.

Personality in a loose sense is an adaptive function of men as social beings. The automatic and compulsory life of the biological organism loses its command over the animal with the development of the central nervous system. A highly differentiated nervous system makes it possible for the individual to exercise inhibitory control over the instinctive patterns of reaction. Choices can be made, immediate pleasures can be deferred in the interest of greater future rewards. With the coming of freedom of choice as a result of the discriminating processes of the central nervous system, it can be said that the individual exercising that freedom has a consciousness. The unconscious life of the biological organism is not lost, but it is modified and controlled to an extent that makes social life possible. When the personality fails in its function, as it does when crimes of passion are committed by otherwise normal, decent citizens, it is because the instinctual life of the individual is no longer under the inhibitory control of the ego or super-ego.

As man passes from the biological phase of evolution into the psychosocial phase, communal experience and organized systems of knowledge determine for him *how* he will adapt to his environment, if not *why*. Unlike other animals, man is no longer content to meet his environment as he finds it but has learned to create artificial environments—physical, social, and mental.

The passage from the biological phase into the psychosocial has not, by any means, been completed, and any satisfactory definition of personality will recognize the process of the socialization of the individual's biological behavior. A definition that emphasizes the biosocial aspects of human experience sees *personality* as *"the dynamic organization of interlocking behavior systems that each of us develops through learning processes, as he grows from a biological newborn to a biosocial adult in an environment of other individuals and cultural products."* [3]

Literature is interested in everything that shapes human destiny, everything that human beings value. Dramatic literature shows a social interest in human affairs because it represents characters in action in an environment where conflicts are invoked. Even lyric poetry, for all its personal subjectivity, often implies a social setting in that there is a suggested situation with a speaker and a listener. Literature expresses a fundamental interest in the unique ways of the individual, in his management of himself and his environment for the satisfaction of his needs, in his conflicts with others as he pursues his ends. Life and literature meet in their common interest—*the forming and testing of personality*. Even *not in itself* a moderate understanding of literature depends upon a working knowledge of the forms and patterns of the psychological life, of man's capacities for interpretation, appreciation, and organization. To gain this knowledge, it will be necessary to consider, at the very least, the self-conscious level of human experience, where the psychosocial aspects of the environment will shape and modify personality.

A sensible objection might be raised at this point. Since life in the individual is continuous, while the life history of a fictional personality is intermittent, how can we rely on knowledge of the former to illuminate the latter? The answer may be stated this way: As in literature, so in life, we must be content with a just *sufficient* formulation of the *complete* formulation of a personality, since a complete formulation either in life or in literature

---

[3] Norman Cameron, *The Psychology of Behavior Disorders: A Biosocial Interpretation*, Houghton Mifflin Company, Boston, 1947, p. 16. Quoted by permission of the publishers.

is impossible. Still it may be asked—sufficient for what? In literature the answer is found in the aesthetic needs of the design of the story; in life the answer is found in the necessity for explaining a given set of facts, predicting future behavior or controlling delinquent behavior. In literature there is little interest in the prediction and control of behavior, but there is considerable in the description and explanation of behavior. Despite improvement in techniques of analysis, there is still little reliance on introspection for evidence of how the personality is formed or how it functions. We are still largely dependent on inferences made from its manifestations in words and other overt acts. These are the very conditions which dramatists and novelists depend on for revealing their fictional personalities.

It would be a mistake to say that there is *no* difference between the personalities met in a literary text and those we meet in life, but there is a danger in concluding that experiences evoked by the works of literature are, as such, distinct from other human experiences. It is as Stella Benson [4] says: "People made of skin and bones are just as incredible as people made out of ink and paper." Arthur Koestler, the novelist, has explored the relationship between the real and the fictional character by examining the way in which we "image" real people, and he concludes,[5] "... the images of *real people* in our memory are not as different from our images of *fictional characters* as we generally believe."

The problems of understanding characters in literature are little different from those of understanding one's friends. In life as in literature, people may be unpredictable or they may be altogether predictable. The law of literature requires that the light of understanding illuminate the inexplicable and make all plausible. In life such conditions are desirable, but not always attainable. Yet the only difference between life and literature at this point

[4] Quoted by Frederic Wertham, "The Dreams That Heal," *New Republic*, Nov. 3, 1947, p. 26.

[5] Arthur Koestler, "The Novelist Deals with Character," *Saturday Review of Literature*, Jan. 1, 1949, p. 31.

is that life does not always allow one to see the pertinent evidence, whereas literature must. Getting to know people through direct experience of them is a lengthy process. It takes time to see people with their changing faces meeting changes in their environment. It takes time to test the generalizations that are so quick to form on first meeting. In life it is a matter of days and months and maybe years before one can be satisfied that he knows for certain some major aspects of his friend's personality. In literature there is neither time nor space for infinite elaboration; evidence must be carefully selected and credibility must be gained through the author's skill in revealing key traits in his characters during significant actions. The reader then builds on this framework, using the laws of personality that say there is congruence in the behavior patterns of human beings. It has been seriously suggested by a reputable psychologist [6] that "a man's conduct at any given moment, his every action, is an expression of the whole man, and ... should enable us to interpret the whole man."

It may be that there *are* forms of action which reveal the whole man in a flash, and it is certain that *some* gifted observers are able to obtain a fairly complete picture of a person from a few brief observations. It is the function of a gifted writer to place his characters in such situations as will bare a character's nature unmistakably. On the other hand, it is the part of the reader to fill out the picture of a character from his brief observations of that character's behavior—behavior which is expressive of individual differences, and hence characteristic. Such behavior is the hallmark of character and reveals quality.

Whether a man's behavior is adaptive, emotional, or conventional, individual differences appear. The individual differences constitute expressive behavior. Infants give the impression of consistency, of being one like the other, because their patterns of behavior are diffused; that is, there is a uniformity in the behavior of all infants. As children mature, differentiation takes place and individualized behavior appears. *A* may sit quietly with a book,

[6] Rudolph Allers, *The Psychology of Character,* trans. with intro. by E. B. Strauss, Sheed & Ward, Inc., New York, 1943, p. 8.

while *B* climbs the walls. As adults, *A* may speak softly, use a gentle handshake, cough silently with his hand over his mouth, close the door quietly; *B* may speak loudly, use more pressure in his handshake, make a loud noise coughing, bang the door. The individual differences between *A* and *B* are apparent in the catalogue of their behaviors, but there is a consistency and uniformity in the behavior patterns within *A* and within *B*. Where there is complete congruence or complete individuality in the expressive movements of *A* or *B*, the personality is integrated and harmonious. Where congruence is lacking (if *B* were to speak loudly and have a *weak* handshake) the personality is unintegrated and the expressive movement self-contradictory.[7]

Literature is interested in both types of characters—the integrated and the unintegrated. When the characters in a literary work are true to type, thoroughly uniform and consistent in their behavior, the work is likely to be allegorical. Characters in most farces and melodramas are entirely predictable once their qualities have been established in the play. Minor characters in prose fiction are likely to be consistent in their behavior, and it is proper that they be so, for they might otherwise distract the reader's attention from the main concerns of the principal figures in the story. Farces and melodramas are generally peopled with uncomplicated characters whose behavior is thoroughly predictable under given circumstances. The complications in such literature are to be found in the plot structure rather than in the psychology of the characters.

In comedy and tragedy one is more likely to find the disturbed, maladjusted, unintegrated personalities who are in conflict with themselves or the social forces that impinge upon them. In the major characters there is almost certain to be contradictory behavior that surprises the reader to some degree. It is proper in comedy or tragedy that the behavior of some principal figure may contradict expectation, but when it does, it must ultimately be explicable, it can never be incomprehensible. Life frequently

[7] Gordon W. Allport and P. E. Vernon, *Studies in Expressive Movement,* The Macmillan Company, New York, 1933, p. 182.

presents us with the inexplicable, but it is the function of literature that the behavior of the characters must, within the limits of art, be lawful.

Characters who never disappoint our expectations, whose behavior is thoroughly reliable, have been called "flat," and those who are capable of behaving in an unexpected fashion which is nevertheless explicable have been called "round." [8]

The creative reader will inevitably extend his attitudinal sympathies and empathies beyond the letter of the patterns set for him by the author because a character that lives for the reader in the pages of a book excites in him visions and speculations about the character beyond the immediate plot needs. It may be a fault that he wonders what course of study Hamlet took at Wittenberg, since the answer to that is nowhere to be found in the play and therefore has no function in his understanding of Hamlet himself; but to say, on the other hand, that the reader has *only* the author's given facts about any character is equally mistaken. Take only the physical features of a major character as given by an author and it will be found that they do not, by any means, add up to a whole human being. If one reads with care and consideration for the laws of consistency in personality, there should be no trouble in filling out the selected details given by the author. The reader relies upon some degree of unity in personality, and he is assured that this unity is reflected in expression and that "for this reason, acts and habits of expression show a certain consistency among themselves." [9]

If human relations are happier than we have any right to expect, in view of their complexity and the margin for error, we have the law of consistency to thank. Social understanding depends to a considerable extent on the reliability of judgments of personality traits and the predictability of human actions. When judgments are faulty and expectations are disappointed, wherein

[8] E. M. Forster, *Aspects of the Novel*, Harcourt, Brace and Company, Inc., New York, 1927. For a discussion of flat and round characters see chap. 4.

[9] Werner Wolff, *The Expression of Personality: Experimental Depth Psychology*, Harper & Brothers, New York, 1943, p. 171.

lies the failure? Is the law of consistency unreliable; are judgments of character too often refracted through the prejudice and bias of the observer? Dr. Werner Wolff has conducted experiments to discover the reliability of forms of expression as indices of personality traits. He observed that people often describe the behavior of others in terms that refer to personality traits. If, for example, a man is seen to smile or laugh, the tendency for the observer to describe him as "happy" is almost universal. This tendency indicates that people generally feel that there is a close relation between the external and the internal personality. The generalization is reinforced by Dr. Wolff's finding that different people seem to agree in their descriptions of the same form of expression. The similarity in the descriptive terms would suggest a similarity of response, though some correction of this notion will be offered later.

There is a degree, then, to which an author can rely upon his readers to have a uniform response to his characters. But an author's lot is not always a happy one in this regard; readers are sometimes intolerant of conflicting behaviors in a character; they resent ambiguities and unresolved complexities. Readers will sometimes *force* congruence on a character whose behavior is deliberately designed by the author to be incongruent. Such readers often make the mistake of projecting onto the writer's work their own predispositions. Projection is dangerous because the writer depends on a reader's willingness to submit to his influence for the duration of the poem, story, or play, so that these literary works may have their way with the reader. On the other hand, insistence that a text mean one thing for all readers will strangle the imaginative play of suggested or implied meanings, the tangential influence of ambiguous interpretations. A writer depends upon the existence of a large area of commonality in the interpretation of human behavior, but his work is the richer for suggesting a variety of interpretations within the limits set by the congruence of human personality.

It is a common experience to be deceived by outward appearances; characters are not always the same on the outside as they are on the inside, and readers must be on their guard against such deceptions. What is more difficult for a reader to accomplish is to get at the true personality when both the overt and private behavior mask the real personality. Often in life it is a task for the psychiatrist; but in literature good writers sometimes give us levels of characterization that permit us to see into the unconscious reality of the human beings they characterize.

The fact that people will agree that a man is happy because he is smiling or laughing means that there is an element of objective reliability in the word *happy* as a description of the man. But it must be remembered that there may be a subjective implication in *happy;* perhaps, when one person uses the word, there is a reference to the virtuous elements in happiness, which are then assigned to the smiling man, but when another person speaks of him as happy, the implication may be that the man is a fool. The reason for the divergent implications may be that the first observer is philanthropic, while the second observer is misanthropic.

The importance for readers of recognizing the subjective aspect of the vocabulary of personality traits is the warning it posts against uncritical acceptance of the descriptions offered by certain characters of the behavior of other characters. Such warning may be unnecessary for those who are already familiar with the social axiom which reads: If you want to find out the truth about Johnny, don't ask his mother. The implication is that Johnny's mother, who should know him best, knows him least.

But even in the narration of a fiction or the personal revelation of a lyric there is an unconscious or perhaps conscious disposition to use the subjective vocabulary. The important thing is that in direct expressions of genuine attitudes, lyric or narrative, there may be "hidden" references to the real personality that underlies the overt *and* the private personality.

A novelist knows that personality is manifold, and he would not content himself with a single descriptive term to establish a character. Nor is he content with a simple enumeration of characteristics. He presents situations in which a trait obtains its definition in relationship to many determinants. A living picture of a personality requires the entrance of the reader into a mood and a psychic condition of receptivity which it is the responsibility of the author to create.

In the large sense a personality is the result of an integration of the physical and psychological processes of the individual. The purpose of such integration is usually designated by social psychologists as *tension reduction*.[10] The tensions develop from a failure on the part of the individual to adjust satisfactorily to his environment or, perhaps, from a failure of his organs to function efficiently because of disease or abuse. There are two important exceptions to this generalization: the desire for food and the desire for sexual pleasure develop independently of environmental stimulus; hence the tensions arise, not from failure to adjust to the environment or from functional failures of the organs, but simply from the dynamic nature of the organs involved. The tensions created—whatever their cause—are often cultivated in anticipation of the pleasure attendant on their release. Tensions of fatigue, for example, are often induced by deliberate exercise in order that the individual may better enjoy a rest.

Apparently a tensionless state of static contentment does not suit men. They want to be engaged continuously in the process of reducing tensions and achieving satisfaction and contentment. They will deliberately develop tensions so that they may have the joy of reducing them.

References to tensions as fundamental to the function of personality suggest an analogy to literature, for it, too, is dependent on tensions, in the form of conflict, suspense, climax, crisis, etc. Personality in its dynamic interpretation is a process of integration; literature is an integrative process, too. Personality is forever adjusting internal demands to external opportunities. If a person becomes sluggish under the impact of dulling monotony, literature provides him with significant forms of symbolic action. The reader enters into an exercise in adaptability and role assumption

[10] Clyde Kluckhohn and Henry A. Murray (eds.), *Personality in Nature, Society, and Culture*, Alfred A. Knopf, Inc., New York, 1949, pp. 12–16.

under controlled conditions. His attitudinal postures do not commit him to a practical identification with the characters or situations, for he realizes that the environments and the characters are only symbolically designated. The necessity of the active reader to submit to the characterizations of a number of different characters makes it inevitable that he will maintain some objectivity, for he will see himself in each of the characters as he views them through different eyes.

It should be remembered that personality in literature is expressed, not only in fictional characters, but also in terms of the author, who often expresses *himself* in lyric poetry or in prose narration. Bonamy Dobrée recognizes among the delights of reading the special delight of coming in contact with the author's personality. His view of the experience is that we hear the author's voice through his style. Dobrée compares two prose passages, one from *Lay Thoughts of a Dean* by Dean Inge and the other from the Preface to *John Bull's Other Island* by George Bernard Shaw: [11]

...how wide apart the voices are! Dean Inge, with the suspicion of a pulpit drone, speaks with a level flow, on the slow side (he is a little fatigued we feel) giving a slight air of portentous solemnity by ending the clause or the sentence on a long syllable...he likes the "dying fall." Mr. Shaw, on the other hand, speaks with a lively voice; there is no fatigue there; it is all vigour. The prose is swift; you naturally raise and drop your voice as you read it; there is no sense of solemnity, though it is serious enough, and Mr. Shaw prefers to end the clause or sentence sharply, like a hammer-tap, or rattle....

Dobrée's appreciation of the differences in the two passages is highly impressionistic, and the recognition of the differences of style as a matter of differences in voice is surely metaphorical—and yet he says of Shaw's prose that "you naturally raise and drop your voice as you read it." The suggestion here is that the notion of style as voice is something more than metaphorical. The inference is that if you read aloud you will "naturally" transform

[11] Bonamy Dobrée, *Modern Prose Style,* Oxford University Press, New York, 1934, p. 13. Quoted by permission of the Clarendon Press, Oxford.

written style into vocal style and so make plain to yourself the character or personality of the author. Dobrée [12] advises the reader to "listen for the voice which betrays individuality, the personality which no writer who goes to work honestly can keep out of anything he writes...."

Summary

The view of life maintained here is largely that of the behaviorist. The character of human activity, whether mental or emotional, has been seen as fundamentally motor. The avenues of experience for the individual have been characterized as "attitudinal"; that is, to learn something about an object, it is necessary to assume the attitude of the object (animate or inanimate). To discover the true nature of a man's behavior is to understand *him*. The structure of human personality follows essentially the same laws in life and literature; consequently, the participator in life and the reader of literature alike adopt the attitudinal method of appreciation and realization. One strong advantage in regarding life and literature from the social behaviorist's point of view is that the reader of literature *participates* in the experience of reading literature; he no longer takes a static position on the periphery of the text. The reading of literature, like the writing of it, becomes an active revelation rather than a passive toleration.

Exercises

1. From the point of view expressed in this chapter describe in what sense you find literature satisfactory or unsatisfactory as a source of knowledge. Is the knowledge essential to or incidental to the function of the literature?

2. Examine your own constitutional characteristics, and evaluate their cultural modifications. Do the same for a character you are studying in prose fiction, drama, or poetry.

[12] *Ibid.*, p. 14.

3. Do you recognize inconsistencies in your own behavior in life? Can you offer explanations for any or all of them?

4. Consider the ways in which your personality adjusts its internal demands to external opportunities (see page 68). Then consider how some character in literature adjusts his internal demands to external opportunities.

PART 2

The Nature of Literature

6

ℒiterature and ℰxperience

𝒮INCE THE TIME of Aristotle, criticism has been plagued with the word *imitation*. *Plagued* is quite the correct word, because *imitation* refuses to be put out of the vocabulary of critics even though some critics are beyond measure allergic to it.

It is not a bad word. Indeed, since we must find *some* word to serve the purpose which *imitation* has often served, perhaps we should agree to let this word stand. But we must make it our servant and not our master if it is to be useful to us.

Thus far we have talked about experience as it affects the individual and his growth. From this point on, the problem is: How is the experience of an individual (in this case, the poet [1]) expressed through or in the words which the individual uses to describe it?

The point of view assumed here is that the experience is lodged symbolically in the words through which the poet tries to re-present the experience. This act of re-presenting is what we shall

---

[1] It is convenient, and traditional, to use the word *poet* to refer to the writer of either prose or poetry. A poet is a maker.

call *imitation*. In this sense, art imitates life. Indeed, life in its most general sense is all that poetry *can* imitate. Words as symbols can have meaning only when they refer to experience.

Modification of Experience

This does not mean that poetry seeks literally to reproduce life—at least not necessarily, though it may also try to do this. The poet may perfectly properly try as exactly as he can to duplicate his view of, say, sunrise on Mount Shasta in July. What we must remember is that *his* view of Mount Shasta on such an occasion, if he really succeeds in presenting it sharply and fully, is necessarily in some respects distinct from ours, since the experience of one individual can never precisely duplicate that of another individual. What we really get, in the poet's imitation of the sunrise in this case, is a reflection of the scene as it *appears* to the poet, with the particular shades and colors and memories which he images as he looks at the mountain; if he is a good poet, his view will probably tell us things which we should never have seen for ourselves, and we find his view richer than our own— or, if not that, we find the combination of his view and ours richer than ours alone would have been. While we may sensibly speak of the poet's imitation of the scene, we must remember that the scene which he re-presents is only in part a representation of what lies *before* his eyes; it is also in part a creation from what lies *behind* his eyes, in the womb of the brain, the fertile storehouse of all his past experience. It is the coming together of the present and the past which gives birth to the particular experience (compounded of both) which we call the poem. The words of the poem are a fixative, capable of holding, symbolically, the particular coalescence of past and present memories which otherwise would escape into the flux of experience.

Furthermore, it is possible for the poet to imitate things which are quite unlike a visible sunrise on Mount Shasta. He may imitate dreams; he may imitate fancies; he may imitate actions which have taken place far back in the historical past. Here, for example, is a poem, "Rondeau" (an *imitation*), by the English poet Leigh Hunt (1784–1859):

> Jenny kissed me when we met,
>   Jumping from the chair she sat in;
> Time, you thief, who love to get
>   Sweets into your list, put that in:
> Say I'm weary, say I'm sad,
>   Say that health and wealth have missed me,
> Say I'm growing old, but add,
>   Jenny kissed me.

It is said that the "real" Jenny was Jane, the wife of Thomas Carlyle. Leigh Hunt had been ill for several weeks, and Mrs. Carlyle had been seriously worried about him. When, one day, he suddenly appeared at her home, well again, she impulsively jumped up and kissed him. The poem is said to have been based on this incident. But the experience which results from Hunt's re-presenting of this literal experience is both less than and more than the original experience. It is less because it does not give us all the details of the original; it is more because, while it gives us *some* of these details, it involves more than the immediate pleasure of being kissed by Jenny. It creates a whole new environment for the experience and involves attitudes which may well not have been in the original experience at all. In this sense, the poem is creative even while it imitates, because it is imitating something other than the immediate experience of being kissed by Jenny. We do not need to know that Jenny was Jane Welsh Carlyle—that detail becomes irrelevant to an appreciation of the poem, though for students of English literature it is a very interesting irrelevancy. Poems are not to be used as documents in the biography of poets unless one is interested in something other than poetry—in personal history, let us say, or social history. We learn nothing of *essential* value to the poem by learning that it was suggested by an incident in Hunt's immediate experience.

But the poem does necessitate our paying attention to certain unique details. The speaker ("me"), who need not be identified with the poet at all, has been kissed by Jenny, who had been sitting in her chair when he came in. The kiss is enough to weigh heavily in the balance against such melancholy possibilities as weariness, sadness, ill-health, need, and increasing years. What we do in reading the poem is to move from the particular experience to the generalization that Time, that old thief, cannot take away such memories as Jenny's kiss, though the kiss itself remains in time past. In this way, man defeats Time. The poem begins and ends with the *particular* statement "Jenny kissed me," but between the two lines come the reflections which make all the difference between the weight of the first line and the weight of the last. The poem ends in a return to the opening statement (that is why it is called a rondeau), but the *experience* does not return to the opening statement because it is now modified by all that intervenes. The poem is dynamic, and it is at once particular and universal: a *concrete universal.*[2]

The experience of defeating Time through happy memories is just as real, just as true, just as "accurate" as the experience of being kissed by Jenny. Hence it is fair to say that the poet is imitating experience of both kinds. But by bringing the two experiences together into a new poetic experience, he is *distorting* the particular event in life which prompted the poem. Poets and poems always distort life. Art in general distorts life by both adding to it and abstracting from it. One of the pleasures of poetry is that poems bring order and meaning to experiences which often in real life seem to have little of either.

There is, of course, much else to be said about Leigh Hunt's "Rondeau." We have only begun to indicate the things which give the poem its particular values. But while you may find it profitable in your discussions in class to look now at other aspects of the whole experience of the poem, we will move on to another poem to examine once more the relationship between "real life" and poem.

[2] The phrase is used by W. K. Wimsatt, Jr., in an essay included in his book *The Verbal Icon,* University of Kentucky Press, Lexington, Ky., 1954, pp. 69-83.

Point of View as Modification

In "Song," by Sir John Suckling (1609–1642), we have again a dramatic situation involving a man and a woman. But here the speaker is not the happy man who has been kissed, but someone trying to soften the griefs of a melancholy lover who has apparently *not* been kissed.

> Why so pale and wan, fond lover?
>   Prithee, why so pale?
> Will, when looking well can't move her,
>   Looking ill prevail?
>   Prithee, why so pale?
>
> Why so dull and mute, young sinner?
>   Prithee, why so mute?
> Will, when speaking well can't win her,
>   Saying nothing do't?
>   Prithee, why so mute?
>
> Quit, quit, for shame, this will not move:
>   This cannot take her.
> If of herself she will not love,
>   Nothing can make her:
>   The devil take her!

Here it is again the matter of what has happened between the man and the woman (or rather, in this instance, what has *not* happened) which provides the initial movement for the poem. But again the experience in the poem shifts its center—this time not to the man involved in the event, but to the sympathetic speaker of the poem. The *point of view* through which we look at the preliminary experience is thus somewhat more objective. The poem is rhetorical in that it attempts to persuade. In "Rondeau," the speaker was looking back on an experience, so that the poem itself was an imitation of a *memory;* in "Song," the speaker is looking in on an experience. The fond lover, pale, dull, and mute, may be imagined as standing dolefully lamenting his state.

Cheer up, says our spirited speaker; if you can't win her by looking well, you certainly won't win her by looking ill. Apparently his words have no effect, and he tries again: Don't stand there with your foot in your mouth! If you can't win her by speaking well to her, you certainly won't win her by playing dumb. No response again. So the speaker begins anew with what sounds like a third attempt to make the lover more cheerful: Stop acting this way! She won't be moved by your looking ill, nor by your standing mute. If she won't love of her own free will, nothing will make her. (And then he makes the unexpected reversal:) The devil take her!

This turn at the close, with its amusingly unexpected advice to the lover to leave her to the devil, is what an earlier century would have called *wit*. It is this witty close which pulls the whole experience within the poem into focus by limiting properly for us the attitude of the speaker and thus telling us the position from which we are to view the poem. The "surprise ending," which is not a "trick ending," is one of the things which gives uniqueness to the fairly conventional experience being reported upon—unrequited love. It doesn't matter in the least whether Suckling was re-presenting a particular real-life experience. He was re-presenting, imitating, an experience common in real life, but modifying it and giving it particular point here by choosing a certain point of view, a certain attitude, by which to measure the experience. What, for example, would have happened to the poem had the last stanza been left off? The attitude of the lover must, for the sake of the poem, be brought together with a somewhat different attitude on the part of the speaker; out of this juxtaposition of a present experience with attitudes derived by the speaker from other sorts of experience comes the particular *environment* of Suckling's "Song." Like Leigh Hunt's "Rondeau," "Song" presents us with a dramatic situation, with a speaker and a person or (in "Rondeau") a personification (Time) spoken to. In "Song," of course, the presence of the person spoken to (the lover) is much more strongly felt. Indeed, it is the lack of responsiveness on the part of the lover that gives the poem its rhetorical movement, as the speaker keeps working away with his questions and amused advice.

In both the poems we have been speaking about thus far, we can grant a certain distortion in the poet's imitation of experience. All literature thus modifies experience—or almost all. It is very rare for a real-life situation to take the shape of a poem without distortion. The choice of a point of view is central to the particular modification of experience achieved by any work of art.

Extension of Experience

Much literature not only modifies but also extends experience. We have seen, in earlier chapters in the book, how vicarious a great deal of our experience is. We feel that we know, for example, through observation and report, and through knowledge of life processes, at least something of what is involved in the concept *death*. A student who had been only lightly bitten by semantics once said that we can know nothing of death until we have experienced it—and that, having experienced it, we are in no position to talk about it. Hence, he concluded, *death* is of no use to us as a word. This is the kind of nonsense semantics is meant to cure, of course, not to propagate. All of us know a good deal about things which have not in immediate fullness befallen us at all. If this kind of knowledge were not possible, the world would be in a sad way indeed. Much of man's humanity must come to him in this sense indirectly.

Here is a poem by the American poet Emily Dickinson (1830–1886):[3]

> I heard a fly buzz when I died;
>   The stillness round my form
> Was like the stillness in the air
>   Between the heaves of storm.

[3] Quoted by permission of the publishers from *Poems by Emily Dickinson*, ed. Martha Dickinson Bianchi and Alfred Leete Hampson, Little, Brown & Company, Boston, 1948, pp. 212–213.

> The eyes beside had wrung them dry,
>   And breaths were gathering sure
> For that last onset, when the king
>   Be witnessed in his power.
>
> I willed my keepsakes, signed away
>   What portion of me I
> Could make assignable,—and then
>   There interposed a fly,
>
> With blue, uncertain, stumbling buzz,
>   Between the light and me;
> And then the windows failed, and then
>   I could not see to see.

Here experience is not only modified but extended in a very real way to something the poet could not "really" have known without going through the process of dying itself. But the fact that Emily Dickinson did not have to die in order to write the poem does not mean that the experience is false or valueless. The peculiar force of the poem lies at least in part in the juxtaposition of two very common experiences: hearing the buzz of a fly, and sensing the weighted silence about the bed of one who is dying. Again the context is dramatic; there is a scene, there is a speaker. First we are introduced to the buzzing of a fly, but at almost the same moment we are introduced to the notion of death. The statement in the first line seems flatly literal: When I died, I heard the sound of a fly buzzing. The remainder of the poem is devoted to giving meaning to this simple juxtaposition of events. Down to the last line of the third stanza, the poet turns her attention to the dying: the air is still, charged with expectation; the people watching beside the bed wait with bated breath the onset of death; the last acts of the dying speaker have been performed—will written, mementos assigned to others—leaving now only the physical presence to be taken (without the active willing by the speaker) by death. And then again comes the fly, breaking the silence, interposing this small, active voice from life between the speaker and death. It seems at first *ironical* that at so solemn a moment the attention of one dying should center upon so slight and inconsequential a thing. But it is the last thing the dying person remembers. Blue, uncertain, stumbling, the buzzing creature may itself seem to the reader a little out of life; but the suggestion of weakness in the buzzing certainly underscores the failing of the speaker, and the little fly becomes the first part of "that last onset," as the light dies. Death seems thus slight, usual, insignificant on the one hand, and intensely momentous on the other—both at once. It is the irony implicit in the juxtaposition of the two experiences which gives the poem its particular freight of meaning. And it is *as if* we had experienced with the speaker the moment of death. By the experience of reading such an account we *vicariously* know something of what death might mean in such circumstances.

Juxtaposition of Experiences

It is of course not only the writer of poetry who functions in this way. A somewhat similar juxtaposition of slight and weighty experiences is achieved by John Donne (1572–1631) in his capacity as a preacher. Donne was also a poet; he came near to being the first poet to live in America, because he sought (but did not get) the position of secretary to the Virginia Company when it was reorganized for the purpose of colonizing America. Instead, Donne remained in England and eventually became Dean of St. Paul's, in London. In one of his magnificent sermons, we find this passage: [4]

When we consider with a religious seriousness the manifold weaknesses of the strongest devotions in time of Prayer, it is a sad consideration. I throw my selfe downe in my Chamber, and I call in, and invite God, and his Angels thither, and when they are there, I neglect God and his Angels, for the noise of a Flie, for the ratling of a Coach, for the whining of a doore; I talke on, in the same posture of praying; Eyes lifted up; knees bowed downe; as though I prayed to God; and,

[4] Sermon LXXX in *Eighty Sermons.*

if God, or his Angels should aske me, when I thought last of God in that prayer, I cannot tell: Sometimes I finde that I had forgot what I was about, but when I began to forget it, I cannot tell. A memory of yesterdays pleasures, a feare of tomorrows dangers, a straw under my knee, a noise in mine eare, a light in mine eye, an any thing, a nothing, a fancy, a Chimera in my braine, troubles me in my prayer. So certainely is there nothing, nothing in spirituall things, perfect in this world.

Part of our response to this piece may lie in our knowledge (which lies *outside* the text in this case) that the speaker is a distinguished dean of the Church of England. The knowledge that such a shepherd suffers from the same frailties as his flock is perhaps in itself moving. But to some readers, this view may seem naïve or commonplace.

In any event, what we are concerned with here is the way in which Donne juxtaposes the seriousness of prayer and the humdrum sounds of everyday life in such a way as to intensify the experience of *trying* to pray. The *irony* is certainly heavier here than in the poem by Emily Dickinson; the weakness of mankind in spiritual matters is the point Donne is making. The *comment* in this piece is far more explicit than the comment in the poem. While the images (that is, the sense impressions—the visual or other sense responses called forth by such details as the noise of the fly, the rattling of the coach, the whining of the door hinges, the straw under the knee, etc.) are perhaps equally sharp and precise in the two pieces, it is fair to say that Emily Dickinson relies on the images to *carry the comment,* while Donne chooses in addition to make the comment explicit. This distinction is one which may frequently be made between prose and poetry; but it is wholly inaccurate to say that this is a necessary distinction between the two forms of writing.

Imitation

So far in this chapter, we have been concerned with explaining in what sense it may be said that literature is *imitation*. It may be of interest here to quote a definition set down by Ronald S. Crane,[5] whose concern with modern interpretations of Aristotle is well known:

In the stricter sense an "imitation" is brought about whenever we succeed, by means of art, in producing an analogue of some natural process or form, endowed with similar powers to affect other things or us, in materials which are not naturally disposed to assume of themselves any such process or form; any poem can thus be said to be an "imitation" when it is sufficiently intelligible, as a concrete whole, on the assumption that the poet, in making it, was intent on using certain possibilities of language in order to create in us, by certain devices of technique, the illusion of human beings more or less like ourselves doing or undergoing something, for the sake of the emotional effects naturally evoked by such characters, passions, or actions in real life when we view them as disinterested but sympathetic spectators.

This is a carefully qualified definition—so qualified that it may for the moment seem abstruse. But Crane is as anxious to make clear what imitation does *not* mean as to make clear what it *does* mean. Imitation in this sense is not an argument for "realism" in art; it is not a denial of novelty in a poem or of creative powers in the poet. Poems as imitations may differ in their medium of imitation, in their object of imitation, and in their manner of imitation. In Crane's view of Aristotle, the degree of excellence of a poem is the degree to which it *actualizes,* "within the necessary limits of its matter," what it is by nature capable of actualizing. Unity and order and fullness of development or appropriate size are the standards by which to measure beauty in poetry. It is not the *communication* of experience but the *imitation* of experience which is the goal; communication is subsequent to and secondary to the function of the poem. The worth of the poem is not limited to the degree to which it communicates to a single and perhaps limited reader. While a reader may be too modest in assuming that his inability to understand a poem is due to his *lack* of understanding, it is also possible for a reader to be

---

[5] From *The Languages of Criticism and the Structure of Poetry,* University of Toronto Press, Toronto, 1953, p. 48. Quoted by permission.

so immodest as to ascribe to the poem itself his own limitations as a reader. While we may say of a public speech or a piece of rhetoric that it fails of its purpose if it fails to reach the audience to whom it is delivered, it is not equally clear that a poem fails if a single reader fails to grasp the fullness of its imitation. The hope in the education of literary tastes is that readers may be led to stretch and extend themselves in the act of criticism rather than to lie too soon and too comfortably boxed in by critical prejudices.

Imitation and the Texture of Poetry and Prose

It has frequently been said, and perhaps it was once truer than it seems now, that the *density* of poetry is greater than the density of prose. Another way of putting it is to say that the *texture* of poetry is *tighter* than the texture of prose. Compared with prose, that is, poetry has seemed often to contain a tighter, closer weaving of its fabric; each word in the poem has seemed to weigh more heavily, to enter more largely into the meaning than was the case with the word in prose. This is at least one of the attitudes which have frequently led people to assert that the experience of poetry is more largely emotional than the experience of prose, because its impact has seemed to them more concentrated. While, as with all generalizations, it is difficult to sustain the argument constantly, it is probably nevertheless true up to a point. It is also true that the modern short story and the modern novel have tended to move closer to the poem in their texture, so that earlier works of prose fiction often seem to us nowadays loose or thin in their fabric. Some readers, as a result, become impatient with prose fiction of earlier times; but it seems too bad to feel that prose which *differs* from ours is necessarily weaker. We are concerned here with differences between two ways of imitating experience rather than with making final value judgments, which must come after an appreciation of the respective merits of two sorts of style. It is one of the functions of education in literature to increase our taste. The reader who is so highly refined that he can no longer read anything other than *King Lear* and the Bible is not to be envied but rather to be pitied.

Two short stories are reprinted in the next few pages. One of them, from the raucous *Satyricon* of Petronius Arbiter (written sometime before A.D. 66), was a popular tale even before Petronius put his hand to it. The text given here is a translation of the Latin *Satyricon*. The other story is by one of the acknowledged masters of our own century, who has been also one of the primary influences at work in shaping the style of contemporary prose fiction. James Joyce's "Araby" is one of an integrated collection of stories called by him *Dubliners*. Read the two stories— for enjoyment! Let your critical faculties rest until you have finished reading, at least for the first time. It has been said, with no little truth, that a reader, even the critical reader, must be *receptive* before he becomes critical. Give the writer a chance to tell his story before you break in with your own ideas.

THE WIDOW OF EPHESUS [6]

A certain matron of Ephesus was so renowned for her chastity that she drew the women even of nearby nations to come and view her as a spectacle. Now when her husband died, she was not content with the ordinary customs of following the funeral train with her hair dishevelled and beating her bared bosom before the multitude, but she even followed her dead husband into the tomb, and when his body was placed in an underground vault, according to the Greek fashion, she proceeded to keep guard and to weep there night and day. As she thus afflicted herself and invited death by fasting, neither her parents nor her relatives could get her away. The city officials finally withdrew rebuffed, and this woman of unique example, lamented by all, was now prolonging her fast the fifth day. Beside her in her weariness sat a very loyal maidservant, who both patterned her tears after those of her grieving mistress and renewed, as often as it burned low, the light placed in the tomb. So there was only one topic of conversation in the whole city, and people of every class were agreed that this

[6] Quoted by permission of the publishers from the translation by Clarence A. Forbes in *Latin Literature in Translation,* by Kevin Guinagh and Alfred P. Dorjahn, Longmans, Green & Co., Inc., New York, 1946, pp. 623–625.

was the only true and shining example of love and chastity ever known.

In the meantime the governor of the province gave command for some robbers to be crucified near the chamber in which the matron was mourning over the corpse of her late husband. Now the next evening a soldier, assigned to guard the crosses so that no one should take down any of the bodies for burial, observed a light burning brightly among the tombs, heard the groaning of a mourner, and in his human weakness he was curious to know who it was or what was afoot. So he went down into the tomb and, on seeing this woman of striking beauty, at first he halted in confusion, as if it were a portent or an apparition from the infernal regions. Then as he saw the corpse lying there and marked the woman's tears and her face torn by her nails, he guessed what was indeed the truth, that she missed the dead man so intensely that her loss was too much to bear. Bringing his bit of dinner into the tomb, he began to urge the sorrowing woman not to persevere in her fruitless grief and not to rend her heart with unavailing groans. All of us, he said, have the same end and the same last home; and he added the rest of the arguments which are wont to cure despairing hearts. But she, wounded by a stranger's consolations, only smote her breast the more, and plucking out her hair she cast it on the body of the dead. Still the soldier did not give up, but with the same pleading he tried to offer the woman food, until the maidservant, tempted by the odor of the wine, first gave in and reached forth her hand to accept his proffered kindness, and then, refreshed by eating and drinking, she too began to assail her mistress' obstinacy. "What good will it do you," she said, "if you faint with hunger, if you bury yourself alive, if you throw away your spirit uncondemned, before the fates demand?

'Think you the ashes or ghosts of the buried know?'
Will you not return to life? Will you not shake off this womanish perversity and enjoy the sweets of existence as long as you may? Why, the very corpse lying there ought to admonish you to live."

No one is unwilling to listen when he is being compelled either to partake of food or to live. So the woman, starving from her several days of abstinence, suffered her obstinacy to be broken, and she sated herself with food no less greedily than the maidservant who surrendered first. But you know what temptation is generally wont to assail a person replete with food. The blandishments by which the soldier won the matron over to the will to live served also to undermine her chastity. The youth seemed to the chaste lady not to be lacking in either comeliness or eloquence, and the maidservant urged his suit and kept saying:

"E'en to a pleasing love will you demur?
Reck you not in whose lands you're come to dwell?"

Why do I prolong the tale? The woman yielded this part of her body, too, and the victorious soldier won both arguments.

Now they spent not only that night together, when they made their marriage, but also the next and the third, closing the doors of the vault, of course, so that if any friend or stranger came to the tomb he would suppose that the most chaste wife had expired on her husband's corpse. But the soldier, delighted alike with the woman's beauty and with his secret, kept buying whatever good things his means allowed and immediately at nightfall he would bring them to the tomb.

So when the parents of one of the crucified men saw that the guard was relaxed, by night they took down his hanging body and gave it the last rites. But when the soldier, undone by his sloth, saw on the next day one cross lacking a corpse, he was in dread of torture and told the woman what had happened; he said he would not await the judge's sentence, but with his sword would render justice to his own worthlessness. Let her, therefore, grant a place to him who was about to die, and make the tomb the fateful resting-place of lover and husband alike. The woman, who was no less merciful than chaste, answered: "God forbid that I should behold at the same time the two deaths of the two men most dear to me. I would rather have the dead hang than the living perish." So saying, she bade the corpse of her husband be taken from the coffin and nailed on the vacant cross. The soldier adopted the scheme of the most wise woman, and on the next day the people wondered how a dead man had mounted onto the cross.

ARABY [7]

North Richmond Street, being blind, was a quiet street except at the hour when the Christian Brothers' School set the boys free. An uninhabited house of two storeys stood at the blind end, detached from

[7] From *Dubliners* in *The Portable James Joyce*. Copyright 1946, 1947 by The Viking Press, Inc., New York. Reprinted by permission of The Viking Press and of Jonathan Cape, Limited, London, with acknowledgment to the Executors of the James Joyce Estate.

its neighbours in a square ground. The other houses of the street, conscious of decent lives within them, gazed at one another with brown imperturbable faces.

The former tenant of our house, a priest, had died in the back drawing-room. Air, musty from having been long enclosed, hung in all the rooms, and the waste room behind the kitchen was littered with old useless papers. Among these I found a few paper-covered books, the pages of which were curled and damp: *The Abbot,* by Walter Scott, *The Devout Communicant* and *The Memoirs of Vidocq.* I liked the last best because its leaves were yellow. The wild garden behind the house contained a central apple-tree and a few straggling bushes under one of which I found the late tenant's rusty bicycle-pump. He had been a very charitable priest; in his will he had left all his money to institutions and the furniture of his house to his sister.

When the short days of winter came dusk fell before we had well eaten our dinners. When we met in the street the houses had grown sombre. The space of sky above us was the colour of ever-changing violet and towards it the lamps of the street lifted their feeble lanterns. The cold air stung us and we played till our bodies glowed. Our shouts echoed in the silent street. The career of our play brought us through the dark muddy lanes behind the houses where we ran the gauntlet of the rough tribes from the cottages, to the back doors of the dark dripping gardens where odours arose from the ashpits, to the dark odorous stables where a coachman smoothed and combed the horse or shook music from the buckled harness. When we returned to the street light from the kitchen windows had filled the areas. If my uncle was seen turning the corner we hid in the shadow until we had seen him safely housed. Or if Mangan's sister came out on the doorstep to call her brother in to his tea we watched her from our shadow peer up and down the street. We waited to see whether she would remain or go in and, if she remained, we left our shadow and walked up to Mangan's steps resignedly. She was waiting for us, her figure defined by the light from the half-opened door. Her brother always teased her before he obeyed and I stood by the railings looking at her. Her dress swung as she moved her body and the soft rope of her hair tossed from side to side.

Every morning I lay on the floor in the front parlour watching her door. The blind was pulled down to within an inch of the sash so that I could not be seen. When she came out on the doorstep my heart leaped. I ran to the hall, seized my books and followed her. I kept her brown figure always in my eye and, when we came near the point at which our ways diverged, I quickened my pace and passed her. This happened morning after morning. I had never spoken to her, except for a few casual words, and yet her name was like a summons to all my foolish blood.

Her image accompanied me even in places the most hostile to romance. On Saturday evenings when my aunt went marketing I had to go to carry some of the parcels. We walked through the flaring streets, jostled by drunken men and bargaining women, amid the curses of labourers, the shrill litanies of shop-boys who stood on guard by the barrels of pigs' cheeks, the nasal chanting of street-singers, who sang a *come-all-you* about O'Donovan Rossa, or a ballad about the troubles in our native land. These noises converged in a single sensation of life for me: I imagined that I bore my chalice safely through a throng of foes. Her name sprang to my lips at moments in strange prayers and praises which I myself did not understand. My eyes were often full of tears (I could not tell why) and at times a flood from my heart seemed to pour itself out into my bosom. I thought little of the future. I did not know whether I would ever speak to her or not or, if I spoke to her, how I could tell her of my confused adoration. But my body was like a harp and her words and gestures were like fingers running upon the wires.

One evening I went into the back drawing-room in which the priest had died. It was a dark rainy evening and there was no sound in the house. Through one of the broken panes I heard the rain impinge upon the earth, the fine incessant needles of water playing in the sodden beds. Some distant lamp or lighted window gleamed below me. I was thankful that I could see so little. All my senses seemed to desire to veil themselves and, feeling that I was about to slip from them, I pressed the palms of my hands together until they trembled, murmuring: *"O love! O love!"* many times.

At last she spoke to me. When she addressed the first words to me I was so confused that I did not know what to answer. She asked me was I going to *Araby*. I forgot whether I answered yes or no. It would be a splendid bazaar, she said she would love to go.

"And why can't you?" I asked.

While she spoke she turned a silver bracelet round and round her wrist. She could not go, she said, because there would be a retreat that week in her convent. Her brother and two other boys were fighting for their caps and I was alone at the railings. She held one of the spikes, bowing her head towards me. The light from the lamp opposite our door caught the white curve of her neck, lit up her hair that rested there and, falling, lit up the hand upon the railing. It fell over one side of her dress and caught the white border of a petticoat, just visible as she stood at ease.

"It's well for you," she said.

"If I go," I said, "I will bring you something."

What innumerable follies laid waste my waking and sleeping thoughts after that evening! I wished to annihilate the tedious intervening days. I chafed against the work of school. At night in my bedroom and by day in the classroom her image came between me and the page I strove to read. The syllables of the word *Araby* were called to me through the silence in which my soul luxuriated and cast an Eastern enchantment over me. I asked for leave to go to the bazaar on Saturday night. My aunt was surprised and hoped it was not some Freemason affair. I answered few questions in class. I watched my master's face pass from amiability to sternness; he hoped I was not beginning to idle. I could not call my wandering thoughts together. I had hardly any patience with the serious work of life which, now that it stood between me and my desire, seemed to me child's play, ugly monotonous child's play.

On Saturday morning I reminded my uncle that I wished to go to the bazaar in the evening. He was fussing at the hallstand, looking for the hat-brush, and answered me curtly:

"Yes, boy, I know."

As he was in the hall I could not go into the front parlour and lie at the window. I felt the house in bad humour and walked slowly towards the school. The air was pitilessly raw and already my heart misgave me.

When I came home to dinner my uncle had not yet been home. Still it was early. I sat staring at the clock for some time and, when its ticking began to irritate me, I left the room. I mounted the staircase and gained the upper part of the house. The high cold empty gloomy rooms liberated me and I went from room to room singing. From the front window I saw my companions playing below in the street. Their cries reached me weakened and indistinct and, leaning my forehead against the cool glass, I looked over at the dark house where she lived. I may have stood there for an hour, seeing nothing but the brown-clad figure cast by my imagination, touched discreetly by the lamplight at the curved neck, at the hand upon the railings and at the border below the dress.

When I came downstairs again I found Mrs. Mercer sitting at the fire. She was an old garrulous woman, a pawnbroker's widow, who collected used stamps for some pious purpose. I had to endure the gossip of the tea-table. The meal was prolonged beyond an hour and still my uncle did not come. Mrs. Mercer stood up to go: she was sorry she couldn't wait any longer, but it was after eight o'clock and she did not like to be out late, as the night air was bad for her. When she had gone I began to walk up and down the room, clenching my fists. My aunt said:

"I'm afraid you may put off your bazaar for this night of Our Lord."

At nine o'clock I heard my uncle's latchkey in the halldoor. I heard him talking to himself and heard the hallstand rocking when it had received the weight of his overcoat. I could interpret these signs. When he was midway through his dinner I asked him to give me the money to go to the bazaar. He had forgotten.

"The people are in bed and after their first sleep now," he said.

I did not smile. My aunt said to him energetically:

"Can't you give him the money and let him go? You've kept him late enough as it is."

My uncle said he was very sorry he had forgotten. He said he believed in the old saying: "All work and no play makes Jack a dull boy." He asked me where I was going and, when I had told him a second time he asked me did I know *The Arab's Farewell to his Steed*. When I left the kitchen he was about to recite the opening lines of the piece to my aunt.

I held a florin tightly in my hand as I strode down Buckingham Street towards the station. The sight of the streets thronged with buyers and glaring with gas recalled to me the purpose of my journey. I took my seat in a third-class carriage of a deserted train. After an intolerable delay the train moved out of the station slowly. It crept onward among ruinous houses and over the twinkling river. At Westland Row Station a crowd of people pressed to the carriage doors; but the porters moved them back, saying that it was a special train for the bazaar. I remained alone in the bare carriage. In a few minutes the train drew up beside an improvised wooden platform. I passed out on to the road and saw by the lighted dial of a clock that it was ten minutes to ten. In front of me was a large building which displayed the magical name.

I could not find any sixpenny entrance and, fearing that the bazaar would be closed, I passed in quickly through a turnstile, handing a shilling to a weary-looking man. I found myself in a big hall girdled at half its height by a gallery. Nearly all the stalls were closed and the greater part of the hall was in darkness. I recognised a silence like that which pervades a church after a service. I walked into the centre of the bazaar timidly. A few people were gathered about the stalls which were still open. Before a curtain, over which the words *Café Chantant* were written in coloured lamps, two men were counting money on a salver. I listened to the fall of the coins.

Remembering with difficulty why I had come I went over to one of the stalls and examined porcelain vases and flowered tea-sets. At the door of the stall a young lady was talking and laughing with two young gentlemen. I remarked their English accents and listened vaguely to their conversation.

"O, I never said such a thing!"

"O, but you did!"

"O, but I didn't!"

"Didn't she say that?"

"Yes. I heard her."

"O, there's a ... fib!"

Observing me the young lady came over and asked me did I wish to buy anything. The tone of her voice was not encouraging; she seemed to have spoken to me out of a sense of duty. I looked humbly at the great jars that stood like eastern guards at either side of the dark entrance to the stall and murmured:

"No, thank you."

The young lady changed the position of one of the vases and went back to the two young men. They began to talk of the same subject. Once or twice the young lady glanced at me over her shoulder.

I lingered before her stall, though I knew my stay was useless, to make my interest in her wares seem the more real. Then I turned away slowly and walked down the middle of the bazaar. I allowed the two pennies to fall against the sixpence in my pocket. I heard a voice call from one end of the gallery that the light was out. The upper part of the hall was now completely dark.

Gazing up into the darkness I saw myself as a creature driven and derided by vanity; and my eyes burned with anguish and anger.

Petronius is interested primarily in telling a fairly cynical joke about the failure of virtue. The characters in the story are "flat" rather than "round": that is, they are not fully developed, they do not have very clearly defined personalities. They exist for the sake of the plot, and are sharply subordinate to it. Anything we need to know about them we are told quite explicitly. Indeed, the story is so matter-of-fact and so simple in its line of development that it may seem to read like a *synopsis* of a story rather than a story itself, like a report of the incidents rather than a mirroring of the incidents themselves. While the plot is compact, the texture of the story is loose. One does not need to look closely or long at the words to see that they are lacking in any great intricacy of design. This simplicity of design, this openness of texture, is characteristic of much prose fiction prior to our own time, though to be sure the development in complexity of the short story and the novel has been gradual and fairly constant. "The Widow of Ephesus" imitates the *surfaces* of life, picking and choosing its elements for the sake of its plot and distorting what would have been the real-life experience by reducing personality to a minor place in the action. Even the narrator of the story is remote from us; his tone is reportorial, omniscient. He manipulates the persons of the story for the sake of the dry chuckle he expects from us when he has finished. In real life, we might be shocked or pained or disgusted by the story of the inconstant widow (unless, of course, we shared the cynicism of Petronius and said, Woman is a weak vessel, and what else could one expect?), but in the story the *point of view* from which we are to look at the tale, the *angle of distortion,* is clearly marked out for us by the teller, and details are so selected as to limit and define the nature of our response. Distortion in art is distortion for a purpose.

James Joyce, in "Araby," tells a story so different in its manner and design that one is tempted to say that we are dealing with an art entirely different, though both stories *are* stories. The incidents in Joyce's story are, on the surface at least, comparatively slight. A sensitive and shy young boy, living on North Richmond Street in Dublin, falls in love with a girl and goes to a bazaar to buy her a present. After getting money from his uncle, he arrives at the bazaar late and is keenly disappointed to find that the greater part of the hall is already dark and that no one else seems to share the sense of excitement with which he had started out. All his anticipated pleasure turns to anguish and anger.

But of course this is not really the story at all. The incidents in Joyce's story are simply the surfaces; in themselves, they would give us a texture as loose as that of Petronius's story. The true story in "Araby" lies in the sharp sense we get of the inner experience of the boy through the close and serried words of the prose.

This time the story is told in the first-person ("I"). It is personal (even, we are told by Padraic Colum, "out of personal memory" of the author); it is *concerned*. The opening of the story is filled with opposite kinds of image. Words like *blind, quiet, uninhabited, imperturbable, musty, long-enclosed, waste, littered, useless, straggling, rusty, sombre, feeble, dark,* and *muddy* give us a strong sense, a strong picture, of decay or paralysis or lifelessness. But along with them, setting up a tension by their very opposition to these images, come such words as *ever-changing violet, stung, played, glowed, shouts, gauntlet, rough, odorous, horse, music, swung, tossed,* all of them suggesting life or action or sound. There is a further complication: this dismal North Richmond Street of the story itself has living, conscious qualities, as though the "inhabited" qualities of the houses were in some way communicated to the inanimate houses and street in turn. That is, the street is "blind"—but blindness suggests life, since one must be alive to be blind; each house has its "neighbours"; each has its "brown imperturbable face"; and one house, the one at the blind end, is "detached from its neighbours." All these examples come from only the first three paragraphs of the story, and it is important to observe that the words in the first group tend to *precede* the words in the second group in their order of appearance. It is in this mixture of light and shadow that the figure of Mangan's sister is first introduced to us, standing in the light of the half-opened door. Against the darkness, the animal vitality of her figure is sharply apparent to the boy who watches her. This detail opens the fourth paragraph, too: the boy, hidden behind the *blind,* watches the girl come out into the morning *light.* The sense of the boy's *life* in *darkness,* with which the story opens, thus intensifies the sentence with which the fourth paragraph concludes: "...her name was like a summons to all my foolish blood." Out of the dimness of this growth, the boy's blood responds to the call of *light,* in the person of the girl. We are, of course, by long convention used to the notion that the female principle, the mother principle, is the *life* element, into which the male principle enters.

Look at the story again, and see with what meticulous care Joyce continues the tension arising from the juxtaposition of opposites: drunkenness and curses, shrill litanies, chalice and prayers. The boy's eyes fill with tears which he cannot understand—but which we, by now, *can* understand, because we have been shown the strange mixture of sensations out of which they arise. At this point the reader is already in possession of more knowledge than the narrator, though it is the narrator who has "told" us the "facts."

Meanwhile, Joyce builds up another series of opposites in the juxtaposition of images dealing with religion and denial and images based upon pagan or exotic or "romantic" appeals. The priest appeared early in the story; he reappears in the sixth paragraph. But the images associated with the priest are those of paralysis, silence, decay, and in this paragraph the light is *distant.* It is the *girl* who provides the life, the vitality—the harp, the music, the flow of the blood are set in operation by her, and not by the awareness of the priest (who is, of course, *dead*). It is the girl whose name springs to the boy's lips in moments of prayer; it is the girl who brings the "single sensation of life." It is per-

haps not blasphemous to say that the worship of Mary would at
this point be more meaningful to the boy than the worship of
God, though his feeling for the girl is clearly in part sexual. In
the room where the priest had died, the boy, in an attitude of
prayer, *presses the palms of his hands together,* trembling, and
cries fervently *"O love! O love!"* many times. And in the next
paragraph, the name *Araby,* the title word, is first introduced,
calling up as it must some sense of the exotic East, of splendor,
perhaps of incense (which would certainly intensify the opposition of pagan and Christian images). The notion of Oriental
luxury, of physical delight in color and wealth and bodily in-
dulgence, is underscored in Joyce's explicit sentence: "The syllables of the word *Araby* were called to me through the silence
in which my soul luxuriated and cast an Eastern enchantment
over me."

You can follow this sequence of images through the remainder
of the story. Perhaps that would be a good exercise for a class
period. All we need do here is to say once again that this closely
considered use of words results in a far greater *density,* a far
closer texture, for Joyce's story than for the tale by Petronius
Arbiter. And the bazaar, to which we finally come, brings all the
many fine threads of the story together. It seems at first to be the
fruit of all the ripening in the boy's hopes—he looks forward to it
wholeheartedly. But it comes actually to be a part of the darkness
with which the story began: the hall is dark, delight is missing,
the bazaar is silent like *a church after a service.* The counting of
money in front of the curtain lighted by colored lamps is like
the clinking of coins in the counting of the church collection—
but it is the sound of something over and done with, now being
added up. A voice cries that the light is out. And the boy, yanked
brutally out of Araby, is again in the darkness of Dublin, and the
sense of the ridiculousness of his position and of his dreams burns
into him in anguish and anger.

This strong sense of revelation at the end of the story, this
sharp and illuminating recognition on the part of the character,
is something Joyce calls an *epiphany,* and the term is useful

enough for us to remember it.[8] The epiphany may, to be sure, exist for the reader rather than for the character. It is also a common occurrence in religious experience, where it also designates a revelation, a manifestation of something *beyond*. Joyce manages, in the epiphany, a particular kind of extension of experience, beyond the sensual surface, beyond the "actual." Like faith, the epiphany is the evidence of things not seen, and the expressive language in which Joyce symbolizes the experience is only a shadow of the Idea. This may sound too highly Platonic in a chapter devoted to Aristotle's concept of imitation—but in art as in life, experience is binary.

We said earlier in the chapter that the contemporary short story and novel often partake of the nature of poetry on the score of density. "Araby" illustrates this claim. The use of images to carry the weight of meaning, the intertwining and progression of images, the *presentation* rather than the *explicit description* of meaningful incidents all seem characteristic of poetry. They are not at all characteristic of, say, "The Widow of Ephesus." Furthermore, "Araby," while it is dramatic as any story must in part be dramatic (that is, it is a story of the development of conflict within characters who have a life of their own), is also lyrical (richly imaged, personal, subjective). Irene Hendry has suggested that Joyce's theory of epiphanies furnished him with a method of characterization which became typical for him—a gradual progression from the personal to the impersonal, from the first person to the third, from the kinetic to the static. That is, "Araby" begins as the personal memory of the narrator; it is highly subjective; it is a motion *toward*. But before the story has reached the final period, the narrator and the reader have parted company, in a sense: we know more than the boy knows, the "I" becomes for us "he." (It is perfectly true, of course, that the *whole* story is written by the mature Joyce, and not by a boy.) And the

---

[8] There is an interesting essay on the subject by Irene Hendry: "Joyce's Epiphanies." The essay appeared originally in *The Sewanee Review,* Summer, 1946; it has been reprinted in Seon Givens (ed.), *James Joyce: Two Decades of Criticism,* Vanguard Press, Inc., New York, 1948, pp. 27–46.

motion of the story reaches a *stasis* (the opposite of motion) in which all the meaning of the earlier motion comes rushing in upon the reader. "Araby" seems wonderfully to combine narrative, dramatic, and lyrical manners—but we must leave those terms for later discussion.

This particular method of imitation is quite characteristic of much of Joyce; it is entirely unlike the method of Petronius Arbiter. The latter imitates the surface of events; the former, while beginning with the surfaces, imitates the *springs* of experience. Joyce's incidents seem at first so simple, so casual, so "clear" that one feels that he is not distorting experience at all, but simply putting it on the page. But our analysis has surely suggested that the distortion is here. While it does not destroy the illusion of "reality," Joyce's carefully controlled manner of distortion lets us experience a reality which we could never otherwise quite know. The experience is now quite literally bound into words in the story; it could not exist without the particular language Joyce employs. Indeed, it may be said that the distortion is responsible for the *intensification of reality*. A newspaper story, a journalistic reporting of an event, is likely to lessen the sense of reality because, in extracting and cutting down and choosing details, it gives us a much looser texture than the texture of the experience it is reporting; a short story, while it also chooses and extracts and cuts down, at the same time amplifies and modifies and extends (hence clarifies) the experience. Things happen in real life which seem totally improbable: truth is stranger than fiction. But the story must make the events which it relates seem *probable:* fiction is less strange than "truth," and frequently truer.

Summary

We have concerned ourselves in this chapter with looking at certain ways in which literature modifies, clarifies, and extends experience through its process of imitation of life. *Imitation* is not flat reproduction; it does not mean copying; it does not deny that the poet is a creative agent. It is the disposing into form, through the use of language, of materials which do not of themselves assume that form, for the sake of certain emotional effects like the emotional effects of real life but differing from them in being contained by and limited to the work of art embodying the imitation. That is, our response to the boy in "Araby," and to his situation, is rooted in the unique situation presented by Joyce. Our "recognition" of the "truth" at the end of the story is a recognition of the truth of *this particular story;* only if Joyce includes in his story the possibility of reference to universals are we permitted to move outside the bounds of the unique situation which is here given. We do not say to ourselves, "Oh, yes, this is very much like the story of that boy who used to live down the street," and proceed to read the story *as if it were* the story of the boy down the street. We recognize that our feelings at this point are peripheral and probably at most points irrelevant, though without our having *some* feeling of the likeness of "Araby" to our own experience we should probably lose interest in the story. While "Araby" as an experience is unique, it has in it elements which are universal.

The process of imitation involves selection of detail through choice of a point of view, choice of language, arrangement of parts, choice of final effect, and so on—many things, indeed, all of them resulting in a distortion of the thing being imitated. As a result, the experience within a piece of literature can never be identical with an experience in real life. It is, on the contrary, ordinarily more meaningful than the experience of real life because it is ordered, limited, and complete. In this way it is safe to say that we learn through literature; we undergo experiences we should not otherwise undergo, we assume dispositions of persons we should not otherwise come to know, we look from points of view different from our own and frequently more penetrating than our own and almost always more complete than our own because they can take in the whole of the thing which is being viewed. In this way, literature is experience.

Exercises

1. It is clear that in its way literature imitates life. Can you think of any ways in which *life* imitates (not copies, but re-forms or re-presents) *literature?* (Consider, for example, the behavior of young children.) How extensive do you take this interaction between literature and life to be?

2. In the discussion of Leigh Hunt's "Rondeau," we have given one instance of the way in which literature *distorts* a real-life experience. Can you illustrate this principle of distortion by referring to similar instances?

3. Emily Dickinson's "I heard a fly buzz when I died" gives us, in literature, an experience of death. Can you give other examples of things we know from literature without having had direct experience of them in life?

4. We have said something in this chapter about *irony* in literature. Many contemporary critics see irony as being at the heart of the experience in literature. Can you give examples of irony from your own daily experience?

5. What is the *irony* in the experience of the boy in "Araby"?

6. What do you understand by *density* in prose style? By *close texture?*

7. As in literature, so in real life the point of view which one takes conditions one's attitudes toward experience. Can you illustrate this fact from your own experience?

7

Literature as Art

THE FIRST CHAPTER of the book centered attention on the nature and quality of our experience of the everyday world and stated that as a matter of record *a reader's experience with a book is no different in its nature than his experience with other objects in life.* While a book is certainly not life, while experience in literature is lodged symbolically in language, while we respond to images rather than to direct sensations in literature, nevertheless the reader of a poem or a play or a story reads as he reads because of his previous experience of the world about him and constantly relates what he reads to that experience, making use of precisely the same human faculties and feelings which he employs in his daily living.

The chapter we have just finished tried to show in part how the poet, in imitating *his* experience of the world, distorts or modifies that experience in the interests of clarifying and extending it. "The poet's vision," says Francis Fergusson,[1]

[1] Quoted, by permission of the publishers, from *The Human Image in Dramatic Literature,* Doubleday Anchor Books, Doubleday & Company, Inc., New York, 1957, pp. x–xi.

is ultimately derived from his human efforts to find his way in the puzzling world we all know, i.e., from experience. But experience, in this sense, is not a matter of literal observation and report; it accumulates slowly within us at some deep level at the very edge of awareness. We can hear its voice only when we are free from the immediate pressures of the environment. It is not easy to be aware of experience: concentration is required as well as detachment. Maritain speaks of the poet, when he tries to fix his inspiration or his vision, as listening with the inner ear. He is listening (or looking) for the accepted experience, which, perhaps because it *has* been accepted, comes to him as a harmony, a form or an order. In this vision, what the poet has wished for and what he has gotten are inextricably mixed: he has a vision of some aspect of human nature *and* destiny. He has no access, as poet, to mystical or supernatural insight. His realm is where we all are, his material a reflection of his own spirit.

The reader, likewise making a human effort to find his way and to make up his mind and to feel a sense of harmony with the world about him, listens to the writer because the writer, if he is good, has in some measure *achieved* this reduction to order, and in such a way that the experience remains vital, vivid, and compelling.

Art as Evaluation of Experience

Literature differs from life in many ways, to be sure; but one of its primary differences lies in the degree of *completeness* with which it presents its particular experiences. A work of literary art has within itself a *unity,* a completed pattern or wholeness which is in itself one of the sources of the particular pleasure given by literature. In this sense it is correct to say that a work of literary art contains within itself all the evidence necessary for its interpretation. To say this is not to suggest that the reader does not have certain responsibilities of his own: he must know the meanings of the words in the work or must be responsible for knowing them; he must be willing to feel a degree of responsibility for allusions within the work; he must be responsible for having in his own head a certain store of historical, traditional knowledge or must be willing to check his knowledge against the facts. No one would ask the poet to define within the poem every word he uses, nor to write only poems which would be immediately comprehensible by children! On the other hand, we do seem to ask of works of literary art that they try not to depend for their full force upon knowledge which most of us do not possess. The more personal and private a writer's language and frame of reference become, the less *universality* we feel to be in the work of art itself. While we may say that the imitation of ex- perience and not the communication of experience is the poet's primary concern, we also tend to believe that a purely personal or private poem is somehow limited.

In imitating experience, by the very process of selecting and arranging the poet necessarily in some degree *evaluates* experi- ence. We may say of two poems that both imitate, but that one, in its imitation, is *better* than another. What we are likely to mean is that the better poem succeeds more fully in conveying the quality of its experience to a reader; or, if both poems convey fully, that the quality of the one experience seems to us richer or more significant than the quality of the other. Just as the poem evaluates experience, so our critical study of the poem involves our evaluation of its imitation of experience.

Experience as Evaluation of Nature

The process of evaluation can be examined even prior to the making of the poem. No one of us, limited as each of us is by his particular make-up, can experience the whole of life. In any literal sense, it is impossible for us to "see life steadily and see it whole." But the whole process of our growth and education is directed toward making us better fitted to evaluate whatever ex- perience we do have of this world. Emily Dickinson, out of her strong sensitivity, had a richer (if *not* wider) experience than many a world traveler, though she spent much of her adult life within the walls of her own home. We are constantly making evaluations of our contact with the world about us: our feelings of happiness or unhappiness, our judgments of good or bad, our sensations of pleasure or displeasure are all parts of our process of evaluating. It is true that our evaluations may be false or wrong-headed, but we keep making them. But in our everyday experience, things are never really finished. After the day there is night, and after the night there is another day; after pleasure there will be pain, and after pain there is likely to be more pleasure: things are in a constant state of *becoming*. While there are likely to be in any life certain large moments where things seem to end, or to come sharply into focus, it is literally true that life on earth ends only with death.

These "large moments" are very likely to be, in our own experiences, the equivalent of the *epiphany* in a work of literature. We do, for the moment, sense unity and order and fullness and perhaps purpose. These moments may very well give us a moment of experience so like the experience of a work of art that we think of it as being *aesthetic* in its nature. A sharp sense of the ability to *evaluate* accompanies such moments. We seem to *know,* and the knowledge seems dramatic in its sharpness.

Meanwhile, our daily knowledge is frequently dim and blurred; we go about our tasks with somewhat duller responses, less alive to life than in these less frequent "moments." But each individual's life is different from the life of his fellow men. If each were able to record his own experience in words, the record of each individual would be unique.

The record would not necessarily be a work of art. Indeed, it is in the highest degree unlikely that it *would* be a work of art. A record of what *is* would be a reproduction, not an imitation in the sense in which we are using the word. Its evaluation would be bound by the experiences actually undergone, and limited to the incompleteness of those experiences. In this sense a journal, a diary, an autobiography is not and cannot be a work of art; the more faithfully it remains an account of the life *as actually lived,* the further it departs from the condition of art, which involves selection and distortion and arrangement. This view does not suggest, of course, anything about our interest in the work. We are interested in many things which appear in words but which we should not call works of literary *art*. In plain fact, many of us are torn in the reading of autobiographies between the desire to know what "actually happened" and our willingness to let the autobiography approach the condition of a work of art: to omit or truncate experience, to alter chronology, to give shape to the life story being set down. A good autobiography frequently resembles a work of prose fiction—but perhaps at the same time it loses specificity as a life record.

At the end of the first chapter, we suggested that the good reader seeks in literature the opportunity to grow, to make changes in himself. This desire is part of the vitality in his reading. He is not looking, in literature, for the closest equivalent to his own experience so that he may weep or laugh over *himself,* though the large daytime audiences for soap opera on radio and television frequently seek exactly for this sort of pleasure. Rather, just as the traveler seeks to keep a quality of aliveness by entering into and adapting to new environments, the reader *strengthens* his individuality by *enlarging* the sphere of his response to fictional characters within works of art. The degree to which this enlargement takes place and the degree to which it seems worthwhile both enter into our evaluation of the work of art. The word *worthwhile* suggests an important consideration. It probably seems worthwhile for us to enter into the experience of murder vicariously in *Macbeth,* say, or *Julius Caesar;* we should not feel it equally worthwhile to commit murder so that we might know the experience at first hand! There are people who argue that the more direct experience one has, the better, but this is a view which society is not likely in any absolute sense to tolerate, and surely society is at this point right in its insistence.

The Report Compared with the Work of Art as Evaluation of Experience

We have said that experience is an evaluation of nature in so far as it selects, modifies, arranges, and orders nature; that each individual's experience of nature involves evaluation in the process of his growth and education; and that literature, in turn, is an evaluation of the experience of nature by individuals who are artists by virtue of their ability to put their evaluations into order through the imitative process involving the use of the symbols which we call words. Somewhere in this scheme of responses we ought to take account of one of the functions of journalism: the *reporting* of experiences, usually but not necessarily the reporting of experiences undergone by people other than the reporter.

Read the three texts given below.

FROM REPORT ON AN EXECUTION, BY A POLICE REPORTER [2]

On the night of Thursday, March 6, Tom went up to Sing Sing with a Queens judge to witness the execution.

"Suchow came first," he said. "Two husky guards towered over the pint-sized murderer as he walked into the death house, looking dead pan. In the chair, when the current was turned on, his body jolted against the straps with a thickening [*sic*] thump. His head raised higher and his neck looked like a giraffe's. His fingers, the forefinger and thumb, were crossed. His neck and throat turned red and bulged outward and taut. The prison physician stepped up, very mechanical-like, as if he were an umpire at a ball game, and said very solemnly, 'This man is dead.'"

What impressed Tom most about Suchow's death was that when they laid him on the stretcher, his body remained rigid, still in the posture of sitting down.

"Koberski came next. He strutted into the room. His hands gripped the arms of the electric chair in anticipation. When they turned on the juice I heard a singing, burning noise, zz, zz, zz. It was like a flight of bees. The brine on the piece of rubber under the helmet was burning. Kahkoska was last. He too strutted in. He pulled up his slit trouser leg to let the guard fasten the electrode. Like the others he kissed the cross the priest handed him. Then he did a strange thing. He took a deep breath and, as he filled his stomach with air, protruded it just as the current entered his body. He went 'umph' like he felt it and moved a little under his own power. This time the umpire-like physician took a little longer as he listened to his heart with the stethoscope."

[2] From *PM*, Mar. 31, 1947.

AN ITEM FROM *Time,* JULY 15, 1946 [3]

"I reckon dyin' is black. Some folks say it's gold. Some say it's white as hominy grits.... I reckon it's black."

Willie Francis ought to know what color death is. The skinny, slope-headed, 17-year-old Louisiana Negro saw and tasted death on May 3 as he sat and waited for it, strapped in Louisiana's portable electric chair. It tasted "like cold peanut butter," and took on "little blue and pink and green speckles, like shines in a rooster's tail" when the executioner whispered: "Goodbye, Willie."

But the executioner was crowding fate. For the first time in 24 tries, the chair failed to work. Convicted murderer Francis walked back to his cell to pray, and eat candy, and remember:

"They walked me into the room and I saw the chair.... I knowed it was a bad chair. All I could think was: 'Willie, you goin' out'n this world.'

"They began to strap me in the chair, and everything begun to look dazey.... It was like the white folks watching was in a big swing, and they'd swing away and back and then right up close. When they put the black bag over my head, I was all locked up ... with loud thinkin'.

"The electric man ... could of been puttin' me on the bus for New Orleans the way he said 'goodbye,'" Willie recalled, "and I tried to say goodbye but my tongue got stuck in the peanut butter and I felt a burnin' in my head and my left leg and I jumped against the straps.

"When the straps kept cuttin' me I hoped I was alive, and I asked the electric man to let me breathe.... They took the bag off my head...."

While he waited for October and the U.S. Supreme Court to decide whether he would have to face death twice, stolid, stuttering Willie Francis gave the world the sum of his experience. It was "plumb mizzuble."

KING RICHARD THE LION HEARTED ON THE MURDER OF ABBOTS [4]

"Let me impart to you, Hubert," says King Richard, "knowledge of the right method by which murderous abbots ought to be murdered, specially when they are abominably fat. Do, with such an abbot, as

---

[3] Courtesy TIME, The Weekly Newsmagazine; copyright Time Inc., 1946.

[4] An episode from *Hubert's Arthur,* Cassell & Co., Ltd., London, 1935, pp. 120-121. Quoted by permission of the publishers.

you do with a duck when you prepare that filthy fowl for eating.
Catch your abbot, and make him kneel upright. Go behind him; and
take his ribs and arms between your thighs and knees, riding him
close clutched so. Take his face by the dewlap (or goitre), tightly;
and turn it upward, so that his last glance may be toward heaven; and
let him say such prayers as he can remember. Then, wriggle your dag
(a blunt one, if possible), as far down his gullet as it will go, but
gently, as though you love him, and so cut his throat very delicately
and thoroughly from the inside. He will not say a word, nor even
cough at you. This done, cast your dag aside, so that it may stick in
the earth to clean itself. But you stand up, with your hands clasped
below your abbot's middle, letting him droop limply a little forward
to disgorge his life-blood in an unchecked stream. When it slackens,
heave him up and shake him, to encourage the flow: but scatter not
the gouts of blood abroad, nor on his garments, nor on his person.
When it ceases, lay the corpse neatly in a dry situation; and tie up his
jaw till it is stiff; and, if you have been careful over the business, there
will be no sign, not even a blood stain, by which the manner of his
demise may be discerned: excepting the puddle of blood (large, or
small, according to the capacity of your abbot), which you shall take
order to conceal with loose earth and turves well-stamped down."

Frederick Rolfe, Baron Corvo

Violent death is not a pretty subject; nor, of course, is it intended by any of the writers of the pieces just quoted that it
should be. Doubtless parts of these paragraphs have shocked you
in one way or another. While it is not the purpose of the discussion to shock you, we must confess that there are times when
words do shock and distress, and we shall come to a consideration
of that matter after we have taken up the primary question "How
do these accounts of violent death differ, and by what necessity
do they differ?"

The first item, the police reporter's account of the executions at
Sing Sing, is surely the most matter-of-fact. It is an attempt to
report as vividly as possible the actual memories of the reporter.
In this *limited* sense, it is the most "realistic" of the three, if by
realism one means a reproduction of reality, an account of something actually experienced, reported as it actually seemed to hap-

pen. It is an eye*witness* account. It is selective; it does not attempt
to give all the details, but only the most memorable. It is also
reported in the language of everyday speech. (1) Partly because
of the limitations of the reporter's language, (2) partly because
the selection of details is so managed as to leave us out of all but
a small fraction of the experience, and (3) partly because we are
not sure from this excerpt alone whether to center our attention
on Tom or on the men being executed, the first account seems
perhaps the least vivid of the accounts quoted. Suppose we look
at each of these three considerations separately.

1. The *epithets* and descriptive phrases in the report are like
the jargon of sports reporters in one sense: while they are meant
to give vividness, they actually eliminate vividness because they
are worn-out, clichés. Such words and phrases as "husky," "towered over," "pint-sized," "like a giraffe's," "the juice," and "flight
of bees" are so common in our vocabulary that they are almost
literally lifeless. Clichés may, of course, be extremely useful in
writing, but they do not contribute here to the vividness of the
account because they do not carry the weight of feeling they are
meant to carry. The comparison of the physician to an umpire at
a baseball game, too, seems somehow inappropriate. It again re-
duces the vividness of the account. The expression "dead pan," in
the second paragraph, seems particularly unfortunate under the
circumstances being reported. It is one of those puns which all of
us make from time to time without being aware of the incongruity, and hence humor, of our language.

On the other hand, certain things in the language of the piece
do make for vividness. For example, the phrase "burning noise"
(unlike the phrase "singing noise") carries life because we do not
usually think of noises as "burning." Things which burn do make
noises, certainly; but "burning noise" is something a little different—perhaps unintentionally on the writer's part. It is too bad
that the phrase about the bees, which follows, tends to reduce the
impact of the earlier phrase. The sentence "The brine on the
piece of rubber under the helmet was burning" is also vivid because it is a highly concrete image carrying a strong mixture of

sense responses. When the language is trite, the sense response cannot be strong. One of the things triteness means is reduction of response.

2. We learn so little about the man named Suchow that his death remains pretty matter-of-fact to us. He is blurred as an individual, not only by the language of the reporter, but by the selection of details through which we are told of his death. Our only knowledge of him as he walks in is that he is pint-sized and dead pan. It isn't until after the "juice" has been turned on that the description becomes detailed; and then, of course, our attention is turned solely to the simple and obvious physical manifestations of death by electrocution. Of Koberski's death, we remember only the noise and the odor of burning.

With Kahkoska, however, the account takes on a certain vividness which carries through to the end of the article. We *see* the condemned man pull up his trouser leg, we see the guard fastening the electrode. We watch Kahkoska kiss the cross. The account is now connected; the events come in a single related series. It is as if a camera which has been roving about the death chamber, from spectator to victim, interested only in a kind of panoramic view of the scene, has now moved in upon the event. The writer emphasizes the importance of the moment by writing, "Then he did a strange thing." And we watch Kahkoska fill his stomach with air, and catch the "umph" as he expels it under the impact of the electric current. Even the physician, as a participant in the scene, makes something special of this death as he "takes a little longer" to listen to the heart. The details about Kahkoska's death are selected, certainly; not every movement is told to us. But the selection is here purposeful; the details here *cluster* for effect much more sharply than they did in the accounts of the deaths of Suchow and Koberski. Here we watch both the deed and the man; hence we are permitted to enter into the experience more vividly than elsewhere in the article.

3. The first three paragraphs of the article put Tom in a position of importance as the observer. Furthermore, the details about the executions come to us in Tom's words. Otherwise, however,

Tom is of no importance to us in the experience, until the end of the last paragraph. His view seems pretty general, limited, lacking in vividness. But with the death of Kahkoska, Tom takes on new significance, largely because of the sentence "Then he did a strange thing," where suddenly Tom's response to the scene comes alive. Try reading the paragraph and omitting that sentence, and the paragraph loses much of its vitality. As Tom suddenly focuses sharply on the incident, he draws us with him. We, too, lean forward a little (figuratively, of course), watch with particular care, to see this "strange thing." And we hold our breath a little as the physician "takes a little longer" with his examination of the body. The *point of view* (for that is what we have been discussing) makes an enormous difference in the way we respond to the language of the piece and to the particular selection of details.

Point of View as Angle of Distortion

Where we stand to view an experience, and the attitude or frame of mind in which we view it, makes a considerable difference in what we see and feel. The second of the three accounts, the item from *Time,* illustrates with excellent effect the significance of *point of view*.

The account of the "death" of Willie Francis stands somewhere between reporting and story. It *is* a report; but it is a report where details are carefully selected with a given speaker and a given interpretation in mind. From the variety of things which Willie Francis probably said and did, only those details which add up to a particular sharp impression are reported. In this sense the degree of selectivity is much higher here than it was in the first account, and the point of view is of constant importance.

The *Time* account *seems* at first to be more "factual" than the account from *PM*. In the latter, the report is given in Tom's words, and we are intended to see through his eyes. But actually the *Time* account, while it leaves the person of the reporter strictly out of the narration, is less simply factual because it selects details for an intended and deliberate effect rather than reports simply "what happened." In this sense, the *Time* article approaches the condition of a work of literary art. It has a wholeness, a completeness, an intention which the first item essentially lacks.

The story of Willie Francis is a particularly excruciating example of the way in which literature *extends* experience, except that we are dealing here with fact rather than with fiction, and (for Willie Francis certainly) with a real rather than with a vicarious experience. This is one of those rare occasions when something which actually happened, with a minimum of selection and distortion, becomes almost identical with fiction. We said above that it has, by contrast with the *PM* article, a wholeness and a completeness. We must add now that it does not have the completeness of a story, though it has a completeness which is characteristic of much poetry. It is essentially *lyrical* in the sense that it lacks plot but is an emotional whole; it consists in presenting the more or less static position of a speaker moved by what has happened to him, expressing his state of mind.

Willie Francis's language is "poetic," too, in that it is highly figurative and rich in imagery. Willie is the center of the "poem." In contrast to the language of Tom, the language of Willie Francis is extremely vivid. Willie is certainly not an educated man, judging by his grammar, but he is keenly sensitive to colors and tastes and to sensations in general. This basic (even, if you will, primitive) response to events is normally present in children, whose responses tend to outrun their evaluations and reflectiveness, and far too frequently dead in adults, who, as we said in an earlier chapter, tend to lose or to lack vividness in their responses to experience. Literature seeks in part to revive in us this basic awareness of things and events, to vivify life by imitating it. Hence it is fair to say that Willie Francis is, in his use of imagery (though not necessarily in his grammar), a poet. Death is not gold, nor white like hominy grits, but black; and it tastes like cold peanut butter, and it looks like the blue and pink and green shines in a rooster's tail when the electric man whispers, "Goodbye, Willie." Death is goin' out'n this world, and things look dazey, with the white folks swingin' in and out of sight, and the black bag locked over your head. It's plumb mizzuble. Willie Francis was a convicted murderer, and if one believes in capital punishment, perhaps one must admit that he had to die—as he did, eventually; but Willie Francis the poet is not Willie Francis the man. Our sharing of the experience of "death" is a moving and valuable thing here; recognition of that fact does not involve us in anything like approval of murder, nor even of sympathy with Willie Francis *as* a murderer. The Willie Francis who "dies" in *Time*'s article is Willie Francis the poet. It is probably only the *facts* (Louisiana ... electric chair ... convicted murderer ... Supreme Court) which keep the report within the realm of journalism at all.

Selectivity in Art

We have said that in both the report from *PM* and the report from *Time* selection of details is involved. Probably no account of any experience can be literally complete. We have also said, however, that the selection of details in the report of the "death" of Willie Francis is carefully controlled by the particular point of view, the particular angle of distortion, chosen in advance by the writer. The reporter here gives, not just what he happens to remember, but what he thinks of what is remembered. Hence his report gains in vividness, in impact; the experience is probably therefore more meaningful for us because, within the limits of its intention, it is more complete. Because the report is in a news magazine, we expect it also to represent the "truth."

But in the excerpt from *Hubert's Arthur,* despite the fact that we are dealing with a king who existed in time and space, we do not really ask Baron Corvo to limit himself precisely to what did happen. Doubtless we should be offended, if our historical sense is strong, if he were to depart outrageously from what *might* have been said and done by Richard—unless, of course, he aimed frankly at comic effects, when such gross distortion does *not* offend us. Historical fiction depends for part of its appeal on the presence of characters, scenes, and events drawn from real life, but to the writer of such fiction we are normally willing to grant considerable license in the handling of details. It is probably safe to say that the more remote the historical period, the more license we are willing to grant, since our knowledge of remote times, being dimmer, does not stand in the way of our enjoyment of what is imagined to have happened. Hence we permit Baron Corvo to create, within limits, his personal notion of King Richard.

King Richard speaks in his own person—this is a first-person statement. The *PM* report and the *Time* report both employed both first- and third-person narration; that is, in the *Time* report, for example, the direct words of Willie Francis are *first-person* ("I"), the interspersed statements by the reporter are *third-person* ("he"). The person in which the words are written is a part of the point of view or angle of distortion. But only part. Within the general notion of point of view as being here first person, there is a point of view assumed by the character who is *speaking* in the first person. These two ways of discussing point of view are distinct; some critics limit the term *point of view* to the general notion, but it is profitable here to push it further.

In writing of King Richard, Baron Corvo is making use of what one critic [5] has called "negative" emotions, emotions which normally offend or repulse contemporary taste, though earlier centuries were somewhat hardier in their appetites. What the critic has called the "innocent opportunism" of the Widow of Ephesus (studied in the last chapter) could not be tolerated by us, he says, except "in the licensed playground of the classics." Rickword may or may not be right about Petronius's story; but it *is* perfectly true that we are willing to listen, within one sort of context and within one sort of point of view, to things which in another context and from another point of view would outrage our sensibilities.

Murder is no joke—usually. But for King Richard it is—at least in part. And so long as we are adopting the point of view of King

[5] Edgell Rickword, "The Use of 'Negative' Emotions," in R. W. Stallman, *Critiques and Essays in Criticism, 1920–1948.* Copyright, 1949, The Ronald Press Company. Quotations by permission.

Richard, it is for us, also. As Rickword says, literature of "the negative emotions, of those arising from disgust with the object, provides the means for a whole series of responses in parts of the mind which have been lying fallow for nearly two hundred years." We shan't quarrel here about the fallow period of such emotions; we are concerned only with the fact of their existence. There are readers, certainly, for whom the sense of shock at the employment of such emotions is so great as to destroy the experience of the work of literary art. Some people cannot read Swift because he was particularly a master with such materials. But "natural prejudice should not be allowed to obscure, as it too frequently does, the perfection of expression the negative [work] may achieve...."

Why is it that Richard's description of abbot murder does not simply shock us? Because in part it amuses us. And what is the source and nature of our amusement? The point of view assumed by Richard during his description. The incongruity between the subject matter and the attitude of the speaker (which is another way of saying the point of view) is so marked as to lift us quite out of the realm of "normal behavior," though our response is perfectly "normal," and to make us laugh (or at least chuckle) instead of run for the police. King Richard, as instructor in murder, becomes a kind of master cook preparing a fowl for trussing and roasting. Compare the following account from a cookbook written by Alice B. Toklas,[6] the long-time friend and companion of the delightful Gertrude Stein. Miss Toklas, in a chapter entitled "Murder in the Kitchen," writes as follows:

It was in the market of Palma de Mallorca that our French cook tried to teach me murder by smothering. There is no reason why this crime should have been committed publicly or that I should have been expected to participate. Jeanne was just showing off. When the crowd of market women who had gathered about her began screaming and gesticulating, I retreated. When we met later to drive back in the carry-all filled with our marketing to Terreno where we had a villa

---

[6] *The Alice B. Toklas Cook Book*, Harper & Brothers, New York, 1954, pp. 39–40. Quoted by permission of Harper & Brothers and of Michael Joseph, Ltd., London.

I refused to sympathise with Jeanne. She said the Mallorcans were bloodthirsty, didn't they go to bullfights and pay an advanced price for the meat of the beasts they had seen killed in the ring, didn't they prefer to chop off the heads of innocent pigeons instead of humanely smothering them which was the way to prevent all fowl from bleeding to death and so make them fuller and tastier. Had she not tried to explain this to them, to teach them, to show them how an intelligent humane person went about killing pigeons, but no they didn't want to learn, they preferred their own brutal ways. At lunch when she served the pigeons Jeanne discreetly said nothing. Discussing food which she enjoyed above everything had been discouraged at table. But her fine black eyes were eloquent....

Later we went back to Paris and then there was war and after a lifetime there was peace. One day passing the *concierge's loge* he called me and said he had something someone had left for us. He said he would bring it to me, which he did and which I wished he hadn't when I saw what it was, a crate of six white pigeons and a note from a friend saying she had nothing better to offer us from her home in the country, ending with "But, as Alice is clever she will make something delicious of them." It is certainly a mistake to allow a reputation for cleverness to be born and spread by loving friends. It is so cheaply acquired and so dearly paid for. Six white pigeons to be smothered, to be plucked, to be cleaned and all this to be accomplished before Gertrude Stein returned for she didn't like to see work being done. If only I had the courage the two hours before her return would easily suffice. A large cup of strong black coffee would help. This was before a lovely Brazilian told me that in her country a large cup of black coffee was always served before going to bed to ensure a good night's rest. Not yet having acquired this knowledge the black coffee made me lively and courageous. I carefully found the spot on the poor innocent Dove's throat where I was to press and pressed. The realization had never come to me before that one saw with one's fingertips as well as one's eyes. It was a most unpleasant experience, though as I laid out one by one the sweet young corpses there was no denying one could become accustomed to murdering. So I plucked the pigeons, emptied them and was ready to cook

BRAISED PIGEONS ON CROÛTONS

Every cook has probably gone through something of this kind of experience—meat in its uncooked state turns many an un-cook

pale! But women are hardy and practical, and men must eat.
Only the true vegetarian thinks us cannibals.

King Richard is the already hardened cook! To cook an abbot,
first catch your abbot, a good fat one. If the abbot being murdered
were at all real to us, possessed of a particular personality, doubtless the instructions for murder would appall us—just as we would
be appalled at the prospect of killing, for Sunday dinner, a chicken
brought up as a pet. But this abbot is a duck, a "filthy fowl," says
Richard, and the art of doing him in is a fine art. The act is deliberately, carefully, fully described, step by step. There is a certain
relish in the notion of a deed well done, proprieties well observed
("turn [his face] upward, so that his last glance may be toward
heaven; and let him say such prayers *as he can remember*"—
Richard's jibe at the secularity of certain abbots, frequently the
source of medieval comment). The sharp contrast between the
matter-of-fact language, the businesslike attitude, on the one hand,
and the horrifying nature of the deed being committed, on the
other hand, creates the particular tension involved in the use of
negative emotions and causes us on the one hand to chuckle and
on the other to shudder. It is *not* meant, however, to make us
sick, for at that point the literary experience dissolves and dwin-
dles into a real-life experience and we are only repelled. Our response is to be limited to and contained within the literature
itself. We do not rush out to to try the recipe ourselves! Nor do we
say, The murder of abbots is not so bad after all, though Alice B.
Toklas may have said that about pigeons. This is not, in other
words, a cookbook, and the passage in the novel is not really
meant to be instructive to the readers. What it intends to do is to
give us a sharp feeling about the attitude of Richard toward
abbots and some feeling about the cruelties of life in the time of
the king with the lion's heart. Nothing in the language, nothing
in the selection of details, nothing in the handling of point of
view interferes with that carefully controlled purpose. Nor do we,
as we did in the journalistic reports, look outside the piece to Sing
Sing or to Louisiana's prison, for the world of Richard is limited
to the particular world of the novel.

Summary

If literature is experience, it is also art. Hence in this chapter we have been concerned with the ways in which art, as an imitation of experience, is also an evaluation of experience. A work of literary art is in a very real sense self-contained. Furthermore, in being self-contained it is also unified, and in the unified and contained experience there is also in some sense and to some degree universality. The artist's selection and arrangement of material constitute, in their particular distortion of experience, an evaluation of experience, and the strength and quality of the evaluation depend in large measure on the degree of completeness with which the experience is imitated. Unity, order, and fullness result in both clarity and value. To give unity, order, and fullness, the writer must be largely free from "what actually happened," free to decide for himself what ought to have happened or might have happened or might better have happened. Art has a logic which life frequently seems not to possess. In real life attitudes and evaluations are frequently so mixed, uncertain, and confused as to lead to pretty steady frustration, though of course we try to keep the frustrations below a level where they may do serious damage to personality. But the writer has it in him to achieve, through the creative powers by which he manages to imitate experience, the reduction of disorder to order, the reduction of disequilibrium to equilibrium, and hence to provide that sense of satisfaction and completion which is characteristic of the aesthetic experience. Literature is freer than journalism, and both its aim and its method are different. This chapter has tried to show some of the ways— but only *some* of them—in which this is true.

Exercises

1. What determines the degree of "privacy" a poem may seem "properly" to have? Would you say, for example, that a poem containing a phrase in a language which you did not know was too private in its use of language?

2. Would the best biography of a particular man be the one which most faithfully recorded the real-life facts about its subject? What are the critical principles involved in your answer to the question?

3. How may clichés be used to good effect in writing?

4. What is the validity of the *Time* report of the "execution" of Willie Francis as a news report? Compare the report quoted from *PM*. Which has the greater validity as *news?*

8

The Writer and the Reader

As WE HAVE already suggested, the work of literature, as an experience, is only one in a series of experiences which may be assumed to lie behind any reader's experiencing of a particular poem or story or play. First of all, there is, for the writer, the actual or real-life experiences upon which he draws for the raw materials of his imitation. These are always in some way or ways autobiographical; Virginia Woolf has repeatedly suggested that the life of a writer is written at large, no matter how mysteriously, in the pages of his book. Katherine Anne Porter, another distinguished writer of our time, has stated her feeling about the matter in this way: [1]

By the time a writer has reached the end of a story, he has lived it at least three times over—first in the series of actual events that, directly or indirectly, have combined to set up that commotion in his mind and senses that causes him to write the story; second, in memory; and third in the re-creation of this chaotic stuff.

[1] Katherine Anne Porter, "Noon Wine: The Sources," *Yale Review*, Autumn, 1956, p. 22. Quoted by permission from *The Yale Review*, copyright, the Yale University Press.

This is not to suggest that the writer has "actually" lived every-thing which goes into his writing. Much of his experience is vicarious; much of it, indeed, is probably drawn from literature he has read. But the experience is true experience whether or not it is "actual."

It is one thing to say, with Mrs. Woolf, that a writer's own life is somehow written in his books; it is quite another thing to say that every attitude and every opinion and every event in a book is autobiographical—for this is far from being the usual truth. An author can feel with, or *sympathize* with, a character of whom he would not, in real life, "approve." That is, Shakespeare does not ask us to approve of murder, or of Othello's murder of Des-demona, when he clearly expects us to be moved by, and to *sympathize* with (literally, "feel with"), Othello's suffering. It is understanding the writer asks, not approval. Interestingly enough, the more we understand, the harder it is to make simple, flat judgments *against* people and things. Part of the value of an education of one's tastes in literature lies, it is to be hoped, in this broadening and extending of one's sympathies as a human being. To say this is not, of course, to say that whenever one under-stands, one cannot judge. Crimes against society, for example, are crimes against society no matter how fully one understands them, and no matter how much one feels with the offender. But there is a spirit as well as a letter of the law which issues judgments, and the humane man (for literature is one of the humanities) recog-nizes his kinship with other human beings even at moments of judgment. As one of Shakespeare's wise observers puts it (*All's Well That Ends Well,* Act IV, scene 3, lines 83 to 87),

The web of our life is of a mingled yarn, good and ill together. Our virtues would be proud if our faults whipp'd them not, and our crimes would despair if they were not cherish'd by our virtues.

The Writer and the Poem

Behind the particular experience of the poem, then, lie all the many nebulous and fleeting, as well as all the specific and sharp, experiences which make up the writer's life. But in the process of coming to the poem itself, the writer's *memory* of experience is brought into play. Many otherwise unrelated recollections, feelings, attitudes may come together in the course of memory, fusing at the moment of the poem's creation to yield the *unique* experience which is the poem. That is, the thing which is now fixed in language is in its essence unique, though in its various particulars it may duplicate actual earlier experiences. Thus, language acts as a fixative, capturing for us in timeless form something which would otherwise have been evanescent—if, indeed, it had ever come into being at all, since the point of view which tends to hold disparate experiences into a unity in a work of art is at least in part a conscious, deliberate thing on the part of the artist and might never have operated on all these experiences if it had not been for the creative act itself.

Even for the writer of the poem the experience of the poem is unique. It exists only within the poem itself, and the experience cannot be said to have been completed until the poem has been completed. The language is now the medium which must convey the experience to others; potentially, it contains the experience.

The Reader and the Writer

It is unlikely that the combination would ever exist in which the reader of a poem and the writer of that poem shared no similar experiences at all. Simply by virtue of the fact that both reader and writer are human beings with more or less similar physiological characteristics, certain similarities of experience must be agreed to exist. But beyond that general level of shared responses, it is undoubtedly true that reader and writer may differ enormously in the level, degree, and nature of their experiences. No writer can ask—or, for that matter, would think of asking— that his poem be read only by readers whose experience has been identical with his own. It is clear, of course, that without some degree of correspondence in the experiences of reader and writer no base upon which to effect communication can exist. For one thing, a reader cannot read effectively a poem written in a language he does not understand. Nor can he understand a poem in his own language unless he understands the meanings of the words in the poem. For this reason, the poet cannot let his poem consist entirely of words having purely private meanings; or, at least, if he *does,* he must run the risk of having precious few or no readers.

But beyond this, it must be said that just as the experience now fixed within the poem is unique, and hence in essence separate from any single experience in the earlier life of the poet, so it will be *essentially* different from any experience of the reader. It is out of the essential *difference,* based upon a certain degree of *similarity,* in the two experiences that the particular sense of uniqueness and illumination in a work of art arises. The sharper the illumination, the more we value the work.

The Base upon Which Communication Is Effected

One must be wary of employing the word *communication* in talking about a work of art. Communication in any clear sense is not at all a *necessary* part of the definition of a poem or work of art. A poem may be a poem whether or not it happens to communicate to you as an individual reader. Emily Dickinson used to write poems and tuck them away without showing them at all; but they were poems whether or not Emily Dickinson had communication in mind, and they did not have to wait until they found readers before they could be called poems. A poem (that is, a work of literary art) is a construct in language which embodies an experience, and it is the fact that it embodies an experience, giving it wholeness and carefully circumscribing the point of view through which it can be apprehended, which constitutes its being a work of literary art.

Now it is true that for any of us, *as readers,* communication between the work of art and ourselves is a primary consideration. We cannot evaluate a work of art which simply does not speak to us at all: work of art though it may be, it leads us to one of two feelings about it—either, we say, the poet has written a work which is so private as to be negligible in its value, or we are as readers too limited in comprehension to make a proper audience for it. We often, with too great confidence in our own powers of analysis, leap to the first feeling when we ought rather more modestly to admit the possibility of the second.

Communication of the work of art does, then, matter to us when we begin to decide that certain works of art seem to us better than others. This is why it makes sense to say that, of two works of art, one may be better than the other for readers sixteen years of age, even though the "better" one is felt by a reader forty-five years old to be for him inferior. Tastes change, judgments change—with age, with the passing of time, for all sorts of reasons; but presumably "absolute judgments" of works of art are made out of the fullness of mature experience, after attitudes have begun to settle down (not, it must be said, to *harden*). If knowledge of the materials of a craft is essential to being a good judge of a product of that craft, then fullness of experience (real or vicarious) is *one* of the conditions necessary to the judgment of the literary critic. It is to such a judge that the work of art is likely to speak most fully.

But limitations in the quality of experience may hamper the writer as well as the reader. Read the following poem: [2]

> Strange fits of passion have I known:
> And I will dare to tell,
> But in the Lover's ear alone,
> What once to me befell.
>
> When she I loved looked every day
> Fresh as a rose in June,
> I to her cottage bent my way,
> Beneath an evening-moon.

[2] The text is that given by E. de Selincourt in *The Poetical Works of William Wordsworth,* Oxford University Press, New York, 1944, vol. II, p. 29. Quoted by permission of the publishers.

Upon the moon I fixed my eye,
All over the wide lea;
With quickening pace my horse drew nigh
Those paths so dear to me.

And now we reached the orchard-plot;
And, as we climbed the hill,
The sinking moon to Lucy's cot
Came near, and nearer still.

In one of those sweet dreams I slept,
Kind Nature's gentlest boon!
And all the while my eyes I kept
On the descending moon.

My horse moved on; hoof after hoof
He raised, and never stopped:
When down behind the cottage roof,
At once, the bright moon dropped.

What fond and wayward thoughts will slide
Into a Lover's head!
"O mercy!" to myself I cried,
"If Lucy should be dead!"

William Wordsworth (1770–1850)

Presumably the poet is interested in capturing the strangeness of a particular "fit of passion," the moment when the perfectly natural obscuring of the moon seemed to him suddenly to signal the possibility of Lucy's death. Such auguries, such omens are a natural enough part of experience, to be sure; but in Wordsworth's account, there is little to make this particular experience vivid or sharp enough to hold our attention. To begin with, the short, fairly regular lines and the quickly recurring rhymes make the meter of the poem very prominent. But there is not a corresponding tightness or prominence of detail. The freshness of the rose, the cottage, and the moon in the second stanza; the moon, the lea, the horse, and the paths in the third; the orchard-plot, the hill, the moon in the fourth; and the cottage and the moon in the sixth—all these details are very general in Wordsworth's handling of them, and they are sharply subordinate to the narrative element. But the last two lines, and indeed the whole frame of the poem as a statement to *lovers,* depend for effectiveness upon the *significance* of Lucy to the poet; if neither the attitude of the poet nor Lucy takes on clear identity for us, the poem becomes pretty simply a statement of a theme. The prose statement of the theme is here too perilously close to *being* the poem. The narrative elements do not contribute enough to the total weight of the statement to make them seem worth six or seven stanzas, and the meter and rhyme take over at the expense of matters which ought to be more prominent. The attitude and point of view of the poet are too largely fragmented by the specific details rather than underscored and intensified by them. The poem seems to represent details with a matter-of-fact faithfulness to real life ("My horse moved on; hoof after hoof/ He raised, and never stopped"), but these are details not at all necessary to the experience which is intended in the poem, the imitation of a single "strange fit of passion." There is not enough substance to support the accidental detail. Wordsworth reports rather than creates an emotion.

Now read two versions of another of the Lucy poems.[3] The first represents a stage in the development of the poem; the second is the poem as we now read it in collections of Wordsworth's poetry. Compare the two in terms of the poet's success in imitating the quality of an experience.

Draft

> My hope was one, from cities far,
> Nursed on a lonesome heath;
> Her lips were red as roses are,
> Her hair a woodbine wreath.

---

[3] From *ibid.,* p. 30. Quoted by permission of the publishers.

She dwelt among the untrodden ways
    Beside the springs of Dove,
A Maid whom there were none to praise
    And very few to love:

A violet by a mossy stone
    Half hidden from the eye!
—Fair as a star, when only one
    Is shining in the sky.

And she was graceful as the broom
That flowers by Carron's side;
But slow distemper checked her bloom,
And on the Heath she died.

Long time before her head lay low
Dead to the world was she:
But now she's in her grave, and, oh,
The difference to me!

Final Version

She dwelt among the untrodden ways
    Beside the springs of Dove,
A Maid whom there were none to praise
    And very few to love:

A violet by a mossy stone
    Half hidden from the eye!
—Fair as a star, when only one
    Is shining in the sky.

She lived unknown, and few could know
    When Lucy ceased to be;
But she is in her grave, and, oh,
    The difference to me!

Limitations Placed upon Communication

We have seen that there are several steps in the process which results finally in the poem read by the reader. First, there is the real-life experience or the elements of experience in the life and mind of the poet; second, there is the act of memory; third, there is the fusing of present and past experience in the act of creating the imitation; finally, there is the reading of the poem by the reader.

We have been saying that value attached to the reading of the poem depends in part upon the quality and completeness of the experience within the poem itself and in part upon the fitness, as a judge, of the reader. A poem may seem to a given reader not a particularly good poem, either because the poem itself (that is, the degree of success of the poet) is weak or because the reader is limited. It is important for the reader to be receptive to the poem, to give it a fair chance, before he decides that the fault lies with the poet.

But there are other ways in which communication between poem and reader may be hampered.

VOCABULARY

We have already said that one cannot successfully read a poem in a language which he does not understand. Nor can one successfully read a poem in his own language until he knows the words of which it is composed—not simply *a* meaning, but *meanings* of words. Read, for example, the following poem:

> I struck the board, and cry'd, "No more;
> I will abroad."
> What, shall I ever sigh and pine?
> My lines and life are free; free as the road,
> Loose as the wind, as large as store.
> Shall I be still in suit?
> Have I no harvest but a thorn
> To let me blood, and not restore
> What I have lost with cordial fruit?
> Sure, there was wine
> Before my sighs did dry it; there was corn
> Before my tears did drown it;

Is the year only lost to me?
Have I no bays to crown it,
No flowers, no garlands gay? all blasted,
        All wasted?
Not so, my heart; but there is fruit,
     And thou hast hands.
    Recover all thy sigh-blown age
On double pleasures; leave thy cold dispute
Of what is fit and not; forsake thy cage,
      Thy rope of sands
Which petty thoughts have made; and made to thee
  Good cable, to enforce and draw,
      And be thy law,
  While thou didst wink and wouldst not see.
      Away! take heed;
      I will abroad.
Call in thy death's-head there, tie up thy fears;
      He that forbears
    To suit and serve his need
    Deserves his load.
But as I rav'd and grew more fierce and wild
     At every word,
  Methought I heard one calling, "Child";
    And I reply'd, "My Lord."

George Herbert (1593–1633)

The poem is called "The Collar," and of course there is a sense in which our modern word *collar,* meaning "restraint," operates within the poem (see the lines referring to the cable and the rope); but our modern passion for uniformity in spelling (a passion not shared by the seventeenth century) has obscured another meaning of *collar,* which becomes evident only if we spell the word *choler.* The pun is a way of getting at part of the tension in the poem—the poet is *angry* because he is *restrained;* but a collar is not merely a restraint, and the reference to rope and cable and load suggests a still further application of the word. The word *cordial,* too, is complex. It has our modern meaning, "stimulating" or "invigorating," but it also has a literal meaning, "of the heart," from the Latin word *cor*, meaning "heart." A good dictionary is an invaluable asset to a reader; for the variety of meanings of a word over a given period of history, the *Oxford English Dictionary*, a monumental work in a series of volumes which is probably in your library, may be consulted. Check, for example, the word *suit*, which occurs twice in the poem.

Words have varieties and levels of meaning, and the poet may, as here, ask the reader to bear more than a single meaning in mind. The total context of the poem, the totality of attitude within the environment of the poem, demands wide and full response to such varieties of meaning. One reason why paraphrase of a poem, or restatement of a poem's meaning in other words, destroys the poem is that other words really *are* other words, and the double meanings condensed into single terms are separated and diffused when synonyms for two or more meanings have to be found. In explaining the title of Herbert's poem, for example, we destroyed the impact which the title would have for anyone immediately seeing the pun. This weakened impact resulting from *explication* is one of the reasons why older literatures often seem to us remote; the better equipped we are linguistically, the less need we have for footnotes and editorial comment when we read poetry from the seventeenth century, and the more force the poetry is likely to have for us. But the argument is circular—for *one* of the reasons for reading literature is that it helps to equip us linguistically to express experience and to comprehend experience.

DIALECT

Another kind of linguistic difficulty is presented in the following short excerpt from act I of Shaw's play *Pygmalion*,[4] concluding with Shaw's characteristic note in brackets:

THE MOTHER. How do you know that my son's name is Freddy, pray?
THE FLOWER GIRL. Ow eez yə-ooa san, is e? Wal, fewd dan y' də-ooty bawmz a mather should, eed now bettern to spawl a pore

---

[4] *Pygmalion, A Romance in Five Acts*, Penguin edition, Penguin Books, Inc., Baltimore, 1951, p. 13. By permission of the Society of Authors.

gel's flahrzn than ran awy athaht pyin. Will ye-oo py me f'them? [*Here, with apologies, this desperate attempt to represent her dialect without a phonetic alphabet must be abandoned as unintelligible outside London.*]

It is a common thing for Americans to have trouble with English, Irish, and Scotch dialects (and not only these!) when they are reduced either to phonetic spellings on the page, as here, or to speech on the stage. In both instances, a "distancing" of the experience of the literature is likely to take place; the position of an American is likely to differ markedly from that of an Englishman or an Irishman or a Scot as a member of the audience. The reader must read with his ears open if such spellings as "də-ooty" and "spawl" and "athaht" are to be anything but peculiarities to him; as long as they keep thrusting out at him from the print like strange beasts, they will hamper his responses to the piece itself. Any writer making use of localisms and dialects must face the problem of getting the effects he wishes without interfering too sharply with the projection of his meaning to his readers, as Shaw clearly recognized.

The problem is even sharper in the following poem, "Contented wi' Little," [5] by Robert Burns (1759-1796), which is likely to discourage the timid reader by looking like this in a book:

Contended wi' little, and cantie [1] wi' mair,
Whene'er I forgather wi' Sorrow and Care,
I gie them a skelp,[2] as they're creepin alang,
Wi' a cog [3] o' guid swats [4] and an auld Scottish sang.

I whyles [5] claw [6] the elbow o' troublesome-Thought;
But man is a soger,[7] and life is a faught; [8]
My mirth and guid humor are coin in my pouch,
And my Freedom's my lairdship nae monarch daur touch.

[1] Merry.	[3] Cup.	[5] Sometimes.	[7] Soldier.
[2] Slap.	[4] Ale.	[6] Scratch.	[8] Fight.

[5] Quoted by permission from George Benjamin Woods, *English Poetry and Prose of the Romantic Movement*, Scott, Foresman and Company, Chicago, 1929, p. 204.

A towmond [9] o' trouble, should that be my fa',[10]
A night o' guid fellowship sowthers [11] it a':
When at the blythe end o' our journey at last,
Wha the deil ever thinks o' the road he has past?

Blind Chance, let her snapper and stoyte [12] on her way;
Be 't to me, be 't frae me, e'en let the jade gae:
Come Ease, or come Travail, come Pleasure or Pain,
My warst word is, "Welcome, and welcome again!"

[9] Twelvemonth.   [11] Solders; mends.
[10] Lot.   [12] Stumble and stagger.

Perhaps only a Scot can read such a poem without certain agonies
of mind, though it is true that to the ear the Scotch dialect has
or may have a wondrous music. Burns has many, many virtues
as a poet, and probably no true lover of poetry would wish to
lose a drop of him—but meanwhile it is true that anyone who
hopes for more than titillation of the ear, anyone who wants to
know what the poem is saying, must often make a brave effort to
acquaint himself with the Scotch vocabulary of Burns.

A number of American dialects present us with the same problem. Frequently a writer will seek an answer which will permit
him to avoid phonetic spellings, which are almost always cumber-
some to the silent reader. In the following passage from "Freedom's a Hard-Bought Thing," Stephen Vincent Benét successfully
manages to produce the *effects* of Negro speech without resort-
ing to idiosyncrasies of spelling: [6]

He's scared when he hear the dogs, but he ain't scared like he used
to be. He ain't more scared than any man. He kill the big dog in the
clearing—the big dog with the big voice—and he do it with his naked
hands. He cross water three times after that to kill the scent, and he
go on.

He got nothing to help him—no, Lord—but he got a star. The star

[6] From "Freedom's a Hard-Bought Thing," *Selected Works of Stephen Vincent Benét*, Rinehart & Company, Inc. Copyright, 1940, by Stephen Vincent
Benét. Quoted by permission.

shine in the sky and the star shine—the star point north with its shining. You put that star in the sky, O Lord; you put it for the prisoned and the humble. You put it there—you ain't never going to blink it out.

In quite a different style, Gertrude Stein manages something of the same feat in this passage from "Melanctha," [7] one of the most moving of modern short stories:

"I know Miss Melanctha," he began, "it ain't very easy for you to understand what I was meaning by what I was just saying to you, and perhaps some of the good people I like so wouldn't think very much, any more than you do, Miss Melanctha, about the ways I have to be good. But that's no matter Miss Melanctha. What I mean Miss Melanctha by what I was just saying to you is, that I don't, no, never believe in doing things just to get excited. You see Miss Melanctha I mean the way so many of the colored people do it. Instead of just working hard and caring about their working and living regular with their families and saving up all their money, so they will have some to bring up their children better, instead of living regular and doing like that and getting all their new ways from just decent living, the colored people just keep running around and perhaps drinking and doing everything bad they can ever think of, and not just because they like all those bad things that they are always doing, but only just because they want to get excited. No Miss Melanctha, you see I am a colored man myself and I ain't sorry, and I want to see the colored people being good and careful and always honest and living always just as regular as can be, and I am sure Miss Melanctha, that that way everybody can have a good time and be happy and keep right and be busy, and not always have to be doing bad things for new ways to get excited. Yes Miss Melanctha, I certainly do like everything to be good, and quiet, and I certainly do think that is the best way for all us colored people. No, Miss Melanctha too, I don't mean this except only just the way I say it. I ain't got any other meaning Miss Melanctha, and it's that what I mean when I am saying about being really good. It ain't Miss Melanctha to be pious and not liking every kind of

[7] From *Selected Writings of Gertrude Stein*, ed. by Carl Van Vechten, copyright, 1946, by Random House, Inc., New York, pp. 324–325. Quoted by permission of the publishers.

people, and I don't say ever Miss Melanctha that when other kind of people come regular into your life you shouldn't want to know them always. What I mean Miss Melanctha by what I am always saying is, you shouldn't try to know everybody just to run around and get excited. It's that kind of way of doing that I hate so always Miss Melanctha, and that is so bad for all us colored people. I don't know as you understand now any better what I mean by what I was just saying to you. But you certainly do know now Miss Melanctha, that I always mean it what I say when I am talking."

It is true that Miss Stein and Benét achieve quite *different effects* in their handling of Negro speech, though both succeed in giving us the qualities they wish. How would you describe the differences in tone and quality in the two excerpts?

ALLUSIONS

Almost any writer counts, from time to time, on certain identities between his experience and that of his reader. Communication sometimes rests in part upon a common store of knowledge in the two minds which meet in the experience of a work of literary art. Allusion to facts, events, characters, stories outside the work of art itself is so usual with writers that *allusion* has become a technical word in the vocabulary of critics. An allusion is a reference to something; it may be direct or implied, it may be either simple or complex in its application to meaning within the work of art. In the following lines from Thomas Gray's "Elegy Written in a Country Churchyard," for example, the allusions to English figures are direct and simple:

> Some village Hampden that with dauntless breast,
>   The little tyrant of his fields withstood,
> Some mute inglorious Milton here may rest,
>   Some Cromwell guiltless of his country's blood.

The allusions are, of course, to the period of the Commonwealth, and to figures famous in the literary and political life of that time. It is interesting to note that in the first (or at least an early) draft of the poem, the allusion to Hampden was an allusion to Cato, the allusion to Milton was an allusion to Cicero, and the allusion to Cromwell was one to Caesar. Apparently in the final version Gray decided to limit his consideration to his own country. It would be worth your time to read the entire poem to see *why*. An interesting question of *point of view* is involved.

Such direct allusions as these are common in literature. Such "common ground" as the Bible, Shakespeare, Roman and Greek history, English and American history, and so on, used to provide poets with a very valuable kind of raw material. Shakespeare himself could refer to Antony, in *Antony and Cleopatra,* as "the triple pillar of the world," and be sure that his auditors would catch the allusion to Caesar, Lepidus, and Antony as the Triumvirate, the three pillars supporting the weight of the Roman state. Or Sir Thomas Browne (1605–1682), author of the fascinating *Religio Medici,* could write, "I have therefore always endeavoured to compose those feuds and angry dissensions between Affection, Faith and Reason; for there is in our soul a kind of Triumvirate, a Triple Government of Three Competitors, which distracts the Peace of this our Commonwealth not less than did that other the state of *Rome,*" and could likewise count on the value of the allusion for his readers.

Unfortunately for our older writers, readers nowadays are frequently empty of such knowledge. That is why textbooks containing literature from earlier periods are so full of notes! It is not very pleasant constantly to be looking at footnotes in order to comprehend a text, and it is no wonder that students resist them; how much pleasanter if all of us read widely enough so that the allusions found us already prepared to respond! Knowledge begets knowledge; a dry well quenches no one's thirst. We find ourselves growing impatient with a writer whose references are all to such private experiences that we *cannot* respond; is it not quite proper that a writer should be impatient with a reader who has so small a store of knowledge that he *will not* respond? One reads to get an education, but one cannot have much of an edu-

Eliot & Pound

cation until one has read. All of us need to be willing to prod ourselves, so that we shall not miss profitable experience simply as a result of our own laziness of mind.

The hidden or indirect allusion, for example, is exceedingly difficult for the reader who is ignorant. It is perhaps worth the time to include here a whole story (by a writer who stands high in the opinion of her contemporaries) which will illustrate the point. Katherine Anne Porter [8] has said of this writer,

Nearly all the Southern writers I know were early, omnivorous, insatiable readers, and Miss Welty runs reassuringly true to this pattern. She had at arm's reach the typical collection of books which existed as a matter of course in a certain kind of Southern family, so that she had read the ancient Greek and Roman poetry, history and fable, Shakespeare, Milton, Dante, the eighteenth-century English and the nineteenth-century French novelists, with a dash of Tolstoy and Dostoievsky, before she realized what she was reading. When she first discovered contemporary literature, she was just the right age to find first W. B. Yeats and Virginia Woolf in the air around her; but always, from the beginning until now, she loved folk tales, fairy tales, old legends, and she likes to listen to the songs and stories of people who live in old communities whose culture is recollected and bequeathed orally.

The story we shall read is Eudora Welty's "Shower of Gold."

SHOWER OF GOLD [9]

I

That was Miss Snowdie MacLain.

She comes after her butter, won't let me run over with it from just across the road. Her husband walked out of the house one day and left his hat on the banks of the Big Black River.—That could have started something, too.

[8] "Eudora Welty and 'A Curtain of Green,'" from *The Days Before* by Katherine Anne Porter, copyright, 1941, by Katherine Anne Porter. Reprinted by permission of Harcourt, Brace and Company, Inc.; and Martin Secker & Warburg, Ltd., London.

[9] From *The Golden Apples*, by Eudora Welty, copyright, 1948, by Eudora Welty. Reprinted by permission of Harcourt, Brace and Company, Inc.

We might have had a little run on doing that in Morgana, if it had been so willed. What King did, the copy-cats always might do. Well, King MacLain left a new straw hat on the banks of the Big Black and there are people that consider he headed West.

Snowdie grieved for him, but the decent way you'd grieve for the dead, more like, and nobody wanted to think, around her, that he treated her that way. But how long can you humor the humored? Well, always. But I could almost bring myself to talk about it—to a passer-by, that will never see her again, or me either. Sure I can churn and talk. My name's Mrs. Rainey.

You seen she wasn't ugly—and the little blinky lines to her eye-lids come from trying to see. She's an albino but nobody would ever try to call her ugly around here—with that tender, tender skin like a baby. Some said King figured out that if the babies started coming, he had a chance for a nestful of little albinos, and that swayed him. No, I don't say it. I say he was just willful. *He* wouldn't think ahead.

Willful and outrageous, to some several. Well: he married Snowdie.

Lots of worse men wouldn't have: no better sense. Them Hudsons had more than MacLains, but none of 'em had enough to count or worry over. Not by then. Hudson money built that house, and built it for *Snowdie*...they prayed over that. But take King; marrying must have been some of his showing off—like man never married at all till *he* flung in, then had to show the others how he could go right on acting. And like, 'Look, everybody, this is what I think of Morgana and MacLain Courthouse and all the way between'—further, for all I know—'marrying a girl with pink eyes.' 'I swan!' we all say. Just like he wants us to, scoundrel. And Snowdie as sweet and gentle as you find them. Of course gentle people aren't the ones you lead best, he had that to find out, so know-all. No, sir, she'll beat him yet, balking. In the meantime children of his growing up in the County Orphan's, so say several, and children known and unknown, scattered-like. When he does come, he's just as nice as he can be to Snowdie. Just as courteous. Was from the start.

Haven't you noticed it prevail, in the world in general? Beware of a man with manners. He never raised his voice to her, but then one day he walked out of the house. Oh, I don't mean once!

He went away for a good spell before he come back that time. She had a little story about him needing the waters. Next time it was more than a year, it was two—oh, it was three. I had two children myself, enduring his being gone, and one to die. Yes, and that time he sent her word ahead: 'Meet me in the woods.' No, he more invited her than told her to come—'Suppose you meet me in the woods.' And it was night time he supposed to her. And Snowdie met him without asking 'What for?' which I would want to know of Fate Rainey. After all, they were married—they had a right to sit inside and talk in the light and comfort, or lie down easy on a good goosefeather bed, either. I would even consider he might not be there when I came. Well, if Snowdie went without a question, then I can tell it without a question as long as I love Snowdie. Her version is that in the woods they met and both decided on what would be best.

Best for him, of course. We could see the writing on the wall.

'The Woods' was Morgan's Woods. We would any of us know the place he meant, without trying—I could have streaked like an arrow to the very oak tree, one there to itself and all spready: a real shady place by *day,* is all I know. Can't you just see King MacLain leaning his length against that tree by the light of the moon as you come walking through Morgan's Woods and you hadn't seen him in three years? 'Suppose you meet me in the woods.' My foot. Oh, I don't know how poor Snowdie stood it, crossing the distance.

Then, twins.

That was where I come in, I could help when things got to there. I took her a little churning of butter with her milk and we took up. I hadn't been married long myself, and Mr. Rainey's health was already a little delicate so he'd thought best to quit heavy work. We was both hard workers fairly early.

I always thought twins might be nice. And might have been for them, by just the sound of it. The MacLains first come to Morgana bride and groom from MacLain and went into that new house. He was educated off, to practice law—well needed here. Snowdie was Miss Lollie Hudson's daughter, well known. Her father was Mr. Eugene Hudson, a storekeeper down at Crossroads past the Courthouse, but he was a lovely man. Snowdie was their only daughter, and they give her a nice education. And I guess people more or less expected her to teach school: not marry. She couldn't see all that well, was the only thing in the way, but Mr. Comus Stark here and the supervisors overlooked that, knowing the family and Snowdie's real good way with Sunday School children. Then before the school year even got a good start, she got took up by King MacLain all of a sudden. I think it

was when jack-o'-lanterns was pasted on her window I used to see
his buggy roll up right to the schoolhouse steps and wait on her. He
courted her in Morgana and MacLain too, both ends, didn't skip
a day.

It was no different—no quicker and no slower—than the like happens
every whipstitch, so I don't need to tell you they got married in the
MacLain Presbyterian Church before you could shake a stick at it,
no matter how surprised people were going to be. And once they
dressed Snowdie all in white, you know she was whiter than your
dreams.

So—he'd been educated in the law and he traveled for somebody, that
was the first thing he did—I'll tell you in a minute what he sold, and
she stayed home and cooked and kept house. I forget if she had a
Negro, she didn't know how to tell one what to do if she had. And
she put her eyes straight out, almost, going to work and making cur-
tains for every room and all like that. So busy. At first it didn't look
like they would have any children.

So it went the way I told you, slipped into it real easy, people took
it for granted mighty early—him leaving and him being welcomed
home, him leaving and him sending word, 'Meet me in the woods,' and
him gone again, at last leaving the hat. I told my husband I was going
to quit keeping count of King's comings and goings, and it wasn't
long after that he did leave the hat. I don't know yet whether he
meant it kind or cruel. Kind, I incline to believe. Or maybe she was
winning. Why do I try to figure? Maybe because Fate Rainey ain't
got a surprise in him, and proud of it. So Fate said, 'Well now, let's
have the women to settle down and pay attention to homefolks a
while.' That was all he could say about it.

So, you wouldn't have had to wait long. Here come Snowdie across
the road to bring the news. I seen her coming across my pasture in a
different walk, it was the way somebody comes down an aisle. Her
sunbonnet ribbons was jumping around her: springtime. Did you
notice her little dainty waist she has still? I declare it's a mystery to
think about her having the strength once. Look at me.

I was in the barn milking, and she come and took a stand there at
the head of the little Jersey, Lady May. She had a quiet, picked-out
way to tell news. She said, 'I'm going to have a baby too, Miss Katie.
Congratulate me.'

Me and Lady May both had to just stop and look at her. She looked like more than only the news had come over her. It was like a shower of something had struck her, like she'd been caught out in something bright. It was more than the day. There with her eyes all crinkled up with always fighting the light, yet she was looking out bold as a lion that day under her brim, and gazing into my bucket and into my stall like a visiting somebody. Poor Snowdie. I remember it was Easter time and how the pasture was all spotty there behind her little blue skirt, in sweet clover. He sold tea and spices, that's what it was.

It was sure enough nine months to the day the twins come after he went sallying out through those woods and fields and laid his hat down on the bank of the river with 'King MacLain' on it.

I wish I'd had seen him! I don't guess *I'd* have stopped him. I can't tell you why, but I wish I'd had seen him! But nobody did.

For Snowdie's sake—here they come bringing the hat, and a hullaballoo raised—they drug the Big Black for nine miles down, or was it only eight, and sent word to Bovina and on, clear to Vicksburg, to watch out for anything to wash up or to catch in the trees in the river. Sure, there never was anything—just the hat. They found everybody else that ever honestly drowned along the Big Black in this neighborhood. Mr. Sissum at the store, he drowned later on and they found him. I think with the hat he ought to have laid his watch down, if he wanted to give it a better look.

Snowdie kept just as bright and brave, she didn't seem to give in. She must have had her thoughts and they must have been one of two things. One that he was dead—then why did her face have the glow? It had a glow—and the other that he left her and meant it. And like people said, if she smiled *then,* she was clear out of reach. I didn't know if I liked the glow. Why didn't she rage and storm a little—to me, anyway, just Mrs. Rainey? The Hudsons all hold themselves in. But it didn't seem to me, running in and out the way I was, that Snowdie had ever got a real good look at life, maybe. Maybe from the beginning. Maybe she just doesn't know the *extent.* Not the kind of look I got, and away back when I was twelve year old or so. Like something was put to my eye.

She just went on keeping house, and getting fairly big with what I told you already was twins, and she seemed to settle into her content. Like a little white kitty in a basket, making you wonder if she just mightn't put up her paw and scratch, if anything was, after all, to come near. At her house it was like Sunday even in the mornings, every day, in that cleaned-up way. She was taking a joy in her fresh untracked rooms and that dark, quiet, real quiet hall that runs through her house. And I love Snowdie. I love her.

Except none of us felt very *close* to her all the while. I'll tell you what it was, what made her different. It was the not waiting any more, except where the babies waited, and that's not but one story. We were mad at her and protecting her all at once, when we couldn't be close to her.

And she come out in her pretty clean shirt waists to water the ferns, and she had remarkable flowers—she had her mother's way with flowers, of course. And give just as many away, except it wasn't like I or you give. She was by her own self. Oh, her mother was dead by then, and Mr. Hudson fourteen miles down the road away, crippled up, running his store in a cane chair. We was every bit she had. Everybody tried to stay with her as much as they could spare, not let a day go by without one of us to run in and speak to her and say a word about an ordinary thing. Miss Lizzie Stark let her be in charge of raising money for the poor country people at Christmas that year, and like that. Of course we made all her little things for her, stitches like that was way beyond her. It was a good thing she got such a big stack.

The twins come the first day of January. Miss Lizzie Stark—she hates all men, and is real important: across yonder's her chimney—made Mr. Comus Stark, her husband, hitch up and drive to Vicksburg to bring back a Vicksburg doctor in her own buggy the night before, instead of using Dr. Loomis here, and stuck him in a cold room to sleep at her house; she said trust any doctor's buggy to break down on those bridges. Mrs. Stark stayed right by Snowdie, and of course several, and I, stayed too, but Mrs. Stark was not budging and took charge when pains commenced. Snowdie had the two little boys and neither one albino. They were both King all over again, if you want to know it. Mrs. Stark had so hoped for a girl, or two *girls*. Snowdie clapped the names on them of Lucius Randall and Eugene Hudson, after her own father and her mother's father.

It was the only sign she ever give Morgana that maybe she didn't think the name King MacLain had stayed beautiful. But not much of a sign; some women don't name after their husbands, until they get down to nothing else left. I don't think with Snowdie even *two* other names meant she had changed yet, not towards King, that scoundrel.

Time goes like a dream no matter how hard you run, and all the time we heard things from out in the world that we listened to but that still didn't mean we believed them. You know the kind of things. Somebody's cousin saw King MacLain. Mr. Comus Stark, the one the cotton and timber belongs to, he goes a little, and he claimed three or four times he saw his back, and once saw him getting a haircut in Texas. Those things you will hear forever when people go off, to keep up a few shots in the woods. They might mean something—might not.

Till the most outrageous was the time my husband went up to Jackson. He saw a man that was the spit-image of King in the parade, my husband told me in his good time, the inauguration of Governor Vardaman. He was right up with the big ones and astride a fine animal. Several from here went but as Mrs. Spights said, why wouldn't they be looking at the Governor? Or the New Capitol? But King MacLain could steal anyone's glory, so he thought.

When I asked the way he looked, I couldn't get a thing out of my husband, except he lifted his feet across the kitchen floor like a horse and man in one, and I went after him with my broom. I knew, though. If it was King, he looked like, 'Hasn't everybody been wondering, though, been out of their minds to know, where I've been keeping myself!' I told my husband it reasoned to me like it was up to Governor Vardaman to get hold of King and bring something out of him, but my husband said why pick on one man, and besides a parade was going on and what all. Men! I said if I'd been Governor Vardaman and spied King MacLain from Morgana marching in my parade as big as I was and no call for it, I'd have had the whole thing brought to a halt and called him to accounts. 'Well, what good would it have done you?' my husband said. 'A plenty,' I said. I was excited at the time it happened. 'That was just as good a spot as any to show him forth, right in front of the New Capitol in Jackson with the band going, and just as good a man to do it.'

Well, sure, men like that need to be shown up before the world, I guess—not that any of us would be surprised. 'Did you go and find him after the Governor got inaugurated to suit you then?' I asked my husband. But he said no, and reminded me. He went for me a new bucket; and brought me the wrong size. Just like the ones at Holifield's. But he said he saw King or his twin. What twin!

Well, through the years, we'd hear of him here or there—maybe two places at once. New Orleans and Mobile. That's people's careless way of using their eyes.

I believe he's been to California. Don't ask me why. But I picture him there. I see King in the West, out where it's gold and all that. Everybody to their own visioning.

II

Well, what happened turned out to happen on Hallowe'en. Only last week—and seems already like something that couldn't happen at all.

My baby girl, Virgie, swallowed a button that same day—later on— and that *happened,* it seems like still, but not this. And not a word's been spoke out loud, for Snowdie's sake, so I trust the rest of the world will be as careful.

You can talk about a baby swallowing a button off a shirt and having to be up-ended and her behind pounded, and it sounds reasonable if you can just see the baby—there she runs—but get to talking about something that's only a kind of *near* thing—and hold your horses.

Well, Hallowe'en, about three o'clock, I was over at Snowdie's helping her cut out patterns—she's kept on sewing for those boys. Me, I have a little girl to sew for—she was right there, asleep on the bed in the next room—and it hurts my conscience being that lucky over Snowdie too. And the twins wouldn't play out in the yard that day but had hold of the scraps and the scissors and the paper of pins and all, and there underfoot they were dressing up and playing ghosts and boogers. Uppermost in their little minds was Hallowe'en.

They had on their masks, of course, tied on over their Buster Brown bobs and pressing a rim around the back. I was used to how they looked by then—but I don't like masks. They both come from Spights' store and cost a nickel. One was the Chinese kind, all yellow and mean with slant eyes and a dreadful thin mustache of black horsy hair. The other one was a lady, with an almost scary-sweet smile on her lips. I never did take to that smile, with all day for it. Eugene Hudson wanted to be the Chinaman and so Lucius Randall had to be the lady.

So they were making tails and do-lollies and all kinds of foolishness, and sticking them on to their little middles and behinds, snatching every scrap from the shirts and flannels me and Snowdie was cutting out on the dining room table. Sometimes we could grab a little boy and baste something up on him whether or no, but we didn't really pay them much mind, we was talking about the prices of things for winter, and the funeral of an old maid.

So we never heard the step creak or the porch give, at all. That was a blessing. And if it wasn't for something that come from outside us all to tell about it, I wouldn't have the faith I have that it come about.

But happening along our road—like he does every day—was a real trustworthy nigger. He's one of Mrs. Stark's mother's niggers, Old Plez Morgan everybody calls him. Lives down beyond me. The real old kind, that knows everybody since time was. He knows more folks than I do, who they are, and all the *fine* people. If you wanted anybody in Morgana that wouldn't be likely to make a mistake in who a person is, you would ask for Old Plez.

So he was making his way down the road, by stages. He still has to do a few people's yards won't let him go, like Mrs. Stark, because he don't pull up things. He's no telling how old and starts early and takes his time coming home in the evening—always stopping to speak to people to ask after their health and tell them good evening all the way. Only that day, he said he didn't see a soul *else*—besides you'll hear who in a minute—on the way, not on porches or in the yards. I can't tell you why, unless it was those little gusts of north wind that had started blowing. Nobody likes that.

But yonder ahead of him was walking a man. Plez said it was a white man's walk and a walk he knew—but it struck him it was from away in another year, another time. It wasn't just the walk of any-body supposed to be going along the road to MacLain right at that *time*—and yet it was too—and if it was, he still couldn't think what business that somebody would be up to. That was the careful way Plez was putting it to his mind.

If you saw Plez, you'd know it was him. He had some roses stuck in his hat that day, I saw him right after it happened. Some of Miss Lizzie's fall roses, big as a man's fist and red as blood—they were nod-ding side-to-side out of the band of his old black hat, and some other little scraps out of the garden laid around the brim, throwed away by Mrs. Stark; he'd been cleaning out her beds that day, it was fixing to rain.

He said later he wasn't in any great hurry, or he would have maybe caught up and passed the man. Up yonder ahead he went, going the same way Plez was going, and not much more interested in a race. And a real familiar stranger.

So Plez says presently the familiar stranger paused. It was in front of the MacLains'—and sunk his weight on one leg and just stood there, posey as statues, hand on his hip. Ha! Old Plez says, according, he just leaned himself against the Presbyterian Church gate and waited a while.

Next thing, the stranger—oh, it was King! By then Plez was calling him Mr. King to himself—went up through the yard and then didn't go right in like anybody else. First he looked around. He took in the yard and summerhouse and skimmed from cedar to cedar along the edge of where he lived, and under the fig tree at the back and under the wash (if he'd counted it!) and come close to the front again, sniffy like, and Plez said though he couldn't swear to seeing from the Presbyterian Church exactly what Mr. King was doing, he knows as good as seeing it that he looked through the blinds. He would have looked in the dining room—have mercy. We shut the West out of Snowdie's eyes of course.

At last he come full front again, around the flowers under the front bedroom. Then he settled himself nice and started up the front steps.

The middle step sings when it's stepped on, but we didn't hear it. Plez said, well, he had on fine tennis shoes. So he got across the front porch and what do you think he's fixing to do but knock on that door? Why wasn't he satisfied with outdoors?

On his own front door. He makes a little shadow knock, like trying to see how it would look, and then puts his present behind his coat. Of course he had something there in a box for her. You know he constitutionally brought home the kind of presents that break your heart. He stands there with one leg out pretty, to surprise them. And I bet a nice smile on his face. Oh, don't ask me to go on!

Suppose Snowdie'd took a notion to glance down the hall—the dining room's at the end of it, and the folding-doors pushed back—and seen him, all 'Come-kiss-me' like that. I don't know if she could have seen that good—but *I* could. I was a fool and didn't look.

It was the twins seen him. Through those little bitty mask holes, those eagle eyes! There ain't going to be no stopping those twins. And he didn't get to knock on the door, but he had his hand raised the second time and his knuckles sticking up, and out come the children on him, hollering 'Boo!' and waving their arms up and down the way it would scare you to death, or it ought to, if you wasn't ready for them.

We heard them charge out, but we thought it was just a nigger that was going by for them to scare, if we thought anything.

Plez says—allowing for all human mistakes—he seen on one side of King come rolling out Lucius Randall all dressed up, and on the other side, Eugene Hudson all dressed up. Could I have forgotten to speak of their being on skates? Oh, that was all afternoon. They're real good skaters, the little fellows, not to have a sidewalk. They sailed out the door and circled around their father, flying their arms and making their fingers go scarey, and those little Buster Brown bobs going in a circle.

Lucius Randall, Plez said, had on something pink, and he did, the basted flannelette teddy-bears we had tried on on top of his clothes and he got away. And said Eugene was a Chinaman, and that was what he was. It would be hard to tell which would come at you the more outrageous of the two, but to me it would be Lucius Randall with the girl's face and the big white cotton gloves falling off his fingers, and oh! he had on *my hat*. This one I milk in.

And they made a tremendous uproar with their skates, Plez said, and that was no mistake, because I remember what a hard time Snowdie and me had hearing what each other had to say all afternoon.

Plez said King stood it a minute—he got to turning around too. They were skating around him and saying in high birdie voices, 'How do you do, Mister Booger?' You know if children *can* be monkeys, they're going to be them. (Without the masks, though, those two children would have been more polite about it—there's enough Hudson in them.) Skating around and around their papa, and just as ignorant! Poor little fellows. After all, they'd had nobody to scare all day for Hallowe'en, except one or two niggers that went by, and the Y. & M. V. train whistling through at two-fifteen, they scared that.

But monkeys—! Skating around their papa. Plez said if those children had been black, he wouldn't hesitate to say they would remind a soul of little nigger cannibals in the jungle. When they got their papa in their ring-around-a-rosy and he couldn't get out, Plez said it was enough to make an onlooker a little uneasy, and he called once or twice on the Lord. And after they went around high, they crouched down and went around low, about his knees.

The minute come, when King just couldn't get out quick enough.

Only he had a hard time, and took him more than one try. He gathered himself together and King is a man of six foot height and weighs like a horse, but he was confused, I take it. But he got aloose and up and out like the Devil was after him—or in him—finally. Right up over the bannister and the ferns, and down the yard and over the ditch and gone. He plowed into the rough toward the Big Black, and the willows waved behind him, and where he run then, Plez don't know and I don't and don't nobody.

Plez said King passed right by him, that time, but didn't seem to know him, and the opportunity had gone by then to speak. And where he run then, nobody knows.

He should have wrote another note, instead of coming.

Well then, the children, I reckon, just held openmouth behind him, and then something got to mounting up after it was all over, and scared them. They come back in the dining room. There were innocent ladies visiting with each other. The little boys had to scowl and frown and drag their skates over the carpet and follow us around the table where we was cutting out Eugene Hudson's underbody, and pull on our skirts till we saw.

'Well, speak,' said their mother, and they told her a booger had come up on the front porch and when they went out to see him he said, 'I'm going. You stay,' so they chased him down the steps and run him off. 'But he looked back like this!' Lucius Randall said, lifting off his mask and showing us on his little naked face with the round blue eyes. And Eugene Hudson said the booger took a handful of pecans before he got through the gate.

And Snowdie dropped her scissors on the mahogany, and her hand just stayed in the air as still, and she looked at me, a look a minute long. And first she caught her apron to her and then started shedding it in the hall while she run to the door—so as not to be caught in it, I suppose, if anybody was still there. She run and the little glass prisms shook in the parlor—I don't remember another time, from *her*. She didn't stop at the door but run on through it and out on the porch, and she looked both ways and was running down the steps. And she run out in the yard and stood there holding to the tree, looking towards the country, but I could tell by the way her head held there wasn't nobody.

When I got to the steps—I didn't like to follow right away—there was nobody at all but Old Plez, who was coming by raising his hat.

'Plez, did you see a gentleman come up on my porch just now?'
I heard Snowdie call, and there was Plez, just ambling by with his
hat raised, like he was just that minute passing, like we thought. And
Plez, of course, he said, 'No'm, Mistis, I don't recollect one soul pass
me, whole way from town.'

The little fellows held on to me, I could feel them tugging. And my
little girl slept through it all, inside, and then woke up to swallow that
button.

Outdoors the leaves was rustling, different from when I'd went in.
It was coming on a rain. The day had a two-way look, like a day will
at change of the year—clouds dark and the gold air still in the road,
and the trees lighter than the sky was. And the oak leaves scuttling and
scattering, blowing against Old Plez and brushing on him, the old
man.

'You're real positive, I guess, Plez?' asks Snowdie, and he answers
comforting-like to her, '*You* wasn't looking for nobody to come today, was you?'

It was later on that Mrs. Stark got hold of Plez and got the truth
out of him, and I heard it after a while, through her church. But of
course he wasn't going to let Miss Snowdie MacLain get hurt now,
after we'd all watched her so long. So he fabricated.

After he'd gone by, Snowdie just stood there in the cool without a
coat, with her face turned towards the country and her fingers pulling
at little threads on her skirt and turning them loose in the wind,
making little kind deeds of it, till I went and got her. She didn't cry.

'Course, could have been a ghost,' Plez told Mrs. Stark, 'but a
ghost—I believe—if he had come to see the lady of the house, would
have waited to have word with her.'

And he said he had nary doubt in his mind, that it was Mr. King
MacLain, starting home once more and thinking better of it. Miss
Lizzie said to the church ladies, 'I, for one, trust the Negro. I trust
him the way you trust me, Old Plez's mind has remained clear as
a bell. I trust his story implicitly,' she says, 'because that's just what
I know King MacLain'd do—run.' And that's one time I feel in agreement about something with Miss Lizzie Stark, though she don't know
about it, I guess.

And I live and hope *he* hit a stone and fell down running, before he got far off from here, and took the skin off his handsome nose, the devil.

And so that's why Snowdie comes to get her butter now, and won't let me bring it to her any longer. I think she kind of holds it against me, because I was there that day when he come; and she don't like my baby any more.

And you know, Fate says maybe King did know it was Hallowe'en. Do you think he'd go that far for a prank? And his own come back to him? Fate's usually more down to earth than that.

With men like King, your thoughts are bottomless. He was going like the wind, Plez swore to Miss Lizzie Stark; though he couldn't swear to the direction—so he changed and said.

But I bet my little Jersey calf King tarried long enough to get him a child somewhere.

What makes me say a thing like that? I wouldn't say it to my husband, you mind you forget it.

You will be interested in comparing the method of Miss Welty's story with that of James Joyce's "Araby." How do the structure and texture of "Shower of Gold" differ from the structure and texture of Joyce's story? What do you have to say about the *point of view* of "Shower of Gold"? How does the experience within Miss Welty's story differ from the experience as it might well have occurred in real life?

Our particular interest in this chapter, however, is the extension of the experience *within* the story to include a whole additional set of overtones by reference to experiences *outside* the story. The clue lies first of all in the story's title. Those of you who have studied classical mythology (a particularly rich and fascinating subject) will remember the story of Danaë, daughter of King Acrisius, who was imprisoned by her father in a dark, brazen chamber because of a prophecy that she would bear a child who would slay his grandfather. But Zeus, king of the gods, appeared to her in a shower of gold, and she later bore him a son named Perseus, who did indeed (although accidentally) slay Acrisius.

The shower of gold by which Danaë conceived is like the shower of gold in Miss Welty's story: when Snowdie announced that she was going to have a baby, "It was like a shower of something had struck her, like she had been caught out in something bright. It was more than day." Like Danaë, shut up in her dark brazen chamber, Snowdie is unused to bright light, and the brilliance of daylight makes her crinkle up her eyes. Furthermore, MacLain, like Zeus, is King. Do you remember the "dark, quiet, real quiet hall that runs through her house"? And "King in the West, out where it's gold and all that"? Even the weather on the climactic day has Zeus in it (for Zeus was the one responsible for the sky, for the day and the night, the snow and the rain, the winds and the storm clouds, the lightning and thunder): "The day had a two-way look, like a day will at change of the year— clouds dark and the gold air still in the road, and the trees lighter than the sky was. And the oak leaves scuttling and scattering, blowing against Old Plez and brushing on him, the old man."

As king of the gods, Zeus was supposed to be the supporter of law and order, the protector and keeper of family and social institutions. But he is also famous for his escapades, like the one with Danaë—the irony of his position is one of the sources of amusement in the many stories which have been told of him. The play *Amphitryon* is one such hilarious recounting of the misbehavior of Zeus. Miss Welty, in the figure of Snowdie, is interested in the effect of such a King upon the women (here the figure of *one* woman) so visited. Clearly the story of Leda and the swan is in her mind, too: Zeus visited Leda in the form of a swan, and she bore him twin sons, Castor and Pollux. Snowdie as the mother of bird children is suggested in the sentence "Some said King figured out that if the babies started coming, he had a chance for a nestful of little albinos. . . ." The whiteness of Snowdie echoes the story of the young Io, another beautiful woman loved by Zeus, whom his wife Hera changed into a white heifer to keep her from Zeus. You remember that Mrs. Rainey refers to King MacLain's escapades: "Children of his growing up in the County Orphan's . . . and children known and unknown, scattered-like."

Perhaps enough has been said (though more could be said, and

you may wish to pursue allusions in the story further) to illustrate
the wealth of suggestion, the nature of the overtones, which com-
plement and enlarge the story of Snowdie and King MacLain.
Part of the humor in the story lies in the juxtaposition of the
two Kings, and we are amused here to see Zeus, in the person
of King, get his comeuppance when two of the children he has
fathered in Morgana (for this is a Morganatic marriage: check
with your dictionary!) frighten the daylights out of him! When
he returns, that last Hallowe'en (the story moves from a Hallowe'en courting through springtime and Easter and another
January and several more years and finally back to Hallowe'en
—why?), he stands, for all the world like one of the familiar
statues of Zeus, in front of the house "and sunk his weight on
one leg and just stood there, posey as statues, hand on his hip."
Then, "It was the twins seen him. Through those little bitty mask
holes, those eagle eyes!... They sailed out the door and circled
around their father, flying their arms and making their fingers go
scarey, and those little Buster Brown bobs going in a circle....
They were skating around him and saying in high birdie voices,
'How do you do, Mr. Booger?'... Plez said King passed right
by him.... And where he run then, nobody knows." Zeus is put
to flight by his own eaglets! "Of course gentle people aren't the
ones you lead best, he had to find that out, so know-all."

While "Shower of Gold" will certainly have meaning, as the
story of Snowdie and King MacLain, to the reader who does
not catch the allusions, it will have an enormously greater deal
of fun in it for the reader who is astute enough to catch the
Olympian laughter.

Other Limitations: Historical and Biographical

We have discussed linguistic problems and problems of communication resulting from allusion. Historical knowledge is also
frequently necessary to the adequate comprehension of literature,
for the experience of the literary text is frequently built upon a
knowledge of history *which the writer assumes the reader to*

possess. In a play about Abraham Lincoln's role in the Civil War, for example, it can be expected that, for American readers at least, such names as John Brown, William H. Seward, and Robert E. Lee will have an immediate value. A writer must *begin* somewhere; he cannot do *everything* within his play. Furthermore, such a play as we are postulating ought to be able to assume some knowledge of the causes and issues of the Civil War, since the play *need* not itself take as its concern the rightness or wrongness of the two sides in the conflict. As a matter of fact, such a play as we are talking about has been written—and by an Englishman. John Drinkwater's *Abraham Lincoln* is prefaced by a note which deserves to be quoted here: [10]

In using for purposes of drama a personality of so wide and recent a fame as that of Abraham Lincoln, I feel that one or two observations are due to my readers and critics.

First, my purpose is that not of the historian but of the dramatist. The historical presentation of my hero has been faithfully made in many volumes; notably, in England, by Lord Charnwood in a monograph that gives a masterly analysis of Lincoln's career and character and is, it seems to me, a model of what the historian's work should be. To this book I am gratefully indebted for the material of my play. But while I have, I hope, done nothing to traverse history, I have freely telescoped its events, and imposed invention upon its movement, in such ways as I needed to shape the dramatic significance of my subject. I should add that the fictitious Burnet Hook is admitted to the historical company of Lincoln's Cabinet for the purpose of embodying certain forces that were antagonistic to the President. This was a dramatic necessity, and I chose rather to invent a character for the purpose than to invest any single known personage with sinister qualities about which there might be dispute.

Secondly, my purpose is, again, that of the dramatist, not that of the political philosopher. The issue of secession was a very intricate one, upon which high and generous opinions may be in conflict, but that I

[10] Drinkwater's note is dated 1918. The quotation is from the edition of the play included in Thomas H. Dickinson's *Chief Contemporary Dramatists: Second Series,* Houghton Mifflin Company, Boston, 1921, pp. 91–124. Quoted by permission of the publishers.

may happen to have or lack personal sympathy with Lincoln's policy and judgment in this matter is nothing. My concern is with the profoundly dramatic interest of his character, and with the inspiring example of a man who handled war nobly and with imagination.

Finally, I am an Englishman, and not a citizen of the great country that gave Lincoln birth. I have, therefore, written as an Englishman, making no attempt to achieve a "local colour" of which I have no experience, or to speak in an idiom to which I have not been bred. To have done otherwise, as I am sure any American friends that this play may have the good fortune to make will allow, would have been to treat a great subject with levity.

Drinkwater has raised a whole host of interesting questions for us. He refers explicitly to the order which he has imposed upon the raw materials of history in the creating of his imitation of an action. He distinguishes between the point of view and purpose of the historian and the playwright. He makes clear certain obligations which he feels as a playwright to the materials of a history *widely known.* He indicates that his concern is to make us understand rather than approve: it is important to him to make us *feel with* the character of Lincoln rather than to make us *approve his judgment.* In other words, we are concerned with the fullness of the experience rather than with justification of the Civil War.

Notice that Drinkwater frankly admits his inability to work with local idiom with which he is not familiar. Without raising here the issue of whether a better play would have to take such idiom into account, we can feel that Drinkwater's decision was, for him, quite proper.

The difficulties in communication work both ways here: Drinkwater is bound by certain facts which he cannot traverse (the South cannot win the war, for example); but the reader, too, is required to *know* such facts if he is to experience the play to its fullest. There was a time when writers dealt very freely with the facts of history, but nowadays our historical sense is so lively that we tend to hold the serious writer to account for the *facts;* but if we insist on our rights here, we must also remember that the writer will feel free, in return, to expect some knowledge of us.

Another source of difficulty is biographical. It is sometimes said nowadays that a poem must exist within itself, that knowledge of the writer is unnecessary to an understanding of the work, if the work is really successful. Such a view is a useful antidote to the kind of grubbing into the life of the writer which may become the sole aim of a student of literature. Interest in biography is a perfectly valid and highly useful interest, but it should not become confused with interest in the literary work itself. On the other hand, to deny the usefulness of biographical information in helping us to provide a proper climate for our response to a poem is like denying the usefulness of historical knowledge, of vocabulary, and of mythology. Perhaps we may best illustrate the point by quoting a sonnet:

> When I consider how my light is spent
>> Ere half my days in this dark world and wide,
>> And that one Talent which is death to hide
>> Lodged with me useless, though my soul more bent
> To serve therewith my Maker, and present
>> My true account, lest He returning chide,
>> "Doth God exact day-labour, light denied?"
>> I fondly ask. But Patience, to prevent
> That murmur, soon replies, "God doth not need
>> Either man's work or his own gifts. Who best
>> Bear his mild yoke, they serve him best. His state
> Is kingly: thousands at his bidding speed,
>> And post o'er land and ocean without rest:
>> They also serve who only stand and wait."

There is a Biblical allusion in the third line which you might identify! But our concern is with the words "light" and "dark" in the first two lines of the poem, and with the phrase "Lodged with me useless" in the fourth line. There is no reason why a reader need be left to *guess*. This poem by John Milton is said to have been written when the poet was in his mid-forties, before he went on to write *Paradise Lost* and thus "to serve therewith my Maker," and after he had become totally blind. So significant is the knowledge of the poet's blindness that the sonnet is usually given a title, "On His Blindness." It seems carping to argue that biographical information is irrelevant to consideration of such a poem as this. Indeed, some knowledge of Milton's stature, of his plans as a poet, and of his later achievement enters very largely into a full response to the poem, and there is no reason why we should deny ourselves the pleasure of this full response simply because some theoretical critical position would tell us that we must. Presumably some knowledge of Milton is part of the store of knowledge in the head of any educated man. A reader may find himself much more highly sensitized to the work of a given writer if he knows something about the writer's life. On the other hand, he must be wary of *limiting* the work to the facts of the life, since, as we have seen, a large part of any writer's (or, indeed, any human being's) experience is vicarious and composite in nature.

We might go on listing difficulties in communication based upon one aspect or another of the writer's and the reader's knowledge or lack of it, but probably enough has been said to indicate that there are obligations on both sides of the work of art. While the reader and the writer differ in the fullness and quality of their knowledge in many vital respects, some community of awareness is a prerequisite to the apprehension of the work of art.

Problems in Verification: Fallacies

We have already, in this and other chapters, made mention indirectly of *fallacies* not infrequently to be found in the judgments pronounced upon works of literary art. It is fallacious to treat the poem as if it were a psychological or historical or autobiographical document, for example. The historian, the psychologist, and the biographer have aims which differ from those of the poet, and to assume that the worth of the poem depends specifically upon the accuracy with which it records historical fact, or upon the degree to which it illustrates a particular tenet of psychology, or upon the faithfulness with which it reflects an actual experience of the writer's life is to be guilty of a fallacy of judgment. The psychological critic—that is, the critic with a particular interest in the interrelationships of literature and psychology—may well be an excellent and informative critic for us; the historical critic may well contribute facts necessary to our understanding of poems; the biographer may place a poem for us in the stream of an author's development; all these uses of criticism are valid, of course. But when the poem itself becomes subservient to the interest in psychology or history or biography, the proper sphere of criticism has been usurped.

Fallacies of the Literary Critic

Within the proper sphere of criticism, however, other fallacies may be found. It is perhaps worthwhile here to refer to a supposed fallacy pointed out in the nineteenth century by the English essayist John Ruskin (1819–1900) and to two which are current in our day.

THE PATHETIC FALLACY

Ruskin's "pathetic fallacy" pointed to what Ruskin took to be a false form of expression in literature—the transfer by the writer to inanimate objects of feelings or emotions actually felt only in the writer himself. That is, a writer who uses the phrase "the cruel, crawling foam" to describe the surface of a body of water is attributing to the water attributes of cruelty and crawling which it does not really possess; he is attributing to the water itself attitudes which he holds toward it. Doubtless Ruskin was irritated by excesses which now and then provoke us all—the tree with the nest of robins in her hair, for example, which becomes laughable when one stops to consider it a moment. But we should all agree now that there is nothing *essentially* wrong with the thing Ruskin is condemning, since he is really discussing an aspect of empathy, of "feeling into" an object, which is a perfectly natural aspect of experience, whether in poetry or in actual life. A poet (or any of us, for that matter) may indeed be guilty of sentimentality in excessive emotionalizing in his relations to other things (as when one *suffers* over the death of a housefly), but it is in the excess rather than in the essential fact of empathy that he is guilty.

THE AFFECTIVE FALLACY

The "affective fallacy" has been pointed out by W. K. Wimsatt and Monroe C. Beardsley,[11] who describe it as "a confusion between the poem and its *results* (what it *is* and what it *does*)...."

Suppose, for example (the example is ours and not Wimsatt's or Beardsley's), that a mother who has recently lost a child sees on television a play in which a mother loses a child under similar circumstances. She may, of course, be so reminded of her own loss that the experience is not in the least aesthetic—she may simply dissolve again into the agonies of her own sorrows; under such conditions, she would be much better off *not* seeing the play at all. But let us assume that she is able to be objective enough about herself to realize that the play *is* a play, and that the mother in the play is not herself. She may still be much moved by the closeness of the literary experience to her own experience—much more moved than she might be, let us say, by Shakespeare's *King Lear*. Let us say for the moment that the television play is not so good a play as *King Lear*—that it is a fairly sentimental, fairly stereotyped performance. The real mother, much moved though she may be, need not make the mistake of thinking that the degree of her response proves a high degree of merit in the television play itself. If she *does* make this mistake, and if she judges the worth of the play by the intensity of its appeal to her own emotions, she is being guilty of the affective fallacy. She is being guilty, say Wimsatt and Beardsley, of impressionism in judgment, and the play itself tends to disappear as the proper object of criticism.

[11] See W. K. Wimsatt, Jr., *The Verbal Icon*, University of Kentucky Press, Lexington, Ky., 1954, pp. 21–39.

The point being made by these two scholars is a telling one, and we may all well quake a little when they point the academic finger at us, for no doubt each of us is at times in danger of falling into the trap they have described. We must distinguish, in making literary judgments, between the *grounds* of emotion and the emotion itself. Someone other than the real-life mother, watching the television play we have suggested, might respond quite differently, emotionally, to the script. Nevertheless the play itself has not changed; it is the objective *thing* which must be the source of judgment, and it must not be lost in the welling up of emotion which results from seeing it on the television screen.

This is not to suggest that emotions are irrelevant to a consideration of literature, since literature as the imitating of experience includes the experiencing of emotion. Indeed, as we have been suggesting in various ways throughout this book, the poem is a way of objectifying, fixing, and making permanent emotions and attitudes which are otherwise transient. To say this, however, is not to say that when you find a poem making your pulse quicken and the young man next to you disclaims such a response you and he are necessarily differing in your value judgments of the poem. One must distinguish between relevant and irrelevant emotions in the experiencing of literature. In watching a performance of Shakespeare's *Othello,* or in reading the play silently, we must certainly feel in part as Othello feels—that is, we must share his state of mind so far as is consistent with sharing also the state of mind of Desdemona at, let us say, the moment of the murder. Unless we are compelled by Othello's state, assuming that Shakespeare has succeeded in his intention, we have failed properly to understand the scene. The emotional response is *obligatory,* and probably the more sensitively informed the reader the sharper the emotional response, always within the limits which we described in Chapter 5 as being proper to the aesthetic experience. But the response must arise from, must be dictated by, and must be directed toward the experience *within* Shakespeare's scene. It would be an irrelevant emotion, for example, which you would experience if Othello, holding a light close to

Desdemona's face, should make you feel terror lest the hair of the actress playing Desdemona should catch fire from the flame. This is not part of Shakespeare's scene, though it would be part of the performance on-stage. Great though your emotion on such an occasion might be, you must not confuse it with the emotional power of *Othello*. You must remain free to feel as the characters in the play feel, and if Shakespeare has been generally successful over the centuries in *controlling* the feelings of a large proportion of his audiences, we can surely say that those feelings are not only obligatory but are a responsible measure of the worth of the play itself.

THE INTENTIONAL FALLACY

Probably none of the fallacies we have discussed has had so widespread an acceptance among contemporary students of literature as the "intentional fallacy," by which Wimsatt and Beardsley mean the error of confusing the psychological *causes* of a poem with the poem itself.[12] That is, the naïve intentionalist might argue that a poem is successful if it does what its writer sets out to do. But the psychology of creation is not identical with the completed or created object; a poem once made has a life of its own, and what matters about it is what it *says*, not what its creator *intended* it to say. As a matter of simple fact, we usually have no exact way of knowing *what* the author intended it to say outside the testimony of the poem itself, and it is a very common experience among writers to find that the intention and the created poem frequently differ, even for the writer. A poet may *intend* to shock me; I may like his poem without being shocked by it. If I find his poem to be *good* without being shocked by it, his intention is irrelevant to my judgment of its worth. There is nothing *wrong* about being interested in a writer's intentions, where they can be discovered; but one must remember that this interest is not essentially the interest of artistic criticism. One

[12] *Ibid.*, pp. 3–18. In both this and the discussion of the affective fallacy, we borrow the fallacy names from Wimsatt and Beardsley without necessarily following precisely their analyses of the implications.

does not need to know *who* the Dark Lady is (if she ever existed) to understand a sonnet by Shakespeare which seems to be addressed to a dark lady. The poet may have intended the poem to refer to a particular woman, but that is his concern and not ours, *provided that the poem does not neglect part of its own statement by assuming that we know the lady, and by depending on us therefore to supply part of the experience;* in this case, external evidence is necessary—not for judging *intention,* but for judging the meaning of what is included within the poem. Perhaps the point can be made clearer by referring to Milton's sonnet on his blindness, used earlier in the chapter. What Milton's *intention* may have been in writing the poem is irrelevant to a consideration of the worth of the poem—he may have been trying to bolster his spirits, for example; but the fact that he was talking in part about his blindness matters considerably to an understanding of the thing expressed within the lines of the sonnet, because it is part of the experience of the sonnet. This distinction may seem needlessly subtle. We believe it, on the contrary, to be vital.

A Final Caveat

The fallacy of judging by intent is not entirely unlike another error in critical discussion, which may be illustrated as follows: A critic wishes to talk about a poem by, let us say, a poet named Peter Smith. It happens that nothing is known about this hypothetical Smith outside the poetry he has written. But the poems suggest that he is much interested in the psychological predicaments of individuals, and in particular in manifestations of the Oedipus complex. He may know Freud and Jung and Adler, since he uses terms employed by these analysts. His poems can be arranged so as to suggest a psychological development in which the pressures of modern life become increasingly acutely felt by the subject. In such an arrangement, poems filled with gloom are taken to be late poems.

The critic, arguing, as such a critic might, that knowledge of the poet is an important part of the study of the poem, proceeds now to tell us that Peter Smith is a man widely read in the writings of twentieth-century psychologists, that he has found life increasingly difficult to bear, that he has struggled to extricate himself from his own dilemma by seeking help from the psychoanalyst, but that he has failed. Then the critic says to us, You are now ready to read the following sonnet by Peter Smith—and he gives us the sonnet.

The simple fact is that all the knowledge which the critic parades is drawn from the poetry itself and is highly suspect as evidence; the information is so generalized as to be of no great help in the understanding of a particular poem; the "facts" are of biographical interest only, even if they can be substantiated. While we may indeed be interested in the poet behind the poem, and may want to know something about him simply because we *are* interested, we must remember that the interest in the poem and the interest in the poet are different rather than identical interests, and that the critic is in this case talking nonsense when he presumes to help us read the poem by reporting information which is strictly irrelevant to it. The example hypothesized here may seem exaggerated, but it will surprise no teacher or critic to be told that it is simply a kind of easy paraphrase of examples to be found in school textbooks. Much of the criticism of Shakespeare is poisoned by such circular and vain postulating of biographical "facts" drawn from the evidence of the plays and poems themselves. Although there is a sense in which all art is autobiographical (we began Part 2 by suggesting this), this is not it.

Summary

We have been concerned in this chapter with pointing to relationships existing between the work of art and the reader, to things which the reader may and may not legitimately do in the act of trying to understand and evaluate the work of art. The reader must recognize that the poem itself is the object of inquiry, that it is identical with neither the writer nor the reader, that it is unique. While a poem does communicate, what and how it communicates is what matters—not simply the fact that it communicates. Our limitations as readers, which may lead to difficulties in the poem's communicating to *us*, do not lessen any absolute merits which may exist in the poem as an embodiment of experience, although they may lessen the poem's value *to us*. Readers may be made more sensitive in many ways, by many kinds of knowledge—even by simply growing older; hence all knowledge which comes to us as human beings may profit us as readers. But in the experience of reading a poem, our knowledge is directed to an understanding of the unique experience within the poem; we do not legitimately use the poem as a *document* to increase our other knowledge—or rather, when we *do,* our aim is not the appreciation of literature, but something else.

To be perceptive as readers, we must know words in both their denotations and their connotations; we need to have an ear for varieties of speech; we need a store of information upon which we can draw easily; we need to be fair to the poem, not attributing to it motives and effects which are peculiar to us alone; we must be both willing and able to subordinate the evidence of our own experience to the task of evaluating the experience of the poem. That is, the good reader is sensitive, intelligent, objective, and more or less stable. To say so *much* is perhaps to appear to say nothing; to say less is to say too little.

Exercises

1. Can you locate statements made by other people about the relation of literature to life? You may be interested in checking the following references:

   a. Henry James, the essay entitled "The Art of Fiction."

   b. Henry James, in F. O. Matthiessen and Kenneth B. Murdock (eds.), *The Notebooks of Henry James,* Oxford University Press, New York, 1947; see, for example, pages 33–35, 54–56, 63, 71–72, 76–77, etc.

   c. Katherine Anne Porter, observations on Henry James ("The Days Before"), Willa Cather, Ezra Pound ("It Is Hard to Stand in the Middle"), and Eudora Welty or her observations about herself and her craftsmanship ("Three Statements about Writing"), all in her volume entitled *The Days Before*.

d. Malcolm Cowley (ed.), *Writers at Work: The Paris Review Interviews,* The Viking Press, Inc., New York, 1958.

2. To what extent, if at all, need an author have his audience in mind in writing a piece of literature?

3. To what extent do we hold the writer responsible for complete *accuracy* in his imitation of the facts of real life? For example, would a physician be the best judge of a novel written about the life of a doctor?

4. The authors say of the Wordsworth poem on pages 126 to 127 that "the meter and the rhyme take over at the expense of matters which ought to be more prominent." To what extent and in what sense *do* the meter and rhyme take over?

5. Try to make other comparative studies of various drafts of the same poem (like the comparison of the drafts of the Wordsworth poem in this chapter.) See such books as the following:

a. Rudolf Arnheim, W. H. Auden, Karl Shapiro, and Donald A. Stauffer, *Poets at Work,* Harcourt, Brace and Company, Inc., New York, 1948.

b. Frederick L. Gwynn, Ralph W. Condee, and Arthur O. Lewis, Jr., *The Case for Poetry,* Prentice-Hall, Inc., Englewood Cliffs, N.J., 1954. (See appendix A, pages 405 to 415.)

c. Norman C. Stageberg and Wallace L. Anderson, *Poetry as Experience,* American Book Company, New York, 1952. (See chapter 12, pages 238 to 266.)

6. What did you discover to be the sources of the differences in tone and quality in the excerpts from Benét and Gertrude Stein on pages 134 to 136?

7. What limitations do you find in *yourself* as a good reader of any of the pieces of literature cited in Chapters 6 to 8?

8. In commenting on Drinkwater's play about Lincoln, we decided to overlook the issue of whether or not the use of local idiom would improve such a play. Consider that issue now. Can an English writer successfully write about Lincoln without making use of American speech? What do you know about the speech problems involved in transplanting a contemporary British play to the Broadway stage, or vice versa?

9

Appreciation of Literature: Language

ALL THE THINGS we have been saying about the relationship of literature and life are involved in the act of appreciating literature. In the next two chapters, however, we shall look in some detail at certain aspects of the *craft, or art, of the poet* to see how he achieves that particular *ordering* of the experiences of life which seems to us to merit the name *literature*. We are concerned not with the psychology of creation, but with the relationship of the created object to the reader. This is the particular province of the critic of literature; and, in a good sense, every reader must learn to become his own critic.

Importance of the Impression Made by the Work of Art

It has been said many times that it is the duty of the reader to be *receptive* before he becomes *critical*. Let the work of art have its way with you before you start methodically to analyze it. Be generous in your first approach to a poem or a story or a play. Don't set your head or your heart against the experience of the work simply because it differs from your own experience. Coleridge has said that the reader in approaching a poem must be willing to suspend *disbelief* for the moment; to be capable of an act of faith, as it were, setting aside bias and prejudice and pre-judgments in order to see clearly the experience which the poet is expressing through the symbols which are words, because words permit things to *enter* as well as to *leave*. Coleridge [1] has also posted another warning to the critic: "Until you understand a writer's ignorance, presume yourself ignorant of his understanding."

On the other hand, we must confess frankly at the outset that most of us are blinded at points by limitations so sharp that we do not feel them: hence the virtue of listening (*really* listening) to the responses of others. And we have agreed that one reader's experience of a poem is always, and in a very natural way, in some degree different from another reader's experience of the same poem. But if two sensible and sensitive readers disagree fundamentally on the meaning of a poem it is clear (1) that the poem itself inadequately presents its experience or (2) that at least one of the readers is inadequate in his response. (Value judgments—that is, judgments of the *worth* of particular poems—are another matter; two people may agree on a poem's meaning without agreeing on its worth on an absolute scale of values, perhaps because they start from different critical positions.)

After a reader has given himself as freely as possible to the experience of the poem, he finds that the poem has made some impression on him. (Readers sometimes say that a poem has made no impression on them, but that statement may mean that the poem hasn't been understood, or that it hasn't been "liked," or that the impression has been slight because the experience has been slight or inadequately expressed.) The impression may be as vague as a "feeling"—or as strong as a *feeling*. It may be crystal

[1] *Biographia Literaria*, chap. 12. The passage on the "willing suspension of disbelief" is to be found in chap. 14.

clear as an idea. But whatever it is, that impression is what the reader must start with in his rereading, his criticism, of the poem. In rereading, one tests his impressions by looking for their sources. Frequently one finds that the initial impression was faulty or wrong because it overlooked things in the experience expressed in the poem. The reader who is reluctant to look carefully at a poem because he doesn't want it "destroyed by analysis" may be (although he is not necessarily) lazy; he may prefer his own daydream of a poem to the real poem—but he should realize then that he is a daydreamer and not either a good reader or a reliable critic. On the other hand, each of us will sympathize with the student who is offended by the kind of discussion of a poem which bludgeons it out of shape. No paraphrase, no discussion of a poem's meaning can precisely duplicate the quality of the poem's experience; but that does not mean that discussion and paraphrase are wrong. After all, the only way we have of talking with one another about poems is paraphrase, and the world would be a pretty quiet and lonely place without speech—no matter how much one occasionally longs for silence! If the experience of literature is worth studying, paraphrase and discussion of poems is not only desirable but inevitable.

Decorum as a Literary Principle

We have noticed how literature distorts real life, how it chooses a point of view through which to observe, an angle from which to envision. As soon as a writer chooses a point of view, he begins to discipline his raw materials. Once he imposes upon the experience an attitude, he has in part limited his own powers as God of the world he is creating, because the choice of attitude limits the directions in which the world may expand. In a play or a short story, once the premises of the action have been set down, the writer has further limited the experience by ruling out premises which would violate the ones he has chosen. Once the protagonist of a play has committed a deed, *he has committed it,* and everything thereafter must take that fact into account. In a very real sense it is true that once a work of art gets under way it takes on a life of its own, only in part under the control of the writer (though, to be sure, he nourishes and guides and helps it to its fulfillment). The good writer knows (consciously or not) where his work is going, and he helps it get there. In this sense, every writer must learn to be his own best critic.

Decorum is a word once widely used in criticism to indicate that quality of beauty in a work of art which arises from the congruity or fitness of manner or language to subject. A work of art in which gaps exist between the quality of language and the thing being said in language may be said to *violate decorum*. Unless he meant to be funny, a writer presenting us with a modern child who stubbed his toe and came running to his mother, crying, "Woe is me!" would seem to us guilty of this kind of incongruity, though a tragic hero in Shakespeare might well say it without making us feel that decorum had been disturbed at all. This is, of course, an example so obvious as to be a little silly. But look at the following piece of anonymous light verse: [2]

> A handsome young airman lay dying,
> And as on the aerodrome he lay,
> To the mechanics who round him came sighing,
> These last dying words he did say:
>
> "Take the cylinders out of my kidneys,
> The connecting-rod out of my brain,
> Take the cam-shaft from out of my backbone,
> And assemble the engine again."

Here the intention is clearly humorous. The joke lies in the fact that the vocabulary, while it may be fit or proper for an airman, is incongruous when the airman is dying. The poem achieves its effect of humor precisely because it *is* incongruous, precisely because it violates decorum.

Unfortunately, a poem is sometimes guilty of unintentional

[2] "The Dying Airman," from *A Little Treasury of Modern Poetry,* edited by Oscar Williams, copyright, 1946, 1950, by Charles Scribner's Sons. Reprinted by permission of the publishers.

violation of this principle. For example, the following speech from Shakespeare's youthful play *Henry VI, Part One* (act I, scene 4, lines 73 to 84), is delivered by the valiant English hero Talbot as one of his noble comrades lies dying from a wound received in battle in France:

> Speak, Salisbury; at least, if thou canst, speak.
> How far'st thou, mirror of all martial men?
> One of thy eyes and thy cheek's side struck off!
> Accursed tower! accursed fatal hand
> That hath contriv'd this woeful tragedy!
> In thirteen battles Salisbury o'ercame.
> Henry the Fifth he first train'd to the wars.
> Whilst any trump did sound, or drum struck up,
> His sword did ne'er leave striking in the field.
> Yet liv'st thou, Salisbury? Though thy speech doth fail,
> One eye thou hast, to look to heaven for grace;
> The sun with one eye vieweth all the world.

To the modern ear, Talbot's "encouragement" to the dying Salisbury seems a violation of decorum: It is hard for a dying man to take comfort, when one of his eyes has been put out by a shot, in the notion that heaven itself has only one eye, the sun! Furthermore, it seems pretty ingenious of Talbot, at such a moment, to make the comparison! The gap between the language and the matter here illustrates the particular breach of decorum which we call *sentimentality*.

When people use language not suited to their personality, or to their educational level, or to their situation, we think of them as violating decorum. Poems which permit the use of language in these ways seem to us faulty. Likewise actions or gestures or behavior in general which contradicts other aspects of personality may seem to us incongruous. In the Elizabethan theater, the king who talked like a serf would be violating decorum in style; while we do not nowadays like to *think* of certain modes of conduct as being limited to certain classes of people (our democratic views stand in the way of it, for one thing), we nevertheless continue to *feel* that they are. Ask any imaginative child how a king acts, and then how a beggar acts, and you will see how ingrained these distinctions are. The king who acts or talks like a beggar will be incongruous to such a child—or, as we should say, in violation of the principle of decorum.

Thus we constantly ask that the writer observe decorum in his use of language, in his choice of details, in his attitudes—in every conceivable way. The experience will not seem to us a full one unless the principle is carefully kept.

Figures of Words

We ask that poetic language, or the language of literature, have more than propriety or decorum, of course. In the interests of the experience which it is imitating and creating, we ask that it also have clarity, vitality, and precision. Frequently it achieves these qualities by indirection.

Consider, for example, the differences between the following statements:

1. Alas, King Richard, I suspect that you are going to lose your crown.
2. Alas, Richard, I seem to see your glory plummeting.
3. Ah, Richard, with the eyes of heavy mind
   I see thy glory like a shooting star
   Fall to the base earth from the firmament.

The first statement makes it clear that the speaker is sorry ("Alas"), that he is suggesting something which is still to come ("I suspect"), and that he fears the king will be deposed. The second sentence continues the first two notions ("Alas" and "I seem to see"), but the phrase "seem to see" suggests a *visualization* of what is to come, and this visualization adds a degree of vitality to the statement. Finally, the phrase "lose your crown" becomes decidedly more alive, more active, when it is translated into the notion of glory's plummeting. Glory is given some kind of material form or substance which makes it capable of plummeting, and the verb *plummet* is dramatic in its suggestion of both weight and speed: glory falls as a leaden weight falls through water, for example. This additional vitality given to the notion of Richard's losing his crown is accompanied by an increased perception, on our part, of the speaker's attitude. The first sentence might mean simply that the speaker had a feeling (not necessarily accompanied by any strong emotion one way or another) that Richard was to fall, but the second sentence indicates a rather sharply empathic response to Richard's dilemma. Finally, the third sentence makes it quite clear that the speaker is distressed, for the phrase "with the eyes of heavy mind" not only continues the *visualizing* introduced in the second sentence but specifies that the eyes are the eyes of the mind and that the mind is heavy (that is, literally *sad*). Furthermore, the glory which plummeted in the second sentence is now like a star (a *specific* kind of matter), and it is making a headlong plunge from sky to earth, suggesting that it will die in its blazing fall. The third of these sentences is, of course, the way Shakespeare puts it in the speech of the Earl of Salisbury at the close of act II of *Richard II,* in a scene where portents of the king's coming fall are heavy.

METAPHOR AND SIMILE

We may talk about these sentences in one way by saying that the speaker's attitude, through them, becomes increasingly clearer and more precise, as well as increasingly vital. Another way of looking at them is to observe that the language becomes increasingly *figurative,* and that the *figures* are in accord with the principle of decorum which we have just studied. A *figure of speech* is a form of expression which deviates from the "normal," or from ordinary speech, in the interests of extending, sharpening, and vivifying literal meanings. The phrase "lose your crown" is a literal way of talking about Richard's fall (as in the first of our examples); the notion of glory's plummeting is a figurative way of talking about the same thing, and it is figurative because glory is here not abstract, as in normal or literal speech, but substantial. The figure is incomplete because we do not know just *how* to visualize glory. In the third example, glory is "like a shooting star" in its descent. Here we have a figure in which an explicit comparison is expressed by the use of the word *like*. A figure of speech in which a comparison between two normally dissimilar things is expressed by the word *like* or *as* is called a *simile*. Glory and the star are essentially unlike; they are alike in this case in (1) their brilliance and (2) their plummeting. When the comparison is implied but not expressed (that is, when the word *like* or *as* is omitted), the figure of speech is called a *metaphor*. These two figures are so constantly and so vigorously employed in literature that it is common to speak of literature (particularly of poetry) as *the language of metaphor,* where simile and metaphor are lumped together under the single term. Literature is constantly making comparisons; it is essential, by virtue of its being a process of imitation, that it do so. Hence one cannot well speak of literature without employing the names of figures of speech. Of course our language, our ordinary daily language, is full of *dead* metaphors—dead because the life has gone out of them to such an extent that we no longer respond to them as metaphors. Poets once upon a time wrote poems to the "day's eye," but when we see a *daisy* growing in the field we no longer think of it as the day's eye. Yet that is the origin of the name of the common flower, and it is a metaphor. Such expressions as "mad as a wet hen," "sound as a dollar," "silly ass," etc., have figurative value, but their overuse has tended to dull our ears to the comparisons really being made, or implied. Once a figure has become a cliché, we are less likely to remember that it is (or once was) a figure.

PERSONIFICATION

Our three sentences about King Richard can be made to yield another figure, *personification,* which is the attribution of human or animal qualities to inanimate or abstract objects or ideas. Personification may profitably be thought of as a form of metaphor, for there is always a comparison involved. For example, the third sentence refers to the "eyes of heavy mind." One may think either of *metaphor* here (the process of thinking is the process of seeing — thought = sight) or of *personification* (the mind, like the human body, has eyes, and it is in the *mind's eye* that the sight occurs). This is a rather complex example, but such simple examples as the following from a sonnet by John Donne offer no problems: "Death, be not proud, though some have called thee/ Mighty and dreadful, for thou art not so." Death, an abstraction, is here conceived of as having personality.

All three of the figures thus far discussed enable the poet to talk with greater concentration of energy than we usually employ in ordinary talk, because his figures permit him to include in the experience he is imitating associations which enrich and enlarge the "root" experience. In this sense the *density* of literary language is greater than the *density* of ordinary use of language.

SYMBOL

Another figure, somewhat more complex in its use than any of the figures thus far discussed, is the *symbol*. A symbol is a figure of speech in which one thing is thought of as standing for, or representing, another—usually a material object thought of as representing an immaterial thing. We have already said, of course, that all language is a symbolical expression of gesture, since words have meaning attached to them only by convention. The word *cat* is a symbol for the kinds of animal which we call by that name. But when we talk about a symbol as a figure of speech, we are using it in a somewhat narrower sense. There are many conventional symbols in literature: love is a red rose, life is a weary river, death is a skeleton, the cross is Christianity. Colors, too, have symbolical value for us: black is evil, white is innocence, red is danger, green is envy, yellow is jealousy, purple is rage, brown is autumnal decay, blue is melancholy, etc. Such symbols have arisen through repeated use, and poets rely heavily upon our recognition of such symbols *as* symbols. Symbols are often like metaphors, but metaphors with half the comparison left unexpressed in words, since the poet expects the reader to be able to supply the other half for himself.

Not all symbols are conventional. A writer may establish symbolical value for a thing within the limits of his own poem or story or play; or he may use an object first in its nonfigurative environment and then proceed to give it symbolical value. James Joyce's use of snow in his story "The Dead" is a particularly fine example of the writer's ability to construct his own symbol. When snow is first introduced into the story, it is simply snow on Gabriel's galoshes and on the shoulders of his overcoat when he comes in from outdoors. But notice what it becomes by the time we reach the final paragraph of the story, after Gabriel has felt his own identity fade out "into a grey impalpable world. . . ." [3]

A few light taps upon the pane made him turn to the window. It had begun to snow again. He watched sleepily the flakes, silver and dark, falling obliquely against the lamplight. The time had come for him to set out on his journey westward. Yes, the newspapers were right: snow was general all over Ireland. It was falling on every part of the dark central plain, on the treeless hills, falling softly upon the Bog of Allen and, farther westward, softly falling into the dark mutinous Shannon waves. It was falling, too, upon every part of the lonely churchyard on the hill where Michael Furey lay buried. It lay thickly drifted on the crooked crosses and headstones, on the spears of the little gate, on the barren thorns. His soul swooned slowly as he heard the snow falling faintly through the universe and faintly falling, like the descent of their last end, upon all the living and the dead.

Other Figurative Uses of Language

In Shakespeare's time, the minds of schoolboys were stuffed liberally with horrendous names of figures: zeugma, paralipsis, paromology, prosopopoeia, anadiplosis, chiasmus. (Aren't you glad to be alive *today!*) An excellent book by Sister Miriam Joseph entitled *Shakespeare's Use of the Arts of Language* (Columbia University Press, 1947) will give you details and provide you with examples of a great host of such figures. It will be

[3] *The Portable James Joyce,* The Viking Press, Inc., New York, 1947, p. 242. Quoted by permission of The Viking Press, Jonathan Cape, Limited, and the Executors of the James Joyce Estate.

enough here, perhaps, to concentrate on only seven additional figures: paradox, irony, apostrophe, synecdoche, metonymy, hyperbole, and litotes.

PARADOX

A *paradox* is a seemingly self-contradictory statement or proposition. The Friar, in Shakespeare's *Romeo and Juliet,* says in speaking of the earth that it is both the repository for the dead and the source of life:

> The earth that's nature's mother is her tomb.
> What is her burying grave, that is her womb.

This is a paradox—the kind of statement which, says Browning, "lingers while it mocks." We all know of people who have in their personalities and attitudes such seemingly contradictory elements that we say of them that they seem to be living paradoxes. The paradox is a particularly fruitful way of indicating tensions between experiences. At the close of the play *Richard II,* the new king, Henry IV, is suddenly brought news of the murder of Richard. Henry had wanted Richard out of the way so that his own position on the throne of England might be secure, but the news of the murder brings home to him the horror of his part in this murder. He says, to Exton the murderer,

> Exton, I thank thee not; for thou hast wrought
> A deed of slander, with thy fatal hand,
> Upon my head and all this famous land.
> EXTON. From your own mouth, my lord, did I this deed.
> HENRY. They love not poison that do poison need,
> Nor do I thee. Though I did wish him dead,
> I hate the murderer, love him murdered.

Henry *seemingly* contradicts himself when, having wished Richard dead, he protests that he loves the dead king.

IRONY

Implicit in this last example is another figure which is known by the name *irony.* Irony, strictly speaking, is a figure of speech in which the thing *said* is the opposite of the thing *intended*. Mark Antony, in his oration over the dead Caesar in Shakespeare's *Julius Caesar,* uses heavy irony as he speaks constantly of the "honourable Brutus," since he clearly feels that in joining Caesar's murderers Brutus has been quite *dis*honorable. We use irony when we say to someone who has done something which seems to us *un*friendly, "A fine friend you are!" When irony has a strong bite or cut to it, we frequently refer to it as *sarcasm.*

Irony need not have this cutting edge, however. The irony of King Henry's position in the closing scene of *Richard II* is that he has said one thing and in a sense wanted another. Irony used this way to point up a result the opposite of the thing wished for or expected or admired is called *dramatic irony* because of its constant use by playwrights. To one who knows the outcome of the play *Macbeth,* there is a terrible irony in Lady Macbeth's words immediately following the murder of Duncan, as she bids Macbeth join her to wash the blood off his hands. "A little water clears us of this deed," she says easily, but the ironical fact is that she can *never* wash this blood off her hands; the stain of the sin haunts her bitter sleep during the scene at the opening of act V, where she cries, "All the perfumes of Arabia will not sweeten this little hand," though in her sleepwalking she still says to her husband, in her nightmare, "Wash your hands, put on your nightgown, look not so pale!"

Irony has become so distinguishing a mark in modern literature that some contemporary critics speak as if literature *were* irony. Strictly speaking, it is simply one of the figures of speech.

APOSTROPHE

Much used in literature, *apostrophe* (which means literally a "turning away," from its use in classical rhetoric to indicate a momentary digression within a speech to address a person or thing not actually present) is the addressing of (1) an absent person as though he were present or (2) an inanimate object or thing as if it were capable of hearing. Some definitions of apostrophe include the addressing of persons actually present, but this is not for us a figurative use of language, and so it is not included here. Examples of apostrophe are easily found. Wordsworth addresses the dead Milton as if he were within hearing in the line "Milton! thou should'st be living at this hour," and John Donne speaks to death in "Death, be not proud. . . ." Poets often speak directly to the moon, the sun, and the stars. The example from Donne shows that *apostrophe* and *personification* may and frequently do exist together.

SYNECDOCHE AND METONYMY

These doughty figures are so often run together in the literature of criticism that they are sometimes known collectively as *metonymy*. According to definition, synecdoche is a figure of speech in which (1) an inclusive term is used for one of the parts included or (2) one of the parts is used for the inclusive term. Metonymy is a figure of speech which uses one word for another which it suggests. Shakespeare is using synecdoche in the speech of Henry IV's which we have already quoted: "Exton, . . . thou hast wrought/ A deed of slander, with thy fatal hand,/ Upon my head. . . ." *Hand* is used here in reference to Exton's whole act; *head* is used to refer to the person of Henry IV. The reverse (use of the whole for the part) may be illustrated by such an example as "He pounded the piano," where obviously the *keys* of the piano are meant.

In *metonymy*, the relationship is not that of part to whole, but of one thing to another in some sense calling it to mind. For example, "I see my wife's fine hand in this" (meaning "I see her influence") uses *hand* for something else which the hand or mind might have done; "Autumn bends the boughs of the apple trees" uses *autumn* for the *fruit* of autumn.

While there is a real difference between synecdoche and metonymy, it is probably clear that both terms are used for situations in which one word is used for another to which it is related in meaning; hence we may reasonably decide to use *metonymy* to cover both relationships, just as we said it is possible to use *metaphor* broadly to include both metaphor and simile.

Robert Frost is quoted by Louis Untermeyer as saying that he may be considered a *synecdochist.* This seems to be Frost's way of suggesting that much of his poetry is larger in meaning than the *immediate* experience which it embodies; that is, each poem, each experience within a poem, may in one sense be thought of as being a part of a larger whole. Doubtless it is this sense which gives the real impact to the repetition at the end of the following poem by Frost and which makes it possible to think of "Stopping by Woods on a Snowy Evening" as in itself an example of *synecdoche:* [4]

Whose woods these are I think I know.
His house is in the village though;
He will not see me stopping here
To watch his woods fill up with snow.

My little horse must think it queer
To stop without a farmhouse near
Between the woods and frozen lake
The darkest evening of the year.

He gives his harness bells a shake
To ask if there is some mistake.
The only other sound's the sweep
Of easy wind and downy flake.

The woods are lovely, dark and deep.
But I have promises to keep,
And miles to go before I sleep,
And miles to go before I sleep.

HYPERBOLE AND LITOTES

These two figures are uses of *overstatement* and *understatement,* respectively. Hyperbole is exaggeration for effect: "This package you asked me to carry weighs a ton!"—when probably it doesn't.

[4] From *New Hampshire.* Copyright, 1923, by Henry Holt and Company, Inc. Copyright, 1951, by Robert Frost. By permission of Henry Holt and Company, and of Jonathan Cape, Ltd., London.

Litotes is a figure expressing an *affirmative* position by stating the *negative of its opposite*. For example, suppose one wishes to say that Eugene O'Neill is a first-rate playwright (an affirmative position); he may indicate this by saying, "Eugene O'Neill is no second-rate writer," where *second-rate* becomes the opposite of *first-rate* and is qualified by the negative *no*. We make use of litotes constantly in our daily speech: "She's no dumbbell!" "This candy's not bad!" "That's no small achievement!" The positive meaning is underscored by the negative prefixed to its opposite.

Understatement and overstatement are both devices for heightening meaning in literature. As in life, noise calls attention to itself—but so does silence.

Figures of Sound

Thus far we have been talking of figurative language in terms primarily of its *meaning*. We have discussed *figures of words*. But there are also ways in which language departs from normal usage by employing certain *arrangements* of words in the interests of their aural effects: *figures of sound*. It is doubtless true that all the sounds of all the words in a poem contribute to its music, just as all the notes in a musical composition contribute to *its* music; but *some* sounds in poetry contribute *more* because of some striking quality in the use to which the poet has put them—because of the pronounced way in which they enter into the patterning of sound in the poem. *Any* element of patterning, whether in prose or in verse, is significant; but we shall here discuss only the most usual figures of sound: onomatopoeia, alliteration, rhyme, assonance and consonance, augmentation and diminution, acrostic scrambling, and parallelism and antithesis.

ONOMATOPOEIA

Onomatopoeia is the use of words whose sound suggests their sense. For example, in the popular song containing the line *"zing* went the strings of my heart," *zing* is an onomatopoetic word suggesting the sound made by the plectrum gliding over harp strings (the heart thus being made metaphorically to represent an instrument). An amusing use of onomatopoeia occurs in Browning's poem "Up at a Villa—Down in the City":

> *Bang-whang-whang* goes the drum, *tootle-te-*
> *tootle* the fife;
> No keeping one's haunches still; it's the
> greatest pleasure in life.

Allied to onomatopoeia, but distinct from it, is another all-pervasive aspect of language in literature: *tone color,* or *timbre.* *Timbre* is the resonance quality of voiced sounds, particularly vowel sounds, and it is a vital (though sometimes overstressed) quality of the reading voice. The following stanza from the Choric Song of Tennyson's "The Lotos-Eaters" will illustrate tone color in poetry:

> There is sweet music here that softer falls
> Than petals from blown roses on the grass,
> Or night-dews on still waters between walls
> Of shadowy granite, in a gleaming pass;
> Music that gentlier on the spirit lies,
> Than tired eyelids upon tired eyes;
> Music that brings sweet sleep down from the blissful skies.
> Here are cool mosses deep,
> And through the moss the ivies creep,
> And in the stream the long-leaved flowers weep,
> And from the craggy ledge the poppy hangs in sleep.

Because the stanza is conveying an attitude of sleepiness and pleasant relaxation the reader (and particularly the oral reader) suggests these feelings in his vocalizing of vowel sounds in such words as *softer, falls, petals, blown, roses, grass* in the opening lines and many other words throughout the stanza. These are not onomatopoetic words—it is not the *sound* which suggests the *sense* here, but rather the opposite: the *sense* here suggests the proper *sounding* of the words. Oral readers sometimes act as if tone color were restricted to soft, sleepy sounds, and they sometimes come close to lulling one to sleep (and hence destroying the experience of the literature) by making beautiful sounds. It is probably safe to say that it is almost better not to employ tone color at all than to turn every poem into sound only. Remember that the poet himself has done much of the work of choosing the sounds.

Tone color isn't simply a matter of "beautiful" sounds. It may be used to arouse feelings of buoyancy, vigor, motion, too. In the following poem by Dylan Thomas, for example, the attitude implied toward the journey of life suggests the way in which the poet intends the reader to express, vocally, such phrases as "meat-eating sun," "dressed to die," "sensual strut," and "red veins full of money." Perhaps no reader has ever shown more sharply the amazing animal vitality of our language than Dylan Thomas himself in his own oral performance.

> Twenty-four years remind the tears of my eyes.
> (Bury the dead for fear that they walk to the
>   grave in labour.)
> In the groin of the natural doorway I crouched
>   like a tailor
> Sewing a shroud for a journey
> By the light of the meat-eating sun.
> Dressed to die, the sensual strut begun,
> With my red veins full of money,
> In the final direction of the elementary town
> I advance for as long as forever is.[5]

ALLITERATION

Alliteration is the repetition of the same sound in the accented syllables of consecutive, or nearly consecutive, words. Usually the figure is thought of as applying to consonant sounds, as in the following lines: [6]

> The *s*ea gives her *sh*ells to the *sh*ingle,
>   The earth gives her *s*treams to the *s*ea

The repetition of the *s* sounds, though not in consecutive words, is frequent enough to make a decided appeal to the ear. There is

[5] *Collected Poems of Dylan Thomas.* Copyright, 1952, 1953, by Dylan Thomas. Reprinted by permission of New Directions and of J. M. Dent & Sons, Ltd., London.

[6] From Algernon Swinburne's Dedication to *Poems and Ballads.*

a difference between the *s* and the *sh* sounds; strictly speaking, this modification of sound produces *para-alliteration* rather than true alliteration. Furthermore, the *z* sounds at the ends of words (give*s*, shell*s*, stream*s*) echo the alliterative pattern in a hidden fashion. A clearer example of *hidden alliteration* is to be found in the phrase (from *Macbeth*) "after life's fitful fever," where the true alliteration is to be found in *f*itful *f*ever, where the *f*'s are initial and accented. The hidden alliteration is in the *f*'s of a*f*ter, li*f*e, and fit*f*ul, which are in unaccented positions. Even within such a term as *alliteration,* then, we must permit the existence of kinds. Alliteration may, of course, be used in excess. Sometimes in the work of Swinburne (1837–1909) we find it difficult to concentrate on meaning because of the degree of attention paid by the poet to sound.

RHYME

Rhyme is the repetition of identical or similar accented vowel sounds in combination with identical *succeeding* sounds but differing *preceding* sounds. If the vowel sounds are identical, the rhyme is called *perfect,* or *exact,* rhyme. If the vowel sounds are similar but not identical, the rhyme is called *half*-rhyme, or *slant* rhyme. Rhyme is used by poets both at line ends and within lines (terminal rhyme and internal rhyme). For example:

Exact Rhyme (*Terminal*)

> I will arise and go now, and go to Innis*free*,
>   And a small cabin build there, of clay and wattles *made*,
> Nine bean rows will I have there, a hive for the honey *bee*,
>   And live alone in the bee-loud *glade*.

William Butler Yeats
from The Lake Isle of Innisfree [7]

The rhyme scheme of the stanza would ordinarily be indicated thus:

a *b* *a* *b*
(free made bee glade)

[7] From *Collected Poems,* 2d ed., rev., The Macmillan Company, New York, 1956. By permission of The Macmillan Company.

assigning *a* to the first occurrence of any rhyme, *b* to the second, etc.

Slant Rhyme (*Terminal*)

Speech after long silence; it is right	*a*
All other lovers being estranged or *dead,*	*b*
Unfriendly lamplight hid under its *shade*	*b*
The curtains drawn upon unfriendly night,	*a*
That we descant and yet again descant	*c*
Upon the supreme theme of Art and *Song:*	*d*
Bodily decrepitude is wisdom; *young*	*d*
We loved each other and were ignorant.	*c*

William Butler Yeats
After Long Silence [8]

Internal Rhyme

I bring fresh *showers,* for the thirsting *flowers,*
From the seas and the streams;
I bear light *shade* for the leaves when *laid*
In their noonday dreams.

Percy Bysshe Shelley
from The Cloud

Rhymes are also classified as being either *masculine* or *feminine* (strong or weak—which will not please the young ladies!). Masculine rhymes are those where the rhyming syllables are the final and stressed syllables of the line:

... right
... night

Feminine rhymes are those where the rhyming stressed syllables precede the final syllables of the line:

... *nev*er
... for*ev*er

[8] From *Collected Poems,* 2d ed., rev., The Macmillan Company, New York, 1956. By permission of The Macmillan Company. The slant rhymes are italicized in the text.

ASSONANCE AND CONSONANCE

We have said that alliteration may occur between vowels as well as between consonants. In the phrase *"all the aw*ful *au*guries," the italicized sounds are identical and may be said to alliterate. But writers also employ patterns of vowel sounds in stressed positions other than initial positions or include related but not necessarily identical vowel sounds in the patterns. This patterning device is known as *assonance*. Again from Swinburne's "Super Flumina Babylonis":

> M*o*ther, not m*a*ker,
> B*o*rn, and not m*a*de...

It is true that the alliteration of the *m* sounds heightens the patterning of the vowels, but the vowels themselves (partly identical, partly simply similar) form a pattern, for in each line the two vowels italicized move from back to front in placement. Something like this may be observed, too, in the assonantal pattern in the following line from the same poem:

> By the w*a*ters of B*a*bylon we s*a*t down and w*e*pt.

Assonance operates in many degrees, in wondrously complicated patterns. In some literature (particularly Romance literature) poets employ assonance at the ends of poetic lines to give something of the effect of rhyme.

Or the poet may employ *consonance*, which is a kind of rhyme employing identical consonant patterns with varying vowels: *pitter / patter; partly / portly.*

AUGMENTATION AND DIMINUTION [9]

These two terms refer to the arrangement of repeated sounds in words. When the repeated sounds have an increasing number of other sounds intervening between them, the effect is that of *aug-*

---

[9] These terms and the term following (acrostic scrambling) are borrowed from Kenneth Burke, "On Musicality in Verse; as Illustrated by Some Lines of Coleridge," *Poetry*, vol. 57, pp. 31–40, October, 1940.

mentation—as in the phrase "slow sail," where the initial *sl* is repeated with the intervention of the letters *ai* in *sail*. The opposite effect is that of *diminution*—as in the phrase "sail slow."

ACROSTIC SCRAMBLING

Another arrangement of sounds may be referred to as *acrostic scrambling* (that is, a kind of scrambling achieved by the *crossing* of sounds). Burke gives the example "damsel with a dulcimer"; the scrambling may be indicated thus: d-ms-l (damsel) and d-lc-m-- (dulcimer), where *s* and *c* represent the same sound, though the first is voiced and the second voiceless.

PARALLELISM AND ANTITHESIS

Parallelism is the presence of successive phrases or clauses which are identical in construction or in sense (we are concerned in this chapter with *construction*). Antithesis is the juxtaposition of two phrases or clauses strongly contrasted with one another in sense (and usually parallel in construction). Both parallelism and antithesis make part of their appeal to the ear.

Parallelism is illustrated clearly in these lines from the familiar poem "The Hound of Heaven," by Francis Thompson (1859–1907):

> I fled Him, down the nights and down the days;
>   I fled Him, down the arches of the years;
> I fled Him, down the labyrinthine ways
>   Of my own mind; and in the mist of tears
> I hid from Him, and under running laughter.

The effect of emphasis and continuity achieved through the use of parallelism is here varied, in the fourth line, by the device known as *inversion:* that is, instead of saying, "I hid from Him in the mist of tears," the poet *inverts* the relationship between the verb and adverbial prepositional phrase "in the mist of tears."

Antithesis was a favorite device of the poets of the eighteenth century. Alexander Pope (1688–1744) easily yields examples:

> Fools rush in where Angels fear to tread.
>
> *from Essay on Criticism*

> Here to her Chosen all her works she shows;
> Prose swell'd to verse, Verse loitring into prose...
>
> *from The Dunciad*

> True faith, true policy, united ran,
> That was but love of God, and this of Man.
>
> *from Essay on Man*

Parallelism, antithesis, and inversion are combined (as often in the structural complexity of Pope's poetry) in the following example:

> How shall I lose the sin, yet keep the sense,
> And love th' offender, yet detest th' offence?
> How dear the object from the crime remove,
> Or how distinguish penitence from love?
>
> *from Eloisa to Abelard*

And again in this example:

> So peaceful rests, without a stone, a name,
> What once had beauty, titles, wealth, and fame.
> How lov'd, how honour'd once, avails thee not,
> To whom related, or by whom begot;
> A heap of dust alone remains of thee;
> 'Tis all thou art, and all the proud shall be.
>
> *from Verses to the Memory
> of an Unfortunate Lady*

This complication of appeals to ear and sense marks much that is great in the poetry of a period which has been much too often neglected by our century.

Ambiguity

Thus far in the chapter we have discussed a variety of literal and figurative uses of language and sound in the interests of vitality, clarity, and precision. Literature is not successful when it simply confuses (though the reader has some obligation to suspend judgment until he is sure the confusion is not simply a result of his own laziness or inadequacy as a reader). Even a poem or a play or a story about a *state* of confusion must have clarity in the vision of confusion it presents. That is, ambiguity which results simply from inept use of language must be charged against the writer. But there are ambiguities in writing which serve enormously to increase the effectiveness of the thing written; statements which can be taken two different ways (or three or four different ways) may depend for their effect precisely upon the *complex* of meanings. In Joyce's "The Sisters" (*Dubliners*), when Eliza, one of the sisters of the old priest who has died, says, "The duties of the priesthood was too much for him. And then his life was, you might say, crossed," *she* is using the word *crossed* to mean "disappointed," but Joyce is using it in another sense: the old priest has died under the burden of the cross, and the chalice which ought to represent thanksgiving and renewal rests upon his breast, as he lies in his coffin, as if it were the instrument of his death.

Modern literature in particular depends heavily upon layers of meaning which frequently use ambiguity as a device for increasing the density of the experience being imitated. It would be almost impossible here to do justice to the complexity of the subject. William Empson has written, in *Seven Types of Ambiguity*, what is perhaps the standard discussion of the subject, though he seems to some critics to labor the point a little too hard. Well used, ambiguities in literature function much as do overtones in music, extending the range of the experience being communicated. Ambiguities thus used are to be found in all literatures. On the simplest level, ambiguity may be expressed in the *pun,* or play on words—though we do not mean to suggest that *all* puns are simple.

Imagery

We come finally to an aspect of language which overrides distinctions between literal and figurative speech. *Imagery* has had so much attention in modern literary criticism that it seems some-times to be the whole heart of literature. While a word of caution must be exercised here—too much attention to images may be as bad as too little—it is nevertheless true that image making is *vital* to literature.

Image making, or imaging, may be defined broadly as "the reconstitution of previous experience, minus only the original stimulating object or situation." [10] The *image* itself is the response produced by this activity. For example, once we have seen a tree, we can *imagine* (make an image of) a tree thereafter simply as a result of seeing the word *tree*. It is this imitating of the original experience, rather than the original experience itself, to which the term *imagery* refers. The degree of our response to literature is in large measure related to the degree of our image making in the reading of literature.

Both silent and oral readers, of course, engage in the process of imaging. The words of the literature (the symbols on the page) set off neuromotor-glandular responses on the part of the reader; these responses are in turn reported to the cortex by the appropri-ate sensory nerves, giving the reader his awareness of the images. For the silent reader or the restrained oral reader, the responses are largely implicit; they tend, however, to be explicit for the oral reader, to be in some way visible or audible to an audience. Oral reading encourages the fuller degree of participation, here as in other ways.

It is customary, in some discussions of literature, to classify images according to the senses to which the appeal is made. A usual classification would consider images as visual, tactile, audi-tory, olfactory, gustatory, thermal, and kinaesthetic, in reference to the senses of sight, touch, hearing, smell, taste, temperature, and "motion," or muscle movement. But this list is not exhaustive; such a view of literary images probably ought to include the senses of pain and equilibrium, for example. Synaesthetic images trans-late from one sense into another—one may have a *"brown* taste"

[10] We are indebted to Clarence T. Simon of Northwestern University for the wording of this definition.

in the mouth, for example. The fact is that, while visual images may well be predominant for most readers, people differ enormously in the nature of their responses to images. What is primarily a visual image to one reader may be primarily auditory for another. Unless the literature defines the sense appealed to, and counts on that *particular* sense appeal for its relationship to the rest of the work, readers have much latitude in the sense nature of the response they make; the poet cannot ask that every reader have precisely *his* make-up. This does not mean that every reader is free to do anything he wants with every image.

More important than any oversimple classification of images by their sense appeals is the function of the image making itself in giving life to the experience of literature. More often than not, readers must be encouraged to *see*, to *hear*, to *feel*, to *engage in* the attitudes and actions being expressed in the experience of the poem or the story or the play. Literature is meant, among other things, to *move* the reader. The unmoving reader is the writer's archenemy!

We have said that images override distinctions between figurative and nonfigurative uses of speech; that is, an image may be figurative, or it may be literal. The phrase "the barbed porcupine" calls up an image which may be visual or kinaesthetic or tactile, or a combination of these; in any event, it is a *literal* image. But the phrase "the barbed persistence of his cruelty," used in reference to the porcupine, while it may have the same sense appeal (and may even add the sense of pain), is a *figurative* image; the *quills* have become the *cruelty* of the porcupine, and the barbs on the quills, which keep the quills sinking into the body they have punctured, are now an aspect of the persistent cruelty of the porcupine. The use of the quill to symbolize the porcupine's cruelty is probably to be called synecdoche.

A simpler instance may make the matter clearer. "The tree has a robin's nest in its branches" is literal in its use of images, but "The tree wears a nest of robins in her hair" is figurative—as well as funny!

Sometimes, in encouraging young readers to respond fully to

the sensations in images, we forget that one may get so lost in the vividness of the sense impressions that he loses sight of the meanings which the images are intended to convey. Readers ought not to *wallow* in sense responses to language, at the expense of the unity in the structure of the whole piece of literature. Remember that images in literature are really reconstituted experience and that the reconstitution often involves distortion for a particular point. Images not only vivify; they also help to clarify and to extend experience. By *imitating,* but not by simply *copying,* actual experience, images in literature help to create a new (imaginary) world—which actual life, in its turn, then often tries to imitate in the interests of improving our everyday existence.

Images can be considered in terms of their meaning as well as in terms of their sense appeals. For example, studies have been made of particular image groups in conveying meaning in the plays of Shakespeare. Studies exist of the images of sight and nature in *King Lear,*[11] of clothing and garments in *Macbeth,*[12] of light and darkness in *Romeo and Juliet,*[13] and so on. An examination of images in prose works also yields valuable results; for example, one study [14] reveals interesting *image clusters* as functioning in the structure of William Faulkner's novel *Absalom, Absalom!* Imagery thus becomes a central aspect of literary structure, a vital function in the experience which literature embodies. Notice, for example, how sharply the figurative images derived from law, in the following sonnet (Sonnet 134) by Shakespeare, condition the experience expressed within the sonnet:

> So, now I have confess'd that he is thine
> And I myself am mortgag'd to thy will,

[11] Robert Heilman, *This Great Stage,* Louisiana State University Press, Baton Rouge, La., 1948.

[12] Cleanth Brooks, *The Well Wrought Urn,* Reynal & Hitchcock, Inc., New York, 1947, enlarging upon the discussion by Caroline Spurgeon in *Shakespeare's Imagery and What It Tells Us,* The Macmillan Company, New York, 1935.

[13] Moody E. Prior, *The Language of Tragedy,* Columbia University Press, New York, 1947. Professor Prior's book is valuable on this whole subject.

[14] An unpublished doctoral dissertation by Joseph A. Wigley, written at Northwestern University in 1956.

Myself I'll forfeit, so that other mine
Thou wilt restore, to be my comfort still.
But thou wilt not, nor he will not be free,
For thou art covetous and he is kind;
He learn'd but surety-like to write for me
Under that bond that him as fast doth bind.
The statute of thy beauty thou wilt take,
Thou usurer, that put'st forth all to use,
And sue a friend came debtor for my sake;
So him I lose through my unkind abuse.
    Him have I lost; thou hast both him and me:
    He pays the whole, and yet am I not free.

Summary

In this chapter, we have been concerned with certain literal and figurative uses of language. We have seen some of the traditional ways in which language operates within the context of any style. Language is a highly sensitive instrument in the hands of a good writer; *style* is the term applied to the unique quality achieved by a writer in imitating experience in the symbolic, linguistic form known as literature.

But language, before it can fulfill itself as a part of style, must find expression in forms rather more complex than those examined in this chapter. Hence we shall devote the next chapter to a consideration of at least the basic problems of *structure*, which embraces and subsumes the uses of language which we have just examined.

Exercises

1. The authors have stressed the importance of reading a work of literature *receptively* before reading it *critically*. What differences are there between the two kinds of reading?

2. Can you name any pieces of literature which seem to you sentimental? Do you find that you *like* some of these and *dislike* others?

How is it possible to like pieces which seem sentimental, when sentimentality has been defined as a "breach of decorum"?

3. Write a close literal paraphrase of Milton's sonnet "On His Blindness." Try to say, in your own words, as accurately as possible, exactly what Milton says in his poem. Compare your paraphrase with the poem. What *can* the paraphrase do? What can it *not* do?

4. What figures of words and what figures of sound do you find in Milton's sonnet? What images? What is the contribution made by the figures and images to the meaning of the poem?

10

Appreciation of Literature: Structure

$\mathcal{L}$ITERATURE, we have kept saying, is an imitation of life in the symbols which we call words. We have had a good deal to say about the relationships between literature and life, between "normal" uses and "figurative" uses of language and sound, and between "literary" and "nonliterary" accounts of similar experiences. In this chapter, it is necessary to say more about the particular structures within which literature embodies experience in words.

It is perhaps necessary to remark here, too, that the devices of language considered in Chapter 9 and the aspects of structure to be considered in this chapter are *not* the whole of the work of literary art. It is perfectly clear that *structure* as a fully meaningful term includes both the materials of these chapters and the materials in all the chapters preceding them: that is, structure is the inclusive term which embraces the whole organization of the literary piece—subject, language, point of view or attitude, temporal arrangement, etc. It is impossible to discuss subject except in con-

194

junction with specific pieces of literature, and this we shall do in Chapter 11; meanwhile, we must examine certain traditional and definable forms within which writers constantly choose to work.

It is customary to divide literature into two general classes, poetry and prose, although the distinctions between these two classes sometimes grow very slight. Furthermore, because it poses particular problems of its own, we should like to consider with these two classes a form which may be *either* poetry or prose but is in either case a highly specialized structure of language: drama.

The Structure of Poetry

Poetry is the imitation of experience in language which is based upon *return*. Perhaps the Latin word *versus* (from which we derive our English word *verse*, although *verse*, strictly speaking, means a *single line* of poetry) will help indicate what *return* means. *Versus* means a *turning back;* it is the opposite of *prorsus*, from which we derive our word *prose*, which means *forward* or *straight ahead*. Poetry is written in repeated "sections," and within these sections some form of patterning is taking place. *Prosody* is the word we use to name the art or science of patterning in poetry. One aspect of prosody is the study of meter, and it will be convenient to begin our study of the structure of poetry with this.

Meter

Meter is the patterning of two elements in poetry. It is common practice to define these two elements as being stressed sounds and unstressed sounds or accented and unaccented sounds. But a better way to describe the pattern is to say that it is based on a varied alternation of *conspicuous* and *less conspicuous elements,* because it is not only stress and accent (which are, to begin with, as we shall use the words, two *different* things anyway) but also such things as pitch, inflection, and time which enter into the patterning.

Stress, as it is to be used in this chapter, is the *ictus,* or *beat,*

employed to distinguish one syllable from another by the employment of greater force or loudness of utterance. In the sentence
"The rain has stopped," there are two stresses, one on *rain* and
one on *stopped*, both one-syllable words. In the sentence "The
downpour has stopped," however, the second syllable of *downpour*, while it is "lighter" than the first syllable, is "heavier" than
the words *the* and *has*. In words of more than a single syllable,
the syllable which receives the stress is called the *accented* syllable;
that is, accent is the habitual stress placed in pronouncing upon a
particular syllable or particular syllables of a word containing
more than a single syllable. In this sense, one cannot speak of
accent at all in monosyllables such as *son, strong, day, night,* etc.,
since there is no contrast in syllables, which is necessary to the
existence of accent. But monosyllables may receive *stress,* as we
saw in "The *rain* has *stopped.*" Now in the sentence "The downpour has stopped," we have suggested that *-pour,* while it is not
the accented syllable, receives greater stress than the first and third
syllables in the sentence. We can explain this by saying that the
accented syllable receives the *primary stress* and the unaccented
syllable receives a *secondary stress.* Actually, linguists find at least
four degrees of stress operating in the English language [1] though
we shall not try here to be as detailed as that. Now perhaps is the
time to look at a group of verses, or lines of poetry, to see how
meter operates to pattern language. Here are some lines from
"Annabel Lee," by Edgar Allan Poe (1809–1849):

> It was many and many a year ago
>   In a kingdom by the sea,
> That a maiden there lived whom you may know
>   By the name of Annabel Lee;
> And this maiden she lived with no other thought
>   Than to love and be loved by me.

[1] There is a symposium on the subject of metrics in *The Kenyon Review,* Summer, 1956, which reviews the theory behind the Trager-Smith system (the analysis
of stress, pitch, and juncture in poetry). See particularly the article by Harold
Whitehall in that issue. An interesting earlier account is Wilbur L. Schramm's
"Approaches to a Science of English Verse," University of Iowa Studies: Series
on Aims and Progress of Research, no. 46, 1935.

These verses together make up a six-line *stanza*. Stanzas are another means of patterning, another aspect of prosody. The rhyme scheme of this particular stanza is *ababcb*.

Suppose we begin an analysis of the verses by pointing out the *accented* syllables:

<pre>
              /   /   /
It was <i>ma</i>ny and <i>ma</i>ny a year a<i>go</i>
                /
   In a <i>king</i>dom by the sea,
                /
That a <i>mai</i>den there lived whom you may know
                        /
   By the name of <i>A</i>nnabel Lee;
          /   /
And this <i>mai</i>den she lived with no <i>o</i>ther thought

   Than to love and be loved by me.
</pre>

Now to these accents, let us add *stresses* demanded by the sense in addition to those dictated by the accent:

<pre>
              /   /   /   /
It was many and many a <i>year</i> ago
           /   /
   In a kingdom by the <i>sea,</i>
          /   /   /   /
That a maiden there <i>lived</i> whom <i>you</i> may <i>know</i>
              /   /   /
   By the <i>name</i> of Annabel <i>Lee;</i>
          /   /   /   /
And this maiden she <i>lived</i> with no other <i>thought</i>
            /   /   /
   Than to <i>love</i> and be <i>loved</i> by <i>me.</i>
</pre>

Notice that all these sense stresses are on nouns or pronouns and verbs, which normally carry the significant weight of meaning in an English sentence. The rhyme at the line ends intensifies the stress pattern there, so that the *lines* themselves become a part of the patterning process. (Lines of verse with a clearly defined terminal pause are called *end-stopped;* those not so terminating are called *run-on.*) Now observe that the patterning of stresses within the lines is fairly regular, alternating thus:

4 stresses
2 stresses
4 stresses
3 stresses
4 stresses
3 stresses

Because this pattern sets up a certain expectation in the ear of the reader, the word *by* in the second line tends to take on a stress, although in prose such a preposition would *not* be stressed. Thus it is possible to think of three stresses in the second line, too, making the pattern exact. That group of prosodists (*stress prosodists*) who insist that English meter is based upon a regular patterning of stresses might describe the lines as we have described them above.

Poets sometimes write with a patterning of the syllable count in the lines of verse, too, but a count of the syllables in Poe's stanza will show that this is not *syllabic prosody:* 11, 7, 10, 8, 11, 8.

There is still another way of talking about the patterning within the lines—the way Poe himself would have talked about it here, presumably, since he has left us a treatise on prosody. Suppose, first, that we mark all the unstressed syllables in the poem, and that we break the lines up into *measures,* or *feet,* by putting a bar after each stress:

```
x   x  / | x   x  / | x x  / |x /
It was ma|ny and ma|ny a year|ago

   x x  / | x   / |x   /
In a king|dom by|the sea,

  x x  / | x    x   / |  x    / | x   /
That a mai|den there lived|whom you|may know

  x   x   / |x  / | x x  /
By the name|of An|nabel Lee;

 x   x   / | x   x   / | x   x /| x     /
And this mai|den she lived|with no o|ther thought

    x   x  / | x   x   / | x  /
Than to love|and be loved|by me.
```

Now observe how we have added to the patterning: the first, third, and fifth lines each contain *four feet*. Lines containing four feet are called tetrameter lines (*tetra-,* meaning "four," and *meter*). The second, fourth, and sixth lines each contain *three feet.* Lines containing three feet are called *trimeter* lines (*tri-,* meaning "three," and *meter*). Here are some other terms:

dimeter	two feet per line
pentameter	five feet per line
hexameter	six feet per line
heptameter	seven feet per line
octameter	eight feet per line

You are not likely to get monometer (one foot per line), nor to have lines with more than eight feet, although longer lines are not unknown. At any rate, we must stop somewhere!

We have, then, in "Annabel Lee" (at least the stanza we have quoted), alternating tetrameter and trimeter lines, with the trimeter lines all rhyming with each other. Now notice the feet within each line: they are of two kinds only, x x / and x /. The first of these kinds of feet is called an *anapest*. An *anapest* is a metrical foot made up of two unstressed or less conspicuous syllables and one stressed or conspicuous syllable. The other foot is called an *iambus,* or an *iamb.* An *iamb* is a metrical foot consisting of a single unstressed or less conspicuous syllable and a single stressed or conspicuous syllable. The *iambus* and the *anapest* are two of the commonest feet in English verse. Other common feet are the *trochee* (a reversed *iambus*), the *dactyl* (a reversed *anapest*), the *pyrrhic* (two unstressed syllables), and the *spondee* (two stressed syllables). Here are examples of each:

Trochee

$$/ \quad x \mid / \quad x \mid / \quad x \mid / \quad x$$
Bacchus'|blessings|are a|treasure,
Drinking is the soldier's pleasure;
Rich the treasure,
Sweet the pleasure,
Sweet is pleasure after pain.

*John Dryden (1631–1700)
from Alexander's Feast*

Dactyl

```
 /    x   x |/  x  x |/ x   x |  /
Black were her|eyes as the|berry that|grows
  x   x |  /   x  x | / /
on the|thorn by the|wayside
```

Henry Wadsworth Longfellow (1807–1882)
from Evangeline

Spondee

The last foot in the line from *Evangeline* above is a spondee. Both spondaic and pyrrhic feet are usually found only in mixed meters.

Pyrrhic

```
   x   / |x/| x   / |x x|x  /
This med|iae|val mir|acle|of song
```

Henry Wadsworth Longfellow
from Sonnet II, Divina Commedia

The fourth foot is a pyrrhic foot. Or here, as frequently, the pyrrhic can be regarded as an iambus if one takes the third syllable of *miracle* to have a secondary stress.

Poems written in iambs and anapests are said to be in *rising rhythm* (that is, the foot rises toward the stress); the trochee and the dactyl are employed to produce *falling rhythm* (the foot falling from the stress). It is sometimes said that the English language is essentially a language based upon rising rhythm, and that it is difficult to keep dactyls and trochees from being inverted. Iambs and anapests frequently substitute for one another in poetry; dactyls and trochees substitute for one another. This does not, however, preclude mixed measures, and both pyrrhic and spondaic feet are to be found in either rising or falling rhythm. Prosodists who talk about meter in terms of feet are called *foot prosodists*. We are so accustomed, by long habit, to talking about poetry in terms of feet—partly because our early prosodists were brought up on classical poetry, where feet exist in a somewhat different sense, and partly because poets themselves usually talk about their poetry in terms of feet—that we sometimes forget the possibility of poetry written in simple stress patterns or in simple syllabic groups. It is perfectly possible, of course, to have poetry which may be described by *any* of these systems, though in that case the syllabic system tells us *least about* the poem.

We have said that the stanza of "Annabel Lee" is made up of a mixture of anapestic meter and iambic meter arranged in a certain pattern of lines. The word which we shall use to describe the effect which all these varying elements have upon the music or flow of the poem is *rhythm*. Rhythm is the tension in the prosodic surface of a poem produced by the recurrence of a pattern of sound interrupted or varied by substitutions in the meter, by pauses, by inflections—indeed, by any aspect of sound other than the simple recurrence of the basic metrical unit. Rhythm in poetry is a kind of *counterpoint*. You will observe in the stanza of "Annabel Lee" that the rhythm involves not only the mixing of anapests and iambs but the recurrence of a rise and fall in pitch and in emphasis, the latter based in turn upon an alternation of rhetorically conspicuous and rhetorically less conspicuous words. Incidentally, it is perhaps worth pointing out that the pronoun *she* in line 5 (which might seem normally to be a conspicuous word) is made less conspicuous by virtue of the fact that the maiden's name appears in the line above, and then is referred to again in the noun *maiden* immediately preceding the pronoun. Indeed, strictly speaking, the use of the pronoun *she* here is tautological.

We have said nothing thus far about temporal equivalence in the repeated units. This is a vexed and vexing problem, but it seems likely that the units are *theoretically,* at least, equal or approximately equal in time. That is, regular English verse tends to be *isochronous* in its pattern, though the time pattern may vary remarkably from reader to reader. Thus foot prosody may be looked at as a prosodic system cutting across other prosodic systems such as isochronism, isoaccentualism, isosyllabism.[2]

[2] These dreaded words are not meant to frighten the timid—they are the simplest terms for recognizable features of verse, and once you have learned them they will cease to terrify you. *Isochronism* means "equal time" (the theory

It is usual to say that three-syllable feet are more lilting than two-syllable feet, and quicker in time. There was a time when prosodists thought that the trisyllabic foot lacked dignity! We tend now to like mixtures of feet for the sake of variety in the poetic line, though not all mixtures are acceptable to the ear.

Now let us take a passage of poetry by an English poet who is a master of rhythmic effects, to see how we can best explain its prosodic structure. The stanza is from Shelley's "To a Skylark":

/   / /   /

Hail to thee, blithe *Spi*rit!

/   /   /

Bird thou *nev*er wert,

/   /   /

That from Heaven, or near it,

/   / /

*Pour*est thy full heart

/ /   /   /   /

In pro*fuse* strains of *un*preme*di*tated art.

The stresses have simply been marked with a diagonal (/); the accents have also been italicized. The word *Heaven,* which normally has two syllables, has here, as so frequently in poetry, a single syllable, probably, though taking it as a two-syllable word will not really interfere greatly with the analysis which follows.

Probably the only line where there will be any particular quarrel with this marking of stresses is the third line, where it is a little difficult to decide that *from* rather than *that* (that is, *who*) is to be stressed. This is a question of the *sense* of the line. Is Shelley saying primarily,

/   / /   /   /   / /

Hail to you who from Heaven pour your full heart,

or primarily

---

that the repeated units of poetry are equal in the time taken to pronounce them); *isoaccentualism* means "equal accent" (the theory that the repeated units are separated from one another or isolated by the repetition of stress); *isosyllabism* means "equal syllable division" (the theory that syllable count of the unit—usually the line—is the measuring stick).

/   /   /   /   /   /   /   /
Hail to you who from Heaven—or, if not from, near Heaven—pour

    /   /
your full heart?

It seems to us that it is the latter, though the point is a delicate one. Perhaps one should say that there is a secondary stress on *that,* making this a four-stress line. If we mark all the other syllables "light" or "unstressed" or "less conspicuous," we have the following pattern:

	Syllable count
/ x / / /x Hail to thee, blithe Spirit!	6
/ x / x / Bird thou never wert,	5
/ / / x / x That from Heaven, or near it,	6
/ x x / / Pourest thy full heart	5
x x / / x / x / x x x / In profuse strains of unpremeditated art.	12

There is clearly a syllable pattern here, with the last line doubling the syllable length of lines 1 and 3. There is also a stress pattern— 4, 3, 4, 3, 5. Indeed, in the last line one is tempted to say that the first syllable of *profuse* has a secondary stress, or even a primary stress, making the last line a six-stress line (double the number of stresses in lines 2 and 4, and half again as many as in 1 and 3). Now suppose we try to distinguish between the stresses themselves. Do you have any feeling that in each line certain stresses carry more weight than others? In other words, is there an alternation among the stresses themselves between more and less conspicuous syllables? We would say "yes" to this question, and indicate the matter this way:

         /   /
      Hail to thee, blithe Spirit!

         /   /
       Bird thou never wert,

           /   /
     That from Heaven, or near it,

$$/ \qquad\qquad /$$
Pourest thy full heart
$$/ \qquad\qquad\qquad /$$
In profuse strains of unpremeditated art.

Or

$$/ \qquad\qquad\qquad /$$
In profuse strains of unpremeditated art.

Hence there is a rhythm of stresses as well as of stressed and non-stressed syllables. There is also a rhyme pattern: *ababb*. In the first and third lines, there is also a central pause (*caesura*) in the line after the third syllable, providing still another rhythmic effect.

In terms of feet, the first line of the poem may be described as trochaic-spondaic trimeter (/x // /x), or trochaic trimeter with a spondaic substitution in the second foot. This is falling rhythm. The third line gives us trouble in the first foot, but the second and third feet are trochaic, and the line is a trimeter line. It is sensible to say that the dominant trochaic pattern is one of the things which tends to throw a stress on *that,* making the first foot, too, trochaic, though the sense itself may be pulling us toward a stress on *from.* This tension between the two possibilities is again an effect of the rhythm in Shelley's stanza.

In the other paired lines (the second and fourth), we have a problem because we have only five syllables in each line. We may say that the second line is two trochaic feet with the addition of a single stressed syllable, and that the effect is still primarily that of falling rhythm, or we may say, looking at the placement of the two stresses in our two-stress reading of the line, that the first half of the line is in falling rhythm and the second half is in rising rhythm (something like this: / x x x /). The line hovers between two and three feet, and any foot division of the line is likely to be unsatisfying. The problem in the fourth line is similar, but simpler.

The sixth line is highly complex. We may give in to the temptation to pronounce *profuse* as *pro'fuse* and scan the line thus: x/ x/ x/ x/ xx x/ (iambic hexameter, with a single pyrrhic substitution, where the pattern tends to make an iambus even of the pyrrhic foot). But read this way, the line has none of the intricate rhythmic effects achieved by another way of analyzing it. If read as an anapest, three trochees, and another anapest we get this: xx/ /x /x /x xx/. The effect achieved by defeating the ear's expectation by reversing the pattern in the second foot and again in the fifth foot is known as *syncopation,* a term borrowed from music. It is possible to say that our difficulty in scanning the third line is also an effect of syncopation, and even to describe the effect in the middle of line 1 and at the end of line 4 as being that of syncopation. Looked at this way, the *bouncing* effect of the rhythm (which may not too fancifully be looked upon as a characteristic of the mounting bird in the poem) is deliberate and useful.

This analysis is a way of getting at the *sound* of the poem— whether it is read aloud or whether it is heard only by the mind's ear. Different readers will read the poem in slightly different ways, and the differences will reside in the kinds of answer the readers provide to the problems we have raised here. These problems are not imaginary but real; the differences they result in when the poem is read aloud are significant differences. The best readings will be those which accept the variations provided by Shelley without permitting the variations to obscure the regularities. The mixture of *rising* and *falling* effects (reversals in expected patterns) is part of the tension in the prosodic surface of the poem. *It is important not to let an arbitrary pattern of analysis override the variations which so clearly characterize Shelley's rhythm.*

From the discussion foregoing, we may conclude that poetry is that form of literary art in which the words conveying the imitation of experience are arranged in a repeating pattern of units which are more or less equal to one another. The arrangement of elements determining the equalities may vary from poem to poem, from poet to poet, from period to period; but within any given poem, it is likely to be constant. The elements themselves are essentially stress, accent, pitch, and time (including pause). In the poetry we have looked at thus far, the units *tend* to be equal either in time or in stress-accent patterning, or in some combination of these.

Free verse, however, complicates our analysis. No brief account can, of course, take cognizance of all the varieties of free verse (any more than it can examine all kinds of regular verse). Some kinds are so free as no longer to constitute verse at all, but only prose set down in a kind of "verse picture" on the page—bad free verse, and usually bad prose, too.[3]

At its "freest," free verse does not employ rhyme, nor does it employ regular meter. It does, however, have rhythm. Free verse may, on the other hand, employ rhyme and move fairly close to regular metrical effects. Suppose we look at a few passages of free verse to single out at least the most obvious elements of patterning.

T. S. Eliot's "The Waste Land"[4] begins thus:

> April is the cruellest month, breeding
> Lilacs out of the dead land, mixing
> Memory and desire, stirring
> Dull roots with spring rain.
> Winter kept us warm, covering
> Earth in forgetful snow, feeding
> A little life with dried tubers.

It is difficult to see any precise patterning in syllable count, in stressing, or in kinds of feet employed. There is a clear syntactical patterning, however:

[3] We do not mean here to exclude visual prosody as a proper form, however, but only to single out a kind of inferior free verse which, not based on visual prosody, is divided into lines to help it "look" like verse. Visual prosody has a long history; poems on the page may be arranged to look like wings, like a cross, like a diamond, like a kite and its tail, etc. The oral reader is helpless with this aspect of prosody, of course; furthermore, it is doubtless fair to say that most poetry written in this prosody is characterized more by ingenuity than by the quality of the experience it provides. But such a modern poet as e. e. cummings now and again achieves striking and pleasurable effects with it.

[4] From *Collected Poems, 1909–1935* by T. S. Eliot; copyright, 1936, by Harcourt, Brace and Company, Inc., and reprinted by their permission and by permission of Faber and Faber, Ltd., London.

April is the cruellest month, / breeding
Lilacs out of the dead land, / mixing
Memory and desire, / stirring
Dull roots with spring rain.
Winter kept us warm, / covering
Earth in forgetful snow, / feeding
A little life with dried tubers.

This patterning may be described thus:

> Subject phrase participle
> object phrase participle
> object phrase participle
> object phrase
> Subject phrase participle
> object phrase participle
> object phrase

Furthermore, while the syllabic count of the lines is certainly not even, the lines are not strikingly uneven in length. The syntactical patterns (the *isosyntactical* units) are not lost sight of simply because the number of syllables per line varies. Notice that there is considerable patterning of assonance and alliteration here, too, with augmentation and diminution and with acrostic scrambling. There is even a kind of alliteration which we have not hitherto considered: transverse alliteration ("*w*inter *k*ept us *w*arm, *c*overing"), where the alliterating pairs are alternated. It is difficult to think of verse so richly patterned as being in any sense "free" verse!

The patterning in free verse may be syntactical, then. The lines immediately following these in "The Waste Land" are even more complex in their syntactical pattern:

Summer surprised us, coming over the Starnbergersee
With a shower of rain; we stopped in the colonnade,
And went on in sunlight, into the Hofgarten,
And drank coffee, and talked for an hour.

The lines are again broken (as are many of the subsequent lines of the poem), but the break is not based upon repetition of so obvious a syntactical pattern. Still, there *is* a pattern: "[verbal] over ... Starnbergersee, with ... shower of rain, [verb] in ... colonnade, [verb] in sunlight, into ... Hofgarten, [verb] for ... hour." Furthermore, the verb-preposition-object pattern is accompanied by a sound pattern:

$$s \ldots s \ldots z \ldots s \ldots St \ldots z$$
$$sh \ldots . st$$
$$s$$

One might go on, but it is dangerous to push the notion of sound repetition too far as an argument for distinguishing verse from prose, since prose, too, has repetitions of sounds. After all, there are only a certain number of sounds in the language, and they are bound to repeat! It is only when clear *patterns* are discernible that comment is particularly helpful.

But there is another aspect of patterning in the four lines from Eliot's poem: each line is made up of two speech phrases, or cadences. A *cadence,* literally, is a *fall;* it takes its name from the fall of the voice at the end of syntactical units, though, to be sure, the voice does not *always* fall at such points. The cadences in the four lines of "The Waste Land" are:

> Summer surprised us,
> coming over the Starnbergersee
> with a shower of rain;
> we stopped in the colonnade,
> and went on in sunlight,
> into the Hofgarten,
> and drank coffee,
> and talked for an hour.

Strictly speaking, the second and third phrases constitute a single phrase rather than two phrases, and you will notice that Eliot does not punctuate the line ending with *Starnbergersee*. All these phrases are *roughly* of the same length, with the shortest ("and drank coffee") probably making up for its shortness by taking longer to pronounce because of the juncture in *nk c* ("dran*k* cof-

fee"). Notice that the effect of the lines when the speech phrases
are written in separate lines is not at all the effect of the lines
when two cadences are written in a single line. Eliot's own arrangement is less monotonous (because more varied in flow)
than the simple use of a line for each cadence.

Much of the free verse in "The Waste Land" approaches the
condition of blank verse—a kind of "as-if" iambic pentameter,
which is itself a rhythmic effect. References to Shakespeare, and
even quotation from Shakespeare in the text, heighten this illusion
of blank verse (unrhymed iambic pentameter). There are also
tags from ragtime music and from other poetry which set up
rhythmic echoes:

> O O O O that Shakespeherian Rag
> It's so elegant
> So intelligent

Or:

> Sweet Thames, run softly, till I end my song

Again, in the same poem, still another kind of patterning by
repetition of words:

> Here is no *water* but only *rock*
> *Rock* and no *water* and the sandy *road*
> The *road* winding above among the *mountains*
> Which are *mountains* of *rock* without *water*
> If there were *water* we should *stop and drink*
> Amongst the *rock* one cannot *stop or think*

The pattern here is elaborate and balanced:

water	rock			
	rock	water		
			road	road
			mountains	mountains
rock	water			
	water	rock		

This is complicated, in the last two lines, by the combination of
repetition and rhyme in "stop and drink" and "stop or think."

Such echoing, balance, hesitation, and allusion are characteristic of the poetic voice of T. S. Eliot. Examine the remainder of this section of "The Waste Land," and see how the pattern continues: [5]

Here is no water but only rock
Rock and no water and the sandy road
The road winding above among the mountains
Which are mountains of rock without water
If there were water we should stop and drink
Amongst the rock one cannot stop or think
Sweat is dry and feet are in the sand
If there were only water amongst the rock
Dead mountain mouth of carious teeth that cannot spit
Here one can neither stand nor lie nor sit
There is not even silence in the mountains
But dry sterile thunder without rain
There is not even solitude in the mountains
But red sullen faces sneer and snarl
From doors of mudcracked houses
                        If there were water
    And no rock
    If there were rock
    And also water
    And water
    A spring
    A pool among the rock
    If there were the sound of water only
    Not the cicada
    And dry grass singing
    But sound of water over a rock
    Where the hermit-thrush sings in the pine trees
    Drip drop drip drop drop drop drop
    But there is no water

Perhaps enough has been said to show that free verse can be described as patterned. It is probably safe to say that unless verse

[5] *Ibid.*, from the section entitled What the Thunder Said. Why do you think Eliot has used no punctuation in this passage?

is patterned, it is not verse at all, since by definition verse is based upon *return*. Poetry, whether regular or free, comes in *waves* of sound and sense, rising and falling and falling over its own rising, and mixing and mingling its parts in its rising and falling, from boundary to boundary. But the figure will not express all: a poem, like a story or like a play, tends to reach the peak of its movement somewhere *not too far from* its close but not *at* its close. All the temporal arts—music, song, dance—follow this pattern, which is again an alternating of tensions and a *return*. But this must be illustrated in the next chapter, when we actually come to extended analyses of particular pieces of literature.

Perhaps we should close this section on the structure of poetry by giving you the names of the most frequently encountered stanzaic patterns. You will find a good discussion of the major *types* of poetry (popular ballad, literary ballad, metrical romance, dramatic poem, lyric—including sonnet, ode, elegy—epic, and mock epic) in James R. Kreuzer's *Elements of Poetry,* published by the Macmillan Company in 1955. Some of the stanzaic patterns we have already described in preceding pages and chapters, but (since repetition is the mother of studies!) it will do no harm to repeat them here:

couplet	two rhyming lines of verse
heroic couplet	a couplet in iambic pentameter lines, or decasyllabic lines
tercet	three rhyming lines of verse
terza rima	tercets in a pattern rhyming as follows: *aba bcb cdc ded* (etc.)
quatrain	four-line stanza; a special form is the ballad stanza (alternating iambic tetrameter and trimeter rhyming *abcb*)
quintet	five-line stanza
sestet	six-line stanza
sestina	a special kind of sestet arrangement: 6 six-line stanzas, the last word in each of the six lines repeated in a different order in each stanza, and a three-line *envoy* using all six of these six words

septet	seven-line stanzas; a special form is called *rime royal* because it was used by King James I of Scotland: it is seven lines of iambic pentameter rhyming *ababbcc*
octave	eight-line stanza (the Italian sonnet, for example, is made up of an octave and a sestet); *ottava rima* is rhyme in eight-line stanzas arranged *abababcc*
Spenserian stanza	a nine-line stanza made up of eight-lines of iambic pentameter followed by a hexameter line (an Alexandrine), rhyming *ababbcbcc*

Other highly specialized forms from the French are the rondeau, rondel, villanelle, and triolet, all of which appear occasionally in English verse.

The Structure of Prose: Fiction

Like poetry, prose employs both literal and figurative language, and it may make use of all the devices of language suggested in Chapter 9. It is possible to feel that the more richly figurative prose is, the nearer it approaches the condition of poetry, where language tends to have a greater *density*. It has been said that poetry is the language of emotion, but in most senses this distinction between poetry and prose (if the suggestion means that prose is *not* the language of emotion) will not really hold. Like poetry, prose may be highly charged in its emotional tone.

But it *is* true that prose is less regularly patterned than poetry; its rhythms are not based upon so apparent a *return*. Coleridge has said [6] that meter in poetry owes its existence to a state of increased excitement in the poet—apparently as if in a feeling of excitement one should burst into *song*. This state of excitement calls for language appropriate to it, in the interests of decorum. The poet wilfully and designedly arranges the language into

[6] The discussion by Coleridge is to be found in chap. 18 of *Biographia Literaria*.

meter "for the purpose of blending delight with emotion." Meter increases "the vivacity and susceptibility both of the general feelings and of the attention." If the language employed does not live up to the expectations aroused by the metrical arrangement, the poem suffers. The poem by Wordsworth to which we called attention earlier, in Chapter 8, is probably to be criticized on this score.

On the other hand, we tend not to want prose to approach metrical regularity too closely. If the prose which approaches such regularity carries with it density in its use of language and a strong degree of emotionality, we say it is "really poetry." If it lacks these elements, we say it is "self-conscious" or "monotonous." If it has richly figurative language but seems sentimental (that is, without a proper balance of emotionality), we say it is "purple" or "flowery." Underneath all such judgments lies a feeling that prose is prose and poetry is poetry, though some prose is very poetic and some poetry is very prosaic. Probably the best we can do to make a distinction is to say, as we have already said, that poetry is more closely patterned, normally more figurative and condensed, and higher in its degree of emotionality. It seems likely that this greater emotional freight is kept properly distanced, in the aesthetic experience, by the high degree of pattern or formality in the structure of poetry. In life, too, it can be observed that increase in emotion can lead to more rhythmic behavior—jumping up and down, beating with one's fist, pronounced pounding of the heart, tapping with the foot, repetition of words such as "no no no," etc. Apparently this patterning of behavior helps avoid the disruptive effects which might otherwise accompany the emotion.

Space forbids our taking a novel for analysis in the same way in which we analyzed poetry in the first part of this chapter. And since a short story is to be analyzed in detail in the next chapter, perhaps it will not be necessary here to examine even a story, though any generalizations made here must be tested against the actual example when we come to it.

The vocabulary and the methods for discussing prose fiction are less clear-cut than those used for discussing poetry, which is the main reason for beginning this chapter with poetry. But the twentieth century has made clear strides in discussing prose, particularly the short story.

Prose fiction is the imitation in language of experience, so arranged through scene and summary and description as to narrate a *complete action* in a *unique world* which is the world of the story or novel. Traditional terms for describing elements in the narrative are *plot* (made up of incidents so articulated as to yield a beginning, a middle, and an end), *setting* (environment, in its broadest sense), and *characterization* (which involves all those aspects of personality described in the first half of this volume). Like poetry, prose fiction ordinarily reaches the peak of its movement somewhere near, but not at, the close, though the position varies greatly from story to story. The moment at which the action reaches its peak may be called the *climax* of the story. There may or may not be, along the way (since a narrative takes place in *time*), a clear moment which marks a crucial limitation in the direction which the plot may thereafter take; when such a moment exists, it may be called the *crisis* of the story. Both the crisis and the climax in modern short stories tend to be quieter and less obtrusive than in earlier short stories.

Now let us examine these terms by looking at an example furnished us by one of the greatest masters of fiction—Henry James. On Thursday evening, January 10, 1895, James attended a dinner. (It is fascinating to observe how frequently James received food for the artist as well as food for the man when he went out to dine—as he did constantly.) At this particular dinner, the Archbishop of Canterbury repeated to James a story told to him by "a lady who had no art of relation, and no clearness." An undisclosed number of children of undisclosed age had been left in the care of wicked and depraved servants in an old country house after their parents had died. The servants corrupted the children and made them evil to a "sinister degree." Then the servants died. Afterward, the servants' apparitions returned to haunt the house and children and to tempt them to their deaths. They try and try and try, says James in his report, to get hold of the children. "It is all obscure and imperfect, the picture, the story," writes James in his *Notebooks,* "but there is a suggestion of strangely gruesome effect in it. The story to be told—tolerably obviously—by an outside spectator, observer." [7]

Here, then, are incidents to be articulated into a plot which will constitute an action. A setting is suggested—the old country house, and characters—the children and servants. The tone or atmosphere of the setting, which will be a strong element in the particular world to be created, is also here: evil, depravity, wickedness, temptation. This suggests a strong element, too, of suspense leading to a *climax:* the success or lack of success of the servants. The action of the story will be the totality produced by the union of plot, setting, and characterization arranged in a sequence which is temporal. No piece of prose fiction lacks an *action*—that is, a progression from one position or one point of awareness to another. *Someone* must undergo a change in awareness because a story *cannot be* (though a poem *may be* and a pure lyric poem *is*) in this sense static. The change in awareness may or may not be in a character or characters within the story: it may be produced within the reader alone, while the characters remain unaware. But it is this revelation (this "revealing"—which in Joyce is sometimes so strong as to constitute an epiphany) which is basic to the life of the story and which constitutes its design, its action. Indeed, it may perhaps be said that the pattern of poetry resides primarily in its arrangement of language, and the pattern of prose fiction primarily in its arrangement of action. This is not to deny (we need hardly say!) that language and action are interdependent.

Now observe that James even this early in his work on the story seizes upon the position, or *point of view,* from which the story is to be told. In Chapter 5, we discussed point of view as

<hr />

[7] James's *Notebooks* have been edited by F. O. Mathiessen and Kenneth B. Murdock and published by The Oxford University Press, New York, 1947. The quotations here (from pp. 178–179) are by permission of the publisher. No avid student of prose fiction can afford to be ignorant of these *Notebooks,* which tell in fascinating detail the progress of James as a writer of prose fiction.

being a significant aspect of imitation in *any* form of literary art, but in prose fiction it is for Henry James a crucial matter. The particular quality a story takes on, the nature of its action, is strongly influenced by the angle or position from which the events and characters are seen. James says that his story must be told by an outside spectator. Why? Presumably because neither the children nor the servants could give us an *impartial* picture of the matter, nor a *complete* picture of it. James counted heavily, in his best work, on the presence of a sensitive, intelligent spectator who could function as a kind of *thinking camera* to let us see what was happening; and to this spectator he gave the name of *the central intelligence*. Once a reader has granted the great demands in attention and compassion placed upon him by James, he finds that perhaps nowhere in fiction is action rendered with greater lucidity and beauty than in this writer's mature work. On the other hand, some of James's early work, before he had developed his own style as a writer, is incredibly bad.

In writing this particular story, which he called *The Turn of the Screw,* James chose to use the *first-person* point of view, but not quite that of an *outside* spectator. The story begins, "I remember the whole beginning as a succession of flights and drops, a little see-saw of the right throbs and the wrong." The first-person character (the "I") is a young governess. The children are put under her charge—a little girl named Flora and her brother Miles, about ten years old. Also in the country house is a housekeeper, Mrs. Grose. What happened you must read for yourself, since no summary can report the real action which James manages to evolve.

It is clear that the *first-person* point of view limits what is to be seen to the particular person seeing it. Furthermore, the person here, the governess, is *subjective* rather than *objective* in her views, since she is responsible for the children and is thus involved in the action. She cannot be detached. One may have a first-person point of view with an *objective* position when the story permits detached observation.

The point of view may, again, be that of an *omniscient nar-*

rator—someone, frequently the author himself, who has it in his power to know all about what is going on in the minds of all the characters in the story. This narrator may or may not be identified in the story.

The point of view may be that of a character within the story (but *third-person* rather than first-person)—James's *central intelligence*. The third-person point of view may be subjective or objective.

The second person ("you") is rarely used for point of view, though amateur writers frequently experiment with it. It tends to place a needlessly intimate burden upon the reader, who may well object to being told how he is to think and feel (for example, "You look at her and you say, 'I hate you.'").

So crucial a matter is the choice of point of view that the "same" plot told from two different points of view becomes two quite different actions. Very young writers frequently choose the wrong point of view from which to tell a story and then wonder why the story seems to lack "significance" or life.

When the story incidents have been arranged, the setting chosen, the characters assembled, and the position of *authority* (that is, the *point of view*—on whose authority is the story told?) determined, the rhythm of the action is determined in part by the particular way in which the writer uses *scene, summary,* and *description.*[8] This is not to say that a writer must sit down and arrange the "parts" of his story as he might arrange the pieces of a puzzle; he *may* work largely without conscious deliberation, he *may* begin with anything in the story which appeals to his imagination first; he may do anything in any order he chooses, probably. But the point is that all these elements are somehow involved in the process.

Suppose the story begins:

That solemn piece of upholstery, the curtain of the Comédie Française, had fallen upon the first act of the piece, and our two Ameri-

[8] The terms are borrowed from the excellent small volume by Phyllis Bentley, *Some Observations on the Art of Narrative,* The Macmillan Company, New York, 1947.

cans had taken advantage of the interval to pass out of the huge, hot
theatre, in company with the other occupants of the stalls.

> *Henry James*
> *from The Siege of London* [9]

This is *summary:* it summarizes in a single sentence something
which has been going on in time for considerably longer. It is
useful for hurrying over events and information which are needed
in the story but not worth a great deal of the reader's time. Summary is frequently used for *exposition,* or for tying together or
cementing together more significant moments in the action.

Now suppose that the writer wishes to give a picture of something important to the story (in this case, a character):

She turned . . . and presented her face to the public—a fair, well-drawn
face, with smiling eyes, smiling lips, ornamented over the brow with
delicate rings of black hair and, in each ear, with the sparkle of a
diamond sufficiently large to be seen across the Théâtre Française.

This is *description.* It looks more closely and hence more slowly
at things than summary.

Now suppose that the writer wishes us to see and hear the
characters of the story as if they were dramatized on the stage
before our eyes. We watch and listen very closely:

Littlemore looked at her; then, abruptly, he gave an exclamation.
"Give me the glass!"

"Do you know her?" his companion asked, as he directed the little
instrument.

Littlemore made no answer; he only looked in silence; then he
handed back the glass. "No, she's not respectable," he said. And he
dropped into his seat again. As Waterville remained standing, he
added, "Please sit down; I think she saw me."

This is *scene.* It involves dialogue and detailed "stage" business.

As Miss Bentley puts it, *scene, summary,* and *description* involve the tempo, or rate, at which a writer unfolds the world he
is creating. Summary moves rapidly; scene moves in normal time;

[9] From Philip Rahv, *The Great Short Novels of Henry James,* The Dial
Press, Inc., New York, 1944. Quoted by permission.

description is cessation of movement. Or, to use the analogy of the motion-picture camera, summary is panorama, description is close-up, scene is close-up with an audible sound track of voices. It is perfectly clear, of course, that scene, summary, and description frequently and normally appear *mixed* rather than *pure* in writing. But the nature of the mixture has a pervasive effect on the rhythm of the story. Tempo is part of a writer's style. It is perhaps obvious, too, that the point of view affects the tempo because it affects what *can* be seen and heard.

Just as the nature of the action affects the choice of setting, the arrangement of episodes, the tempo, the point of view, the quality of language, and the number of characters (for unity in the work of literary art demands that all these elements cohere and coalesce in the story), so it affects the nature of the characterization. Characters may be *static* or *dynamic, flat* or *round.* The flat or static character seems to possess a single dominant and unchanging trait; he may or may not seem so sharply outlined as to be a caricature, but certainly flat characterization moves in the direction of caricature. The rounder a character is, the more dynamic he is—we watch him changing, exhibiting aspect after aspect of personality as we have illustrated it in the first half of this volume. One must be careful not to insist that flat characters are inadequate; a story makes excellent use of flat characters as part of the imitation of life. One need object only when a flat character is used where a round character is needed—or vice versa, since there are times when a round character is needlessly complex for its place in the story: if the villain in a melodrama were made a round character, the melodrama would probably disappear! Flat characters are usually identified with *types* or *stock characters,* though doubtless both round characters and all living people must be said to be made up of certain mixtures of type and stock traits. In his sonnets, Shakespeare takes delight in making his lady dark and brunette when blonde, blue-eyed beauty is regarded as the ideal in poetry.

This would be a good time to go back to the story "The Widow of Ephesus," in Chapter 6, to test your knowledge of the terms we have been examining. In that story, are the characters flat or round? Does the writer make use of scene, summary, and description, or only one or two of these? What is the point of view? Is there a crisis? A climax? Explain the significance of the setting in relation to the action (the change in awareness) of the story. How would you describe the "world" of this particular story?

Now compare Eudora Welty's "Shower of Gold." Some of the essential differences between an "early" and a "modern" short story may be illustrated quickly in a comparison of these two examples, using the questions above.

The Structure of Drama

As long ago as the opening chapter of this book, we suggested that *all* literature is in a sense dramatic in its nature, involving a speaker, a situation, and a listener. This view can be carried too far, but it contains a strong element of truth. In a pure lyrical poem, the speaker is simply the poet (or one person) speaking aloud; the situation may be a single moment of subjective reflection; the listener may be only the reader, who is "overhearing." Fiction moves closer to the realm of the drama itself: it involves a more extended action, it includes usually a group of characters, and it makes use of dialogue. It is true, of course, that some modern fiction moves in the direction of lyrical poetry, and hence in the direction of simplification of both action and speech; it is also true that some poetry—so-called dramatic poetry is a marked example—moves in the direction of fiction and extends both its notion of action and its notion of characterization, involving speech.

Fiction also makes use of narrative material, and of a narrator who mediates between the action and the reader. Poetry, too—for example, the kind of poetry which is for that reason called "narrative" poetry—may make use of narrated (that is, "told" or "related") material. But drama in its pure form imitates solely through the use of characters speaking lines and engaging in actions which advance an articulated plot.

Like a poem or a story or a novel, a play has a beginning and a middle and an end. That is, it has a necessary form shaped by the plot being embraced; it is more or less self-contained; it begins at a point which will permit all else to be developed from it, moves through a crisis, and reaches a climax at or near its close. It may be written in either poetry or prose; when it is written in poetic form, it makes use of the principle of pattern or return characteristic of all poetic rhythms. It is commonly felt that poetic drama has a greater emotionality than drama written in prose, but this generalization is *only* a generalization and must be made with a full recognition of the varieties of emotionality possible in prose.

Since the drama makes use of visible and audible characters when it is enacted, the play tends to make fuller use of certain of those aspects of character and personality discussed in the first part of this book than does other prose or poetry. For example, gesture *without* language now becomes a very valuable tool for the expression of meaning. In prose and poetry, gestures may be described, but in the play they may be *seen;* hence our experience of movement and response is more immediate, more direct in the play, because the text is *oralized for* us. It is at this point that a limitation in the art of the playwright arises. While it is true that something in the words of the text tends to dictate to the actor or reader what his movement and gesture are to be, the control over gesture and movement is less clearly possible to the playwright than to the writer of fiction and poetry. In his *re-imitation* (or his re-presentation of the playwright's imitation of an action), the actor is in part a creative agent in his own right. Our silent readings vary from one individual to another, but we usually have no way of knowing this except through exchange of critical opinions—and this is at a remove from the aesthetic experience. But oral performances demonstrate in all the immediacy of the aesthetic experience how great is the flexibility of literature, for equally satisfactory performances may vary considerably from one another because of the variations in the personalities acting as instruments for conveying the experience. This does *not* mean that the performances contradict one another at crucial points; if they did, we should not be calling them "equally satisfactory." The performer must be in the service of the text he is performing; he is not there to make the text serve him. The drama in particular sometimes suffers from the desire of the director or the actor to assume the role of the playwright. Perhaps the greater the playwright is, the more successfully he dictates or controls the acts of the performer and director.

A play exists entirely in *scene.* Summary may appear, but only in terms of *scene.* In the opening act, one of the characters may, for example, narrate certain information needed for further development of the plot: his summary (called *exposition* in the drama) exists within the scene we are watching. Or a character may employ description; but again, it exists within the scene we are watching. Perhaps this is what we mean when we sometimes say that drama is the most *vital* of the arts. In a real sense, it *lives* before our eyes and ears.

Tempo in drama is regulated partly by the use of exposition and description, but it is regulated more sharply by the degree of emotional tension existing within scenes. A scene where the excitement is high will have a quicker tempo for the viewer than the scene where characters are relaxed and quiet. Characters in a play, as in fiction, may be flat (stock) or round (three-dimensional), but the effect of drama resides almost entirely in the success with which the playwright gives clarity and intensity to his imitation of a social situation involving conflict between two or more human beings. A poet may write a poem, a novelist may write a novel, and the poem or the novel may be put away in a desk drawer and never have a reader other than the author; this lack of communication to a second reader does not in any way affect the essential excellence of the work of art: but a playwright who never shares his play is almost inconceivable to us, since direct communication has always been an essential aspect of the playwright's craft. That is, the playwright has a particular audience problem; he must make his appeal to an audience assembled in a *social* situation. In view of our interest in literature as experience, this has particular significance, since the attitudes of individuals and their responses to events are frequently rather different when they are members of an assembled *group* than when they are alone. An act expressed in a story or a play manuscript, when we read about it alone in our room, may seem mild enough; but that same act, made immediate and visible and audible on the stage of a theater, may seem shocking or offensive or painful to us as a member of a group. To be sure, a play may be read in the quiet of one's own study, but any play fully worthy of the name of *play* must meet the test of the theater. This does not mean that the best plays are those which make the most money!

Does point of view enter at all into the experience of drama? We have already said that drama does not ordinarily make use of a narrator—though it may (the chorus in Greek drama, the narrator in Thornton Wilder's *Our Town*, characters who step out of the scene to speak directly to the audience are all examples of narrative techniques). Point of view is nevertheless present, though frequently we are not aware that our angle of vision is being carefully controlled. The playwright may be highly *objective*, as Shakespeare usually is; that is, his own personal feelings about the characters in action may be submerged in the life of the characters themselves, so that we are not consciously aware of the personality of the writer. Such a playwright lets the characters "speak for themselves," pointing the way himself only through the arrangement of incidents and the attitudes expressed through characters in the action. Or he may employ a character in the play as a commentator, letting us see how that single character *as a character* sees the rest of the action of the play, letting us adopt that character's opinions. Or he may employ a character as a mouthpiece for his *own* (that is, the playwright's own) point of view, subordinating interest in the life of the character himself to interest in the point of view being expressed. In the so-called propaganda play, indeed, the playwright may subordinate the life of all the characters to the thesis or argument he is presenting; but this unwillingness to *free* the characters from his own predilections seems to most critics a weakness in the playwright, a denial of literature in the interests of propaganda. In this sense even so distinguished a playwright as George Bernard Shaw may seem at times less playwright than critic.

Plays are normally divided into acts, partly for the convenience and comfort of audiences but more significantly for structural considerations. The acts of a play are like the waves of return gathered into stanzas in poetry, or into sections or episodes or chapters in fiction. The modern short story frequently seems to have, in the sections in which it is printed (sometimes numbered sections), a dramatic structure: that is, the sections mount and grow as acts grow within the play.

There are one-act plays, and they are much seen in student performances throughout the country, but the professional theater has rarely made extensive use of them. There is a feeling, only partly justified, perhaps, that the one-act play is too brief to permit full development, through dialogue, of significant action. Television now makes great use of short scripts, but it is interesting to observe that many such scripts concentrate on plot alone and are not particularly concerned with significant enrichment of characterization. Normally, the successful interaction of character and event requires greater length than the short play permits. At its best (probably Synge's *Riders to the Sea* has become the classic example) the one-act play is highly compressed, beginning at a moment *close* to its climax and resulting in what we have called, in connection with Joyce's short stories, an epiphany.

Of longer forms, the three-act and the five-act form are best known, though there have been many four-act plays. Two acts are rare, though in production many of Shakespeare's plays, for example, are performed with a single intermission. The action may be reduced to a pattern: the play begins with necessary exposition, singles out in the lives of its characters a particular conflict pointed to by this exposition, introduces complications into the conflict, reaches a moment of crisis, after which the line of action is somehow limited in the direction it may take, faces these limitations, and issues in a climax, after which the action is quickly brought to a close. The crisis is usually found in the third act of a five-act play, and late in the second or early in the third act in a three-act play. But a warning is in order: Let the crisis be where it *is,* rather than where some rule suggests it *ought* to be. One way of getting at the structure (and hence the meaning) of a play is to ask oneself what in the action constitutes the climax toward which the whole play has moved; then, what *the* critical moment is which functions as a turn in direction in the action. (Remember that this kind of analysis can come only after one has read the play receptively; don't torture the play by dissecting it as you give it a preliminary reading or viewing.) In *Romeo and Juliet,* for example, the death of the lovers (with the resulting cessation of the feud) is the climax (followed by its resolution); the slaying of Tybalt by Romeo is the crisis. The crisis is a result of Romeo's attempt, because of his marriage to Juliet, to treat Tybalt as a kinsman dear to him; the attempt fails because of Mercutio's and Tybalt's passion; and Romeo's killing of Tybalt is the particular incident which produces the remainder of the action—Romeo's banishment, Juliet's engagement to Paris, the use of the potion, and death. The crisis, incidentally, need not be an external action; it may be some decision taken by the leading character of the play, or even a *failure* to act.

Just as poetry may be divided into kinds, or genres (epic, elegy, sonnet, ode, dramatic monologue, etc.), and as prose fiction may be divided into kinds (short story, novel, novella, exemplum, fable, and so on), so drama falls into kinds: comedy, tragedy, history, farce, melodrama, tragicomedy, pastoral, etc. All these kinds (and even, it must be said, *kinds* of kinds) involve judgments of subject and attitude as well as of structure. These judgments are in many ways the most fascinating of all literary judgments, but no book such as the one we are engaged in can possibly hope to explore such matters briefly. Our interest has been in a sense much cruder; we are interested in the "primitive" question of the relationships existing between experience in literature and experience in our own daily lives. Once literature as a mode of experience has become clear to us, once we are sophisticated enough in our knowledge and in our judgments to know how poem and story and play differ, as well as how they compare, we can go on to the larger questions of literary kinds. The complexities of the literary art are enough to provide any individual, no matter how brilliant, with a lifetime of study, even though it must be said clearly on the other hand that the experience of literature is available within limits to *any* of us.

Summary

Traditionally, there are three great categories of literary works: lyric, epic, and dramatic. Aristotle suggested the initial distinction; James Joyce's Stephen Dedalus more recently held forth on the subject; the categories are still illuminating.

The *lyric* is that form in which the writer stands in the most immediate relation to himself; the *epic* is that form in which the writer is equidistant from himself and from others; the *dramatic* is that form in which the writer stands in the most immediate relation to others. Another way of putting it: in the lyric, the writer speaks directly in his own person—the "rhythmical" cry such as ages ago cheered on the man who pulled at the oar or dragged stones up a slope." [10] In the epic, the writer speaks partly in his own person or in the person of his narrator and partly through other characters. In the dramatic, the writer submerges his own person in the persons of the story. The three categories move along a continuum from the completely subjective to the completely objective form.

It is probably already clear to you that these categories override distinctions between poetry and prose, for poetry may be lyric, epic, or dramatic in this sense, and so may prose. The lyrical poem, however, is probably the clearest example of the lyric as an ultimate category; the novel or short story is probably the clearest example of the epic; the play is probably the clearest

---

[10] Quoted by permission of The Viking Press and of Jonathan Cape, Limited, from *A Portrait of the Artist as a Young Man,* Compass Edition, The Viking Press, New York, 1956, p. 214. Acknowledgment is made to the Executors of the James Joyce Estate. See Joyce's whole discussion.

example of the dramatic. These are all aspects of structure as conditioned by point of view. You will remember that we found *all three* of these categories reflected in the development of Joyce's story "Araby" long ago, in Chapter 6. That is why it makes perfectly good sense to talk about, for example, a "lyrical novel," or a "dramatic poem," or an "epic drama." It was clearly an awareness of the fundamental aesthetic problem here which led Shakespeare, in *Henry V,* to employ the chorus in order that he might achieve epic proportions within the dramatic form.

Just as a house or a horse or a human being has a structure by which it can be recognized and within which it performs its function, so works of literature have recognizable structures within which they exist and work. No serious student of the art of literature can afford to be ignorant of at least these basic aspects of structure which condition and determine the aesthetic experience of any literary kind.

Exercises

1. Give the meter, rhyme scheme, and stanza form of Milton's sonnet "On His Blindness." Distinguish between *stress* and *accent* in the poem. Between *rhythm* and *meter.* Do you find any *definable* relationship between these elements in the poem and the impact of the poem on you as reader?

2. Can you locate the climax in Eudora Welty's story "Shower of Gold"? The crisis? Can you define the point of view? Can you describe the relative importance of scene, summary, and description in the narrative? Are the characters round, flat, or mixed?

3. It is sometimes said that reading the text of a play is like reading a musical score or looking at an architect's plans for a house. In what sense is such an observation true? What demands does such reading of a play make on the reader?

4. Can you give any examples of television scripts where narrative techniques (for example, the use of a narrator to establish point of view) are employed? Why do you find such devices more frequently on television than in stage plays or motion pictures?

11

Analysis of a Poem, a Story, and a Play

Now THAT WE have considered in some detail the human aspects of the art and craft of the writer, and the human beings who respond to the experience of the writer as it is symbolized in literature, we surely owe it to ourselves to look more extensively at certain specific pieces of literature to see how all our study works for the vital comprehension of the literature itself. For unless it does this, critical analysis is useless, and literary study itself deprived of its reason for being. We undertake the partial analyses in this chapter to point *a* way of looking at a poem, a story, and a play—a way issuing from the attitude toward literature which this book takes to be particularly fruitful. It is hoped that the stages of analysis will seem by now fairly natural. Remember only that you are not to be limited by the analyses which are given here: whatever you find to add to them, to the valid enrichment of the literature itself, the writers of this volume will certainly welcome.

Analysis of a Poem

We have chosen, first of all, a poem by a writer significant enough to merit the attention of any student of modern literature: D. H. Lawrence. Read the poem *receptively*. Read it simply for the experience which it expresses. Don't worry, during the initial reading, about *anything* except your own enjoyment of the poem.[1]

SNAKE

A snake came to my water-trough
On a hot, hot day, and I in pyjamas for the heat,
To drink there.

In the deep, strange-scented shade of the great dark carob-tree
I came down the steps with my pitcher
And must wait, must stand and wait, for there he was at the trough
    before me.

He reached down from a fissure in the earth-wall in the gloom
And trailed his yellow-brown slackness soft-bellied down, over the
    edge of the stone trough
And rested his throat upon the stone bottom,
And where the water had dripped from the tap, in a small clearness,
He sipped with his straight mouth,
Softly drank through his straight gums, into his slack long body,
Silently.

Someone was before me at my water-trough,
And I, like a second-comer, waiting.

He lifted his head from his drinking, as cattle do,
And looked at me vaguely, as drinking cattle do,
And flickered his two-forked tongue from his lips, and mused a
    moment,

[1] From *Collected Poems* by D. H. Lawrence. Copyright, 1929, by Jonathan Cape & Harrison Smith, Inc.; 1957, by Frieda Lawrence Ravagli. Reprinted by permission of The Viking Press, Inc., New York, and Wm. Heinemann, Ltd., London.

And stooped and drank a little more,
Being earth-brown, earth-golden from the burning bowels of the earth
On the day of Sicilian July, with Etna smoking.

The voice of my education said to me
He must be killed,
For in Sicily the black, black snakes are innocent, the gold are ven-
    omous.

And voices in me said, If you were a man
You would take a stick and break him now, and finish him off.

But must I confess how I liked him,
How glad I was he had come like a guest in quiet, to drink at my
    water-trough
And depart peaceful, pacified, and thankless,
Into the burning bowels of this earth?

Was it cowardice, that I dared not kill him?
Was it perversity, that I longed to talk to him?
Was it humility, to feel so honoured?
I felt so honoured.

And yet those voices:
If you were not afraid, you would kill him!

And truly I was afraid, I was most afraid,
But even so, honoured still more
That he should seek my hospitality
From out the dark door of the secret earth.

He drank enough
And lifted his head, dreamily, as one who has drunken,
And flickered his tongue like a forked night on the air, so black,
Seeming to lick his lips,
And looked around like a god, unseeing, into the air,
And slowly turned his head,
And slowly, very slowly, as if thrice adream,
Proceeded to draw his slow length curving round
And climb again the broken bank of my wall-face.

And as he put his head into that dreadful hole,
And as he slowly drew up, snake-easing his shoulders, and entered
    farther,
A sort of horror, a sort of protest against his withdrawing into that
    horrid black hole,
Deliberately going into the blackness, and slowly drawing himself
    after,
Overcame me now his back was turned.

I looked round, I put down my pitcher,
I picked up a clumsy log
And threw it at the water-trough with a clatter.

I think it did not hit him,
But suddenly that part of him that was left behind convulsed in
    undignified haste,
Writhed like lightning, and was gone
Into the black hole, the earth-lipped fissure in the wall-front,
At which, in the intense still noon, I stared with fascination.

And immediately I regretted it.
I thought how paltry, how vulgar, what a mean act!
I despised myself and the voices of my accursed human education.

And I thought of the albatross,
And I wished he would come back, my snake.

For he seemed to me again like a king,
Like a king in exile, uncrowned in the underworld,
Now due to be crowned again.

And so, I missed my chance with one of the lords
Of life.
And I have something to expiate;
A pettiness.

Taormina

    It is probably safe to say that a snake is for most people an object of both horror and fascination. All literature bears witness to the constant ambivalence in our attitudes toward snakes. The Biblical function of the snake as (paradoxically) persuader to both evil and knowledge, counseling Eve in the Garden of Eden, embodying Satan himself; the idea of the snake as a hidden danger lurking in the grass ("snake in the grass," or Shakespeare's "Look like the innocent flower, but be the serpent under it"); the hypnotic picture of the deadly cobra swaying to the pipe of a snakecharmer; the knowledge of the tremendous muscular strength of the boa constrictor, with his ability to expand or to contract his length; the dreadful *silence* with which the serpent moves—such notions as these are buried somewhere in the consciousness of most readers, together with feelings of revulsion taught us from our childhood. It is safe to say that some of these notions, and the emotions attached to them, are called up even by the title of Lawrence's poem, and are with us as we begin reading.

But the poem itself begins matter-of-factly: a snake comes to drink on a hot, hot day, a day so hot that the "I" of the poem (the point of view is selected at once) is wearing pyjamas. The visual and thermal images are primary in the opening three lines.

The second section (in addition to setting up sound patterns, to which we shall return, and perhaps yielding additional sensory responses for certain readers) introduces notions of *depth* and *strangeness* and *darkness*. Doubtless the word *carob,* too, which will send most readers to the dictionary, creates a sense of the strange or exotic. Otherwise the section is again rather matter-of-fact: the speaker must come down to the water trough—he, too, for water against the heat—and must wait. Why? Because *he* (not *it,* but *he:* why?) is already there. The second section is weightier in its content than the first; it is also longer, though both sections have only three lines. The effect in these first sections is that of moving from summary to scene in narrative. And now the tempo becomes very slow as we move in close to watch.

The speaker is no longer the center of the picture; the snake, "he," is what we watch—we and the narrator, who establishes the point of view for us.

Now the darkness and the strangeness and the sensation of depth barely suggested in the second section begin to take shape as direct sensory responses for us: the snake reaches down, in the gloom; he trails his slackness down into the stone trough; then, so quietly that one must only *imagine* he hears it, the snake drinks. The sense of movement, of reaching, of trailing, of resting, of sipping, of drinking is sharply underscored by the narrator; but everything is in the silence. The snake has dignity here; like the human being who observes him, he needs water against the heat. And he is here first. The snake is invested with a life of his own, needs of his own, before the poem presents us with other considerations. But with our own feelings about snakes, we may well be feeling already the sensation of horror as we watch this creature of the earth at the water trough.

The fourth section sharply restores the speaker to our sight. It is brief, simple: it punctuates the vision, sums up the fact; at the same time, it arouses a certain amount of apprehension. What will happen now? The poem gathers itself for a forward movement.

In the fifth section, we return to the snake himself. Again we watch. The reference to cattle (which is not figurative, but literal) again underscores the snake's likeness to other creatures. Only the reference to his "two-forked tongue" reminds us that he *is* a snake. He takes his time, muses, drinks. Then, with a reference again to the heat, we return to the speaker, who sees this golden creature as a snake from the bowels of the earth—and we are again aware of the snake as snake, for (paradoxically, again) the goldness (rather than the blackness) of the serpent is a sign of venomousness: this is the subject of section 6, which says that here in Sicily (where the poem takes place) educated sense tells the speaker that poisonous snakes ought to be put to death.

The seventh section repeats this notion, but more compellingly. The compulsion to kill is urged on by the intelligence. Self-preservation is a basic consideration. The poem gathers again. But the snake is no longer for the speaker (nor is he for us) simply a snake. The eighth section makes this explicit: the speaker, almost despite himself, "likes" the snake, feels a kinship with him in his need to drink—though, not being human, the snake will depart "thankless" again into the burning bowels of the earth.

Now the poem, midway in its course, poses the questions: Is the speaker afraid? Is it some perversity in him which makes him feel kinship with the snake? Is it even some sense of personal abasement or lowliness which makes him feel honored in the presence of this strange guest? The fact remains that he *does* feel honored; that is the truth behind the question. And yet—.

The short tenth section repeats the voices, italicizing their words: *If you were not afraid, you would kill him!* The strong sense of hatred and fear which most of us feel in combination, out of a long history of responses, is very much shared by the speaker, at least on the side of fear.

Fear—but even more, honor. Honor that the snake has visited him, partaken of his hospitality, "from out the dark door of the secret earth." We are back again to the darkness and the strangeness, and it is almost as if, with the speaker, we were leaving the world of men (with its obligation to kill golden snakes) and entering some world where all creatures minister to the needs of one another: the *secret* earth, which keeps its secrets by concealing them from our sight.

But what of the snake, now? In the next section, the twelfth, we again observe him: something has to be decided, one way or another; he is finishing his drink, he looks about, flickers his tongue, godlike looks about him, and slowly, deep in a kind of trance, proceeds to leave.

The spell cast by the snake's quietly drinking is broken as he departs. Again the sensation of movement is strong in the lines— the drawing, curving, easing, withdrawing, going, drawing of the snake becomes hideous as the snake does that frightful thing— puts his head into the black hole in the earth and begins to enter. This voluntary, deliberate, purposeful return to the condition of *snake* (the evilness of *snake*) violates all the awareness of kinship which the speaker of the poem has created; for the speaker, as for us, this going into the earth is a kind of dying, a return to the subhuman, the nameless blackness. And the speaker retaliates by hurling a log, clumsily, instinctively, hatefully.

The snake, in his snake fashion, responds: no longer godlike, no longer human, no longer a guest, he "convulses in undignified haste, writhes like lightning, and is gone into the black hole."

The poem has now reached the height of its movement. The snake is gone, the spell is broken. The "story" is finished. In a short resolution, covering the last four sections, the speaker draws his own thoughts together: he regrets his act, recognizes that the "voices of his education" have misled him into trying to kill something meaningful and good, suggests kinship between himself and Coleridge's ancient mariner (who killed the albatross and thereby brought a curse upon himself), repeats his sense of the dignity of the snake (king in exile, king of the underworld), and knows that he must do penance for his pettiness.

These last four sections have lost their intensity, their tension— like a spring which has uncoiled, or a snake which has struck, except that it is here the man, and not the snake, who has struck. It is possible to feel, perhaps, that the tension has been *too* greatly relaxed in these sections, that Lawrence has "said" too much— or rather, that he has, by saying more than he needed to, said too little. The comment in the last four sections is less significant than the experience preceding.

Thus far we have been paraphrasing (or saying over again in other words) Lawrence's poem. It is quite true, as we have said in an earlier chapter, that no paraphrase can take the place of the poem, since the poem exists only in the words in which it is set down. On the other hand, the paraphrase is one of the simplest ways of "getting at" the poem; perhaps it is ultimately the only way in which we can verbalize our responses. We must only be careful that our paraphrase does not violate or replace the poem.

We began by saying that we tend to open our reading of the poem with a "feeling" about snakes. It is important that our own feelings be kept, initially, distinct from those of the poet, who may not happen to share them. Lawrence's poem, however, not only permits us to make use of these feelings; it depends on our having them to begin with. Writers almost always rely, although carefully, upon *some* experience or some aspects of experience which they share with their readers. It would be impossible for any work of art to attempt to provide the whole of an experience. It should be abundantly clear by now, of course, that a reader has some responsibility in preparing himself to *be* a reader.

Anything we can say about the poem from this point on ought, if our paraphrase has been accurate, to serve the meaning of the poem as we have described it. Lawrence has given us, within a specific environment, the sensations and thoughts of a specific speaker as he observes the coming, the drinking, and the departure of the snake. The poem is both lyrical and narrative. It is free verse, written in stanzas or "batches." It is first person; it is a scene which contains tempos varying from summary to description. Lawrence also manages wonderfully to combine aspects of the lyrical with aspects of the epic and dramatic here. Can you show how?

Our paraphrase has sought to underscore the degree of *sensation* or *feeling* in the poem; no full reading can result from a totally dispassionate response to "Snake," because the tensions in the speaker of the poem result from the strength of his feelings, which we must therefore share to some degree. The heat, the depth, the strangeness, the shadow, the movement, the suspension of movement, the colors, the sounds, the horror—all these (the list is not exhaustive) are explicitly underscored by the words of the poem, and the reader who feels no muscular responses to them must surely be too remote from the poem. How many kinds of images do *you* find in your own reading of "Snake"?

Of course the reader who has such a horror of snakes in his own actual experience that he cannot subordinate his own feelings to those explicitly directed in the poem is guilty of projection; he, too, is too remote from the poem. We read "Snake," not to confirm our own attitudes, but to experience the attitudes of the poem—presumably, here, the attitude of Lawrence himself. It is what we learn from Lawrence that makes his poem a form of knowledge, though what we learn need not be set down in a topic sentence! The snake we are talking about is *this* snake. The feelings we are talking about are feelings connected with *this* snake, and on *this* occasion. But of course it is equally true that as the sharpness of the immediate sensory experience of this poem begins to wear away, reflection leads us both to a consideration of the *form* of the poem and to some awareness of the poem's universality.

"Snake" owes a great measure of its power to the fact that the experience which it embodies, symbolically, is related to primitive, fundamental drives in each of us. The snake seems immediately to be an enemy, an object potentially destructive of the self. The "voices" speaking to the "I" of the poem are all the educated voices which counsel the self to guard its life—educated, but primitive, since education has here spelled out and underscored the necessity of self-protection. Education has made defense against such an enemy "manly," too; both instinct and education tell this man to kill.

But something equally instinctive, equally primitive (one might say, equally educated—though this is not the point of view of the poet, and hence it is irrelevant here) is at work. A Freudian analyst would notice the sexuality suggested by images in the poem (the heat, the snake itself, the fissure in the earth, the recesses within the earth, the softness and hardness), and would speak of the Oedipus myth at this point, but surely this would eventually limit the poem too sharply. Furthermore, we are interested in literature and not primarily in psychoanalysis, though the psychoanalysts have had a field day with Lawrence. No, the poem is not specifically sexual in its meaning, though its sexuality is a *part* of its meaning. But surely the role of the serpent in myth has *something* to do with the tension felt by the speaker of the poem. Why is the fact of the serpent's being an *under-ground* creature of such weight in the poem? The snake comes out of the burning bowels of the earth; so long as it remains above ground, it seems like a guest, and welcome, but once it begins to withdraw, to go into blackness, the speaker is revolted and the instinctive motions toward self-protection are no longer suppressed. Why is the snake given this double character? And why is the snake's *goldness* (beauty, value), his kingliness, his godliness underscored? Why the speaker's reverence, awe, humility in the face of this creature come out of the dark door of the secret earth? We have already said, in our initial paraphrase, that the snake is *one* creature, and that it reminds the speaker of other living creatures with whom he shares life. This is a literal explanation; but there is a figurative, a symbolical or metaphorical, level on which we may look at the matter, too: the snake is not simply a living creature, but is "one of the lords of life," a king uncrowned in the underworld but now "due to be crowned again." Something about the snake speaks to deep, instinctive things in this man. Some part of life which has been unrecognized, buried, even legislated against by education proves to be valuable and necessary in this "recognition scene" which the poem presents. Jung, the psychoanalyst whose findings have been particularly fruitful for the student of literature, might say that the snake symbolizes those things in the unconscious which have been repressed, and that the recognition of the snake is a recognition of part of the individual which has been buried, a governing part of the self which has been consigned (or has involuntarily consigned itself) to darkness, where it lies uncrowned. The throwing of the log is an attempt at destruction of the newly acknowledged part of the self, in protest against the split in consciousness which its retreat involves. That is, the poem tells us more about the speaker than it does about the snake, and the snake's function in the poem's meaning is *first* of all to be a snake and second to be a symbol which helps us to evaluate the meaning of the poem.

To repeat a criticism we have already suggested, it is possible to feel that the poem expresses these meanings so sharply and so fully in the picturing of the experience that the explicit comments contained in the last four sections are too reductive of the experience, and hence weaken the poem as a poem. Do the last two lines of the poem really underscore (as they seem intended to) the heart of the poem's experience, or do they reduce it? Is "pettiness" a good word for the speaker's act? You may argue (though the argument seems not somehow good enough) that "pettiness" is an example of understatement, and that understatement is an effective positive device here.

We have talked about the poem's movement, about its alternation of tensions and tempos, about its varying lengths of "batches"; suppose we look at the various devices of language which enter into the experience of the poem, and certain of the devices of form.

We have said that the first section is matter-of-fact, but that is a relative judgment. Actually, the ordering of the words in the first sentence differs considerably from the usual prose statement. Can you show how? And notice the patterning of sounds: "*s*na*k*e ca*m*e" (acrostic scrambling, with the nasal sound varying); "wa*ter-tr*ough" (repetition); "*h*ot, *h*ot . . . *h*eat" (alliteration and consonance). Even "*d*ay" and "*d*rink" may not be too far apart to have echo value in the sound patterning. Observe also that the *d* is picked up in the first line of the next section. (Remember always that such patterns exist in prose as well as in verse, but that the patterning is less noticeable in prose, less frequent, and usually less deliberate.) Can you justify the line divisions in this section? (They seem to us rather arbitrary.)

Suppose we list a few of the patterns which follow:

*s*trange-*s*cented *sh*ade	alliteration (or para-alliteration)
scente*d* sha*d*e	hidden alliteration
*g*reat *d*ark *c*arob-*t*ree	a kind of alliteration: *g* and *c* are cognate sounds, the first voiced and the second voiceless; *d* and *t* are similar in relationship; the cognates alternate to produce what is called *transverse alliteration*. Notice in addition the effect of the final stops *t*, *k*, *b* preceding three of these cognates.
d*ee*p, str*a*nge . . .	
sh*a*de . . . gr*ea*t . . . tr*ee*	assonance
*f*rom a *f*issure	alliteration
*y*ellow-bro*w*n . . .	
soft-be*ll*ied *d*own	internal rhyme

Or in the fifth section:

He lifted his head from the drinking,
    as cattle do
                            alliteration and
                             hidden alliteration

flickered ... two-forked tongue
                             transverse alliteration
                             (f t f t)
                             acrostic scrambling
                             (f k r d, f r k d)

mused a moment
                             alliteration and
                             hidden alliteration

earth-brown, earth-golden from the
    burning bowels of the earth
                             assonance:
                             (er-ow, er-ō, er-ow, er)

Continue the list, if you like. You will find that the poem is heavily and skillfully patterned in sound. But you will find that the patterning is heaviest in the long sections, where the tempo is slowest.

The snake is *personified*. Why? You will find, early in the poem, examples of tone color and onomatopoeia. Can you identify the figure involved in "bowels of the earth"? And in "voice of my education"? In the ninth section, can you find an example of consonance? What is the figure involved in "the dark door of the secret earth"? In "flickered his tongue like a forked night"? Why "clumsy log," when it is not the log which is clumsy? What other figures do you find in the poem?

The significant thing, of course, is not simply that there *are* patterns and figures here (although you don't know that unless you know what patterns and figures *are*, to be sure), but that the patterns and figures all operate to give the poem a *closeness of texture*, to call constant attention, by varying the language from its usual nonfigurative nature, or from its looser arrangement of figures, to the experience which the language embodies. What the poet cares about is not some meaning to be derived from the words (as is the case, for example, in expository writing) but the meaning *in* the words themselves. We are meant to savor the sounds of these signs.

We have already suggested that "Snake" is patterned most heavily in the long sections, where description operates most significantly. Because of the closeness of texture apparent in part in the sound patterning, it is probably true, too, that these sections are likely to be the "best" sections for the reader. It may well be true that the patterning is richest here because here the poet himself was most sharply caught up in the response to the experience.

It is also of interest to observe that "Snake" is figured more richly in sound than in words. (We employ here the distinction between figures of sound and figures of words made in Chapter 9.) The comparative scarcity of figurative or metaphorical language helps to give the poem its factual quality. At times the fabric of the language so loosens that it is probably too near to prose —when it is not adequately justified, in other words, in calling itself poetry by being put into verses. Sections 7 through 11 are almost *too* paraphrasable to be good poetry; the *idea* itself here counts for too great a portion of the effect. The questions (largely rhetorical in their intent) are too devoid of emotional impact to carry proper weight. On the other hand, such patterning as exists makes for somewhat richer statement than is to be found in the concluding four sections of the poem, where the emotional load is slight indeed. Aside from certain devices of repetition, these sections are not easily to be distinguished from prose statement. Try putting the lines into straight prose this way:

And immediately I regretted it. I thought how paltry, how vulgar, what a mean act! I despised myself and the voices of my accursed human education; and I thought of the albatross; and I wished my snake would come back, for he seemed to me again like a king, in exile, uncrowned in the underworld, now due to be crowned again. And so, I missed my chance with one of the lords of life; and I have something to expiate: a pettiness.

It sounds like rather disconnected prose, as a matter of fact. It has neither the tight syntactical sequence of prose nor the patterned texture of poetry, though it is figurative.

Perhaps it is not too much to say that the poem as a whole varies from poetry to prose, and that where it is most poetic it is also most effective as the embodiment of experience. Check the division of the sections into lines. Do you find that line endings seem in some sections more arbitrarily placed than in other sections? Which sections *are* these? How are they related to passages where the figurative or symbolical freight of the poem is greatest?

One may say, finally, of "Snake" that despite the brilliance of certain passages, and despite the fascination which the poem exercises, the conclusion it comes to is stated in a rather hollow prose. The insight provided for readers in the descriptive passages is not adequately underscored, at the conclusion, by the poet's *statement*.

Analysis of a Story

We have chosen next to look at a short story. Again we have selected a work by a writer of recognized merit, "A Clean, Well-Lighted Place," [2] by Ernest Hemingway, taken from the third of Hemingway's books of stories, *Winner Take Nothing*. Remember once more that your first reading of the piece should be receptive rather than critical. Read the story for enjoyment.

A CLEAN, WELL-LIGHTED PLACE

It was late and every one had left the café except an old man who sat in the shadow the leaves of the tree made against the electric light. In the day time the street was dusty, but at night the dew settled the dust and the old man liked to sit late because he was deaf and now at night it was quiet and he felt the difference. The two waiters inside the café knew that the old man was a little drunk, and while he was a good client they knew that if he became too drunk he would leave without paying, so they kept watch on him.

"Last week he tried to commit suicide," one waiter said.

"Why?"

"He was in despair."

"What about?"

"Nothing."

"How do you know it was nothing?"

"He has plenty of money."

They sat together at a table that was close against the wall near the door of the café and looked at the terrace where the tables were all empty except where the old man sat in the shadow of the leaves of the tree that moved slightly in the wind. A girl and a soldier went by in the street. The street light shone on the brass number on his collar. The girl wore no head covering and hurried beside him.

"The guard will pick him up," one waiter said.

"What does it matter if he gets what he's after?"

"He had better get off the street now. The guard will get him. They went by five minutes ago."

The old man sitting in the shadow rapped on his saucer with his glass. The younger waiter went over to him.

"What do you want?"

The old man looked at him. "Another brandy," he said.

"You'll be drunk," the waiter said. The old man looked at him. The waiter went away.

"He'll stay all night," he said to his colleague. "I'm sleepy now. I never get into bed before three o'clock. He should have killed himself last week."

The waiter took the brandy bottle and another saucer from the counter inside the café and marched out to the old man's table. He put down the saucer and poured the glass full of brandy.

"You should have killed yourself last week," he said to the deaf man. The old man motioned with his finger. "A little more," he said. The waiter poured on into the glass so that the brandy slopped over and ran down the stem into the top saucer of the pile. "Thank you," the old man said. The waiter took the bottle back inside the café. He sat down at the table with his colleague again.

"He's drunk now," he said.

"He's drunk every night."

"What did he want to kill himself for?"

"How should I know?"

"How did he do it?"

"He hung himself with a rope."

"Who cut him down?"

"His niece."

"Why did they do it?"

"Fear for his soul."

"How much money has he got?"

"He's got plenty."

"He must be eighty years old."

"Anyway I should say he was eighty."

"I wish he would go home. I never get to bed before three o'clock. What kind of hour is that to go to bed?"

"He stays up because he likes it."

"He's lonely. I'm not lonely. I have a wife waiting in bed for me."

"He had a wife once too."

"A wife would be no good to him now."

"You can't tell. He might be better with a wife."

"His niece looks after him."

"I know. You said she cut him down."

"I wouldn't want to be that old. An old man is a nasty thing."

"Not always. This old man is clean. He drinks without spilling. Even now, drunk. Look at him."

"I don't want to look at him. I wish he would go home. He has no regard for those who must work."

The old man looked from his glass across the square, then over at the waiters.

"Another brandy," he said, pointing to his glass. The waiter who was in a hurry came over.

"Finished," he said, speaking with that omission of syntax stupid people employ when talking to drunken people or foreigners. "No more tonight. Close now."

"Another," said the old man.

"No. Finished." The waiter wiped the edge of the table with a towel and shook his head.

The old man stood up, slowly counted the saucers, took a leather coin purse from his pocket and paid for the drinks, leaving half a peseta tip.

The waiter watched him go down the street, a very old man walking unsteadily but with dignity.

"Why didn't you let him stay and drink?" the unhurried waiter asked. They were putting up the shutters. "It is not half-past two."

"I want to go home to bed."

"What is an hour?"

"More to me than to him."

"An hour is the same."

"You talk like an old man yourself. He can buy a bottle and drink at home."

"It's not the same."

"No, it is not," agreed the waiter with a wife. He did not wish to be unjust. He was only in a hurry.

"And you? You have no fear of going home before your usual hour?"

"Are you trying to insult me?"

"No, hombre, only to make a joke."

"No," the waiter who was in a hurry said, rising from pulling down the metal shutters. "I have confidence. I am all confidence."

"You have youth, confidence, and a job," the older waiter said. "You have everything."

"And what do you lack?"

"Everything but work."

"You have everything I have."

"No. I have never had confidence and I am not young."

"Come on. Stop talking nonsense and lock up."

"I am one of those who like to stay late at the café," the older waiter said. "With all those who do not want to go to bed. With all those who need a light for the night."

"I want to go home and into bed."

"We are of two different kinds," the older waiter said. He was now dressed to go home. "It is not only a question of youth and confidence although those things are very beautiful. Each night I am reluctant to close up because there may be some one who needs the café."

"Hombre, there are bodegas open all night long."

"You do not understand. This is a clean and pleasant café. It is well lighted. The light is very good and also, now, there are shadows of the leaves."

"Good night," said the younger waiter.

"Good night," the other said. Turning off the electric light he continued the conversation with himself. It is the light of course but it is necessary that the place be clean and pleasant. You do not want music. Certainly you do not want music. Nor can you stand before a bar with dignity although that is all that is provided for these hours. What did he fear? It was not fear or dread. It was a nothing that he knew too well. It was all a nothing and a man was nothing too. It was only that and light was all it needed and a certain cleanness and order. Some lived in it and never felt it but he knew it all was nada y pues nada y nada y pues nada. Our nada who art in nada, nada be thy name thy kingdom nada thy will be nada in nada as it is in nada. Give us this nada our daily nada and nada us our nada as we nada our nadas and nada us not into nada but deliver us from nada; pues nada. Hail nothing full of nothing, nothing is with thee. He smiled and stood before a bar with a shining steam pressure coffee machine.

"What's yours?" asked the barman.

"Nada."

"Otro loco mas," said the barman and turned away.

"A little cup," said the waiter.

The barman poured it for him.

"The light is very bright and pleasant but the bar is unpolished," the waiter said.

The barman looked at him but did not answer. It was too late at night for conversation.

"You want another copita?" the barman asked.

"No, thank you," said the waiter and went out. He disliked bars and bodegas. A clean, well-lighted café was a very different thing. Now, without thinking further, he would go home to his room. He would lie in the bed and finally, with daylight, he would go to sleep. After all, he said to himself, it is probably only insomnia. Many must have it.

Hemingway's story is a study in empathy, of the impingement of one life upon another in such a way that the second character's humanity leads him to a compassionate awareness of his own loneliness. The action of the story moves toward this awareness by shifting the focus of the writer's "camera" from the old man in the café to the older of the two waiters, about whom the eventual truth is to be told. The younger waiter, without whom Hemingway could not manage the action of the story, is essentially a flat character, which is all the action requires him to be in so brief a narrative.

After the opening paragraph, it will be convenient to divide the story into three sections—metaphorically, the three "acts" of the little drama. The first section will take us to the old man's departure from the café; the second, to the younger waiter's departure from the story; the third, to the story's end. The first paragraph is a kind of "prologue," a setting of the scene, an adjusting of the camera—time, place, characters, opening situation. The paragraph is an excellent combination of elements of summary, of scene, and of description. It is clear at once that the point of view is that of the omniscient narrator, which is dramatic in that it removes the person of the author from the scene entirely, as in the play form.

The dialogue begins. Notice that with his customary economy, Hemingway does not bother to identify the speakers once the first line has been assigned; it is not necessary to do so,[3] and the effect of a conversation overheard is achieved better by his giving us simply the dialogue. The old man is the subject of the conversation, and his predicament is immediately made the object of our curiosity: he has tried to commit suicide, he has been in despair, but he has had no reason for despair because he has had plenty of money. Notice that Hemingway does not yet identify *which* of the waiters says *what,* because we are not yet interested in the waiters. Some feeling of cynicism (or some obtuseness, we do not yet know which) in the waiter who makes the final speech is already suggested to us, since we know that lack of money is not necessarily the only cause for despair. Any awareness we have of this added interest in character, however, is clearly subordinate to our interest in the old man.

Hemingway gives us another paragraph of narrative: a sharp picture of the setting, with the two waiters sitting just outside the door of the café, the old man in the shadow cast by the leaves against the light. A hint of another, more active world, of youth and the pursuit of pleasure, flashes through the paragraph as the girl and soldier pass along the street. The dialogue following in

---

[3] But Hemingway seems to have made one slip; the two speeches "His niece looks after him" and "I know. You said she cut him down" will not work in the alternating pattern. The second seems to belong to the older waiter, but obviously cannot. Why?

the next three speeches gives us some further notion of the story's setting in time, and suggests again either a slight cynicism or a bluntly pragmatic quality about one of the two waiters: "What does it matter if he gets what he's after?" (By the time the story is finished, you will find it possible to go back and assign both these deliberately ambiguous passages to the older waiter. Why?)

Now that the waiters have moved a little more into the center of our consciousness, we return to the old man, and the rest of this section remains rather carefully centered on him, though with enough interest in the two waiters who speak about him so that we take an interest in them as speakers, too. It is the loneliness, the isolation of the old man upon which we focus our attention. His sitting in the shadow is a literal image, but the application is metaphorical, as, eventually, the clean, well-lighted café will take on metaphorical value for us—but first of all the shadow is a shadow, the café is a café. The *reality* of these images is not to be discounted once the symbolical values have been uncovered.

The old man is not only in shadow, but he is also deaf. And he is drunk. The isolation is almost complete; but not entirely complete, or perhaps the need for the brandy would disappear. He is not without relatives—he has a niece. He has money. But he is very old, he has lost his wife, he has nothing better to do with his time. The younger waiter is impatient with him: "An old man is a nasty thing," he says, and it is not hard for any of us to think of very old people who seem, by their very age, isolated from those around them; but the word *nasty,* while we doubtless have pangs of conscience as we recognize precisely what the younger waiter means, seems to us harsh and unfeeling. The younger waiter has a wife, a world to which he belongs, interests beyond his job. He is *not* isolated, no matter how limited his interests may be, though his being "in life" does not move him to any sympathy with the old man. He even dares to say to the old man, who cannot hear him, "You should have killed yourself last week." He is either very young, or very limited in vision, or both. Hemingway tips his hand, as author, when he uses the word *stupid* in remarking upon the younger man's speech.

But the second waiter, specifically identified as the older, is compassionate without being voluble. He seems to speak quietly, as he speaks simply. It is not he, but the younger man, who brings this section to a close by dismissing the old man. Notice how carefully Hemingway has written the dialogue to let us come to our own conclusions about the characters. Except for the word *stupid* he has not taken sides—in his own person, that is, since in another sense he has been wholly responsible for the attitudes we have taken toward the characters. This is the dramatic method. The tempo of the first section is managed by the movement from scene (which is predominant here) to summary-description. The scene itself moves quickly because the dialogue is clipped, brief. As the section ends, we (and the waiter) watch the old man go down the street, "a very old man walking unsteadily but with dignity." *Both* the unsteadiness and the dignity matter very much to this story, for they underscore the uncertainty and the essential humanity of the old man which make possible the action to follow.

Now that the two waiters occupy our interest, Hemingway sharpens the distinctions between them. The one becomes "the unhurried waiter," the other the "waiter with a wife." The younger waiter is hurried because he *has* a wife; the older is without a wife, without youth—without confidence, and unsteady, though surely we would not say without dignity. The young man is young enough (perhaps newly married enough!) that he is easily offended by the older waiter's joke. The two are "of two different kinds."

The older waiter pushes some of the details of the story toward metaphor, now. He speaks of those who need "a light for the night," who need the café and its clean, pleasant air. Cleanliness, light, air, companionship—these are values which the old man wants and lacks, which the older waiter wants and lacks; they are the "life" which the darkness negates. The old do not want *simply* the light, but good light and the shadows of the leaves make a tempting combination.

Really the younger waiter now disappears imperceptibly. He

says, "Good night," the older waiter begins speaking to himself, and soon we realize that the older man has left the café and is standing before a bar. He has begun the old man's search. It is really *his* need, *his* loneliness, *his* uncertainty the story has been moving toward, and not that of the deaf old man. The reasons for his compassion become moving to us, and we suddenly see how deep his sense of the nothingness (the *nada*) of his life goes. He smiles as he stands before the bar, and outwardly there is in him a kind of tolerance and a gentleness toward the nothingness, but the interior dialogue (lyrical in its impact) tells us how bleak his despair really is. Exterior dialogue, conversation with the younger waiter, could never give us this, because the older waiter would never speak so to his colleague. And now the symbolical values of the bar, the light, the shadow, the café, the cleanliness and pleasantness become sharply outlined. Now *we* know far more than the *barman* knows, and the little joke which the waiter makes to him ("The light is very bright and pleasant but the bar is unpolished") has for us a grimness where it has for the barman only irrelevance. And no attempt, in the last two sentences of the story, to shrug off the night's events as being "probably only insomnia" will persuade us—nor, indeed, is it meant to persuade us—that the next night will be any better. But the final line ("Many must have it") drives home with finality the picture of despair shared by this waiter with many others in his world.

Remember that the story is not saying that the world is a dreadful place. It is saying that for *some* people life is empty; in particular, it is empty for a deaf old man and a no longer young waiter whom we are permitted to see and to hear and to watch. Awareness of such experience, compassion for it, understanding of it—these things, rather than any acceptance of despair, are what "A Clean, Well-Lighted Place" asks of a reader.

The sense of the characters in the story is so sharp that it may come to you as something of a shock that Hemingway has told us really nothing of the way these people look. We know their hearts, we feel that we know *them*—but of the color of their eyes, their hair, their clothes (aside from their uniforms) we know nothing at all. They do not even have names. In this respect, all three characters are flat characters. All the details in the story are selected to give us the quality rather than the appearance of the characters. And yet it is safe to say that most readers will feel, after they have read "A Clean, Well-Lighted Place," that they "saw" the story. The dramatic form, the emphasis upon visual and audible detail create a strongly visual image which permits us to fill in such other details as we need to give us the illusion of full scene. But Hemingway himself rules out all detail not strictly necessary to the development of the action on which he wishes to center. The oral reader, of course, would begin to fill out some of these details for an audience; this is both his challenge and his dilemma.

It is the shifts from summary to scene, from exterior to interior, from character to character; it is the repetition of details, the incremental use of detail; it is the terseness of the speeches and the sense of things unspoken—it is these things which give the story its rhythm. The closer kind of patterning which we have observed in poetry is not to be found here, though the second sentence of the story (for example) will yield several examples of alliteration and scrambling of sounds. The metaphors are not set down openly, as in poetry; they uncover for us gradually, they are not explicitly introduced. The rhythms of prose are hidden under the great complexities permitted by the greater freedom of prose. Nevertheless, it would be a mistake to overlook the fact that prose *has* rhythm. The peculiar rhythm of any work of literature is a fundamental aspect of the style of the work. This aspect of Hemingway's style is so marked for most readers that a whole generation of young writers fell into the error of imitating it, hoping thereby to achieve a quality the equal of Hemingway's.

Analysis of a Play

The third of the forms to be discussed is the play. Although in Chapter 10 we discussed the limitations of the one-act play form, we have chosen a play in that form for use here, to show how much can be accomplished when the writer is as skillful as William Saroyan.

HELLO OUT THERE [4]

There is a fellow in a small-town prison cell, tapping slowly on the floor with a spoon. After tapping half a minute, as if he were trying to telegraph words, he gets up and begins walking around the cell. At last he stops, stands at the center of the cell, and doesn't move for a long time. He feels his head, as if it were wounded. Then he looks around. Then he calls out dramatically, kidding the world.

YOUNG MAN. Hello—out there! (*Pause*) Hello—out there! Hello—out there! (*Long pause*) Nobody out there. (*Still more dramatically, but more comically, too.*) Hello—out there! Hello—out there!
(*A* GIRL'S VOICE *is heard, very sweet and soft.*)

THE VOICE. Hello.

YOUNG MAN. Hello—out there.

THE VOICE. Hello.

YOUNG MAN. Is that you, Katey?

THE VOICE. No—this here is Emily.

YOUNG MAN. Who? (*Swiftly*) Hello out there.

THE VOICE. Emily.

YOUNG MAN. Emily who? I don't know anybody named Emily. Are you that girl I met at Sam's in Salinas about three years ago?

THE VOICE. No—I'm the girl who cooks here. I'm the cook. I've never been in Salinas. I don't even know where it is.

YOUNG MAN. Hello out there. You say you cook here?

THE VOICE. Yes.

YOUNG MAN. Well, why don't you study up and learn to cook? How come I don't get no jello or anything good?

THE VOICE. I just cook what they tell me to. (*Pause*) You lonesome?

YOUNG MAN. Lonesome as a coyote. Hear me hollering? Hello out there!

THE VOICE. Who you hollering to?

[4] From *Razzle-Dazzle* by William Saroyan, copyright, 1942, by Harcourt, Brace and Company, Inc., and reprinted with their permission; additional permissions from Pearn, Pollinger, and Higham, Ltd., London.

YOUNG MAN. Well—nobody, I guess. I been trying to think of somebody to write a letter to, but I can't think of anybody.

THE VOICE. What about Katey?

YOUNG MAN. I don't know anybody named Katey.

THE VOICE. Then why did you say, Is that you, Katey?

YOUNG MAN. Katey's a good name. I always did like a name like Katey.
I never *knew* anybody named Katey, though.

THE VOICE. *I* did.

YOUNG MAN. Yeah? What was she like? Tall girl, or little one?

THE VOICE. Kind of medium.

YOUNG MAN. Hello out there. What sort of a looking girl are *you?*

THE VOICE. Oh, I don't know.

YOUNG MAN. Didn't anybody ever tell you? Didn't anybody ever talk to you that way?

THE VOICE. What way?

YOUNG MAN. You know. Didn't they?

THE VOICE. No, they didn't.

YOUNG MAN. Ah, the fools—they should have. I can tell from your voice you're O.K.

THE VOICE. Maybe I am and maybe I ain't.

YOUNG MAN. I never missed yet.

THE VOICE. Yeah, I know. That's why you're in jail.

YOUNG MAN. The whole thing was a mistake.

THE VOICE. They claim it was rape.

YOUNG MAN. No—it wasn't.

THE VOICE. That's what they claim it was.

YOUNG MAN. They're a lot of fools.

THE VOICE. Well, you sure are in trouble. Are you scared?

YOUNG MAN. Scared to death. (*Suddenly*) Hello out there!

THE VOICE. What do you keep saying that for all the time?

YOUNG MAN. I'm lonesome. I'm as lonesome as a coyote. (*A long one*)
Hello—out there!

(THE GIRL *appears, over to one side. She is a plain girl in plain clothes.*)

THE GIRL. I'm kind of lonesome, too.

YOUNG MAN (*turning and looking at her*). Hey— No fooling? Are you?

THE GIRL. Yeah— I'm almost as lonesome as a coyote myself.

YOUNG MAN. Who *you* lonesome for?

THE GIRL. I don't know.

YOUNG MAN. It's the same with me. The minute they put you in a place like this you remember all the girls you ever knew, and all the girls you didn't get to know, and it sure gets lonesome.

THE GIRL. I bet it does.

YOUNG MAN. Ah, it's awful. (*Pause*) You're a pretty kid, you know that?

THE GIRL. You're just talking.

YOUNG MAN. No, I'm not just talking—you *are* pretty. Any fool could see that. You're just about the prettiest kid in the whole world.

THE GIRL. I'm not—and you know it.

YOUNG MAN. No—you are. I never saw anyone prettier in all my born days, in all my travels. I knew Texas would bring me luck.

THE GIRL. Luck? You're in jail, aren't you? You've got a whole gang of people all worked up, haven't you?

YOUNG MAN. Ah, that's nothing. I'll get out of this.

THE GIRL. Maybe.

YOUNG MAN. No, I'll be all right—*now*.

THE GIRL. What do you mean—now?

YOUNG MAN. I mean after seeing you. I got something now. You know for a while there I didn't care one way or another. Tired. (*Pause*) Tired of trying for the best all the time and never getting it. (*Suddenly*) Hello out there!

THE GIRL. Who you calling now?

YOUNG MAN. You.

THE GIRL. Why, I'm right here.

YOUNG MAN. I know. (*Calling*) Hello out there!

THE GIRL. Hello.

YOUNG MAN. Ah, you're sweet. (*Pause*) I'm going to marry *you*. I'm going away with *you*. I'm going to take you to San Francisco or some place like that. I *am*, now. I'm going to win myself some real money, too. I'm going to study 'em real careful and pick myself some winners, and we're going to have a lot of money.

THE GIRL. Yeah?

YOUNG MAN. Yeah. Tell me your name and all that stuff.

THE GIRL. Emily.

YOUNG MAN. I know that. What's the rest of it? Where were you born? Come on, tell me the whole thing.

THE GIRL. Emily Smith.

YOUNG MAN. Honest to God?

THE GIRL. Honest. That's my name—Emily Smith.

YOUNG MAN. Ah, you're the sweetest girl in the whole world.

THE GIRL. Why?

YOUNG MAN. I don't know why, but you are, that's all. Where were you born?

THE GIRL. Matador, Texas.

YOUNG MAN. Where's that?

THE GIRL. Right here.

YOUNG MAN. Is this Matador, Texas?

THE GIRL. Yeah, it's Matador. They brought you here from Wheeling.

YOUNG MAN. Is that where I was—Wheeling?

THE GIRL. Didn't you even know what town you were in?

YOUNG MAN. All towns are alike. You don't go up and ask somebody what town you're in. It doesn't make any difference. How far away is Wheeling?

THE GIRL. Sixteen or seventeen miles. Didn't you know they moved you?

YOUNG MAN. How could I know, when I was out—cold? Somebody hit me over the head with a lead pipe or something. What'd they hit me for?

THE GIRL. Rape—that's what they *said*.

YOUNG MAN. Ah, that's a lie. (*Amazed, almost to himself*) She wanted me to give her money.

THE GIRL. Money?

YOUNG MAN. Yeah, if I'd have known she was a woman like that— well, by God, I'd have gone on down the street and stretched out in a park somewhere and gone to sleep.

THE GIRL. Is that what she wanted—money?

YOUNG MAN. Yeah. A fellow like me hopping freights all over the country, trying to break his bad luck, going from one poor little town to another, trying to get in on something good somewhere, and she asks for money. I thought she was lonesome. She *said* she was.

THE GIRL. Maybe she was.

YOUNG MAN. She was *something*.

THE GIRL. I guess I'd never see you, if it didn't happen, though.

YOUNG MAN. Oh, I don't know—maybe I'd just mosey along this way and see you in this town somewhere. I'd recognize you, too.

THE GIRL. Recognize me?

YOUNG MAN. Sure, I'd recognize you the minute I laid eyes on you.

THE GIRL. Well, who would I be?

YOUNG MAN. Mine, that's who.

THE GIRL. Honest?

YOUNG MAN. Honest to God.

THE GIRL. You just say that because you're in jail.

YOUNG MAN. No, I mean it. You just pack up and wait for me. We'll high-roll the hell out of here to Frisco.

THE GIRL. You're just lonesome.

YOUNG MAN. I been lonesome all my life—there's no cure for that—but you and me—we can have a lot of fun hanging around together. You'll bring me luck, I know it.

THE GIRL. What are you looking for luck for all the time?

YOUNG MAN. I'm a gambler. I don't work. I've *got* to have luck, or I'm a bum. I haven't had any decent luck in years. Two whole years now—one place to another. Bad luck all the time. That's why I got in trouble back there in Wheeling, too. That was no accident. That was my bad luck following me around. So here I am, with my head half busted. I guess it was her old man that did it.

THE GIRL. You mean her father?

YOUNG MAN. No, her husband. If I had an old lady like that, I'd throw her out.

THE GIRL. Do you think you'll have better luck, if I go with you?

YOUNG MAN. It's a cinch. I'm a good handicapper. All I need is somebody good like you with me. It's no good always walking around in the streets for anything that might be there at the time. You got to have somebody staying with you all the time—through winters when it's cold, and springtime when it's pretty, and summertime when it's nice and hot and you can go swimming—through *all* the times—rain and snow and all the different kinds of weather a man's got to go through before he dies. You got to have somebody who's right. Somebody who knows you, from away back. You got to have somebody who even knows you're wrong but likes you just the same. I know I'm wrong, but I just don't want anything the hard way, working like a dog, or the *easy* way, working like a dog—working's the hard way and the easy way both. All I got to do is beat the price, always—and then I don't feel lousy and don't hate anybody. If you go along with me, I'll be the finest guy anybody ever saw. I won't be wrong any more. You know when you get enough of that money, you *can't* be wrong any more—you're right because the money says so. I'll have a lot of money and you'll be just about the prettiest, most wonderful kid in the whole world. I'll be proud walking around Frisco with you on my arm and people turning around to look at us.

THE GIRL. Do you think they will?

YOUNG MAN. Sure they will. When I get back in some decent clothes, and you're on my arm—well, Katey, they'll turn around and look, and they'll see something, too.

THE GIRL. Katey?

YOUNG MAN. Yeah—that's your name from now on. You're the first girl I ever called Katey. I've been saving it for you. O.K.?

THE GIRL. O.K.

YOUNG MAN. How long have I been here?

THE GIRL. Since last night. You didn't wake up until late this morning, though.

YOUNG MAN. What time is it now? About nine?

THE GIRL. About ten.

YOUNG MAN. Have you got the key to this lousy cell?

THE GIRL. No. They don't let me fool with any keys.

YOUNG MAN. Well, can you get it?

THE GIRL. No.

YOUNG MAN. Can you *try?*

THE GIRL. They wouldn't let me get near any keys. I cook for this jail, when they've got somebody in it. I clean up and things like that.

YOUNG MAN. Well, I want to get out of here. Don't you know the guy that runs this joint?

THE GIRL. I know him, but he wouldn't let you out. They were talking of taking you to another jail in another town.

YOUNG MAN. Yeah? Why?

THE GIRL. Because they're afraid.

YOUNG MAN. What are they afraid of?

THE GIRL. They're afraid these people from Wheeling will come over in the middle of the night and break in.

YOUNG MAN. Yeah? What do they want to do that for?

THE GIRL. Don't *you* know what they want to do it for?

YOUNG MAN. Yeah, I know all right.

THE GIRL. Are you scared?

YOUNG MAN. Sure I'm scared. Nothing scares a man more than ignorance. You can argue with people who ain't fools, but you can't
argue with fools—they just go to work and do what they're set on
doing. Get me out of here.

THE GIRL. How?

YOUNG MAN. Well, go get the guy with the key, and let me talk to him.

THE GIRL. He's gone home. Everybody's gone home.

YOUNG MAN. You mean I'm in this little jail all alone?

THE GIRL. Well—yeah—except me.

YOUNG MAN. Well, what's the big idea—doesn't anybody stay here all
the time?

THE GIRL. No, they go home every night. I clean up and then I go,
too. I hung around tonight.

YOUNG MAN. What made you do that?

THE GIRL. I wanted to talk to you.

YOUNG MAN. Honest? What did you want to talk about?

THE GIRL. Oh, I don't know. I took care of you last night. You were
talking in your sleep. You liked me, too. I didn't think you'd
like me when you woke up, though.

YOUNG MAN. Yeah? Why not?

THE GIRL. I don't know.

YOUNG MAN. Yeah? Well, you're wonderful, see?

THE GIRL. Nobody ever talked to me that way. All the fellows in
town— (Pause)

YOUNG MAN. What about 'em? (Pause) Well, what about 'em? Come
on—tell me.

THE GIRL. They laugh at me.

YOUNG MAN. Laugh at you? They're fools. What do they know about
anything? You go get your things and come back here. I'll take
you with me to Frisco. How old are you?

THE GIRL. Oh, I'm of age.

YOUNG MAN. How old are you?—Don't lie to me! Sixteen?

THE GIRL. I'm seventeen.

YOUNG MAN. Well, bring your father and mother. We'll get married
before we go.

THE GIRL. They wouldn't let me go.

YOUNG MAN. Why not?

THE GIRL. I don't know, but they wouldn't. I know they wouldn't.

YOUNG MAN. You go tell your father not to be a fool, see? What is he, a farmer?

THE GIRL. No—nothing. He gets a little relief from the government because he's supposed to be hurt or something—his side hurts, he says. I don't know what it is.

YOUNG MAN. Ah, he's a liar. Well, I'm taking you with me, see?

THE GIRL. He takes the money I earn, too.

YOUNG MAN. He's got no right to do that.

THE GIRL. I know it, but he does it.

YOUNG MAN (*almost to himself*). This world stinks. You shouldn't have been born in this town, anyway, and you shouldn't have had a man like that for a father, either.

THE GIRL. Sometimes I feel sorry for him.

YOUNG MAN. Never mind feeling sorry for him. (*Pointing a finger*) I'm going to talk to your father some day. I've got a few things to tell that guy.

THE GIRL. I know you have.

YOUNG MAN (*suddenly*). Hello—out there! See if you can get that fellow with the keys to come down and let me out.

THE GIRL. Oh, I couldn't.

YOUNG MAN. Why not?

THE GIRL. I'm nobody here—they give me fifty cents every day I work.

YOUNG MAN. How much?

THE GIRL. Fifty cents.

YOUNG MAN (*to the world*). You see? They ought to pay money to *look* at you. To breathe the *air* you breathe. I don't know. Sometimes I figure it never is going to make sense. Hello—out there! I'm scared. You try to get me out of here. I'm scared them fools are going to come here from Wheeling and go crazy, thinking they're heroes. Get me out of here, Katey.

THE GIRL. I don't know what to do. Maybe I could break the door down.

YOUNG MAN. No, you couldn't do that. Is there a hammer out there or anything?

THE GIRL. Only a broom. Maybe they've locked the broom up, too.

YOUNG MAN. Go see if you can find anything.

THE GIRL. All right. (*She goes.*)

YOUNG MAN. Hello—out there! Hello—out there! (*Pause*) Hello—out there! Hello—out there! (*Pause*) Putting me in jail. (*With con-*

tempt) Rape! Rape! *They* rape everything good that was ever born. His side hurts. They laugh at her. Fifty cents a day. Little punk people. Hurting the only good thing that ever came their way. *(Suddenly)* Hello—out there!

THE GIRL *(returning)*. There isn't a thing out there. They've locked everything up for the night.

YOUNG MAN. Any cigarettes?

THE GIRL. Everything's locked up—all the drawers of the desk, all the closet doors—everything.

YOUNG MAN. I ought to have a cigarette.

THE GIRL. I could get you a package maybe, somewhere. I guess the drug store's open. It's about a mile.

YOUNG MAN. A mile? I don't want to be alone that long.

THE GIRL. I could run all the way, and all the way back.

YOUNG MAN. You're the sweetest girl that ever lived.

THE GIRL. What kind do you want?

YOUNG MAN. Oh, any kind—Chesterfields or Camels or Lucky Strikes —any kind at all.

THE GIRL. I'll go get a package. *(She turns to go.)*

YOUNG MAN. What about the money?

THE GIRL. I've got some money. I've got a quarter I been saving. I'll run all the way. *(She is about to go.)*

YOUNG MAN. Come here.

THE GIRL *(going to him)*. What?

YOUNG MAN. Give me your hand. *(He takes her hand and looks at it, smiling. He lifts it and kisses it)* I'm scared to death.

THE GIRL. I am, too.

YOUNG MAN. I'm not lying—I don't care what happens to me, but I'm scared nobody will ever come out here to this God-forsaken broken-down town and find you. I'm scared you'll get used to it and not mind. I'm scared you'll never get to Frisco and have 'em all turning around to look at you. Listen—go get me a gun, because if they come, I'll kill 'em! They don't understand. Get me a gun!

THE GIRL. I could get my father's gun. I know where he hides it.

YOUNG MAN. Go get it. Never mind the cigarettes. Run all the way.

    (Pause, smiling but seriously) Hello, Katey.

THE GIRL. Hello. What's *your* name?

YOUNG MAN. Photo-Finish is what they *call* me. My races are always photo-finish races. You don't know what that means, but it means they're very close. So close the only way they can tell which horse wins is to look at a photograph after the race is over. Well, every race I bet turns out to be a photo-finish race, and my horse never wins. It's my bad luck, all the time. That's why they call me Photo-Finish. Say it before you go.

THE GIRL. Photo-Finish.

YOUNG MAN. Come here. (THE GIRL *moves close and he kisses her*) Now, hurry. Run all the way.

THE GIRL. I'll run. (THE GIRL *turns and runs. The* YOUNG MAN *stands at the center of the cell a long time.* THE GIRL *comes running back in. Almost crying*) I'm afraid. I'm afraid I won't see you again. If I come back and you're not here, I—

YOUNG·MAN. Hello—out there!

THE GIRL. It's so lonely in this town. Nothing here but the lonesome wind all the time, lifting the dirt and blowing out to the prairie. I'll stay *here*. I won't *let* them take you away.

YOUNG MAN. Listen, Katey. Do what I tell you. Go get that gun and come back. Maybe they won't come at all. I'll hide the gun and when they let me out you can take it back and put it where you found it. And then we'll go away. But if they come, I'll kill 'em! Now, hurry—

THE GIRL. All right. (*Pause*) I want to tell you something.

YOUNG MAN. O.K.

THE GIRL (*very softly*). If you're not here when I come back, well, I'll have the gun and I'll know what to do with it.

YOUNG MAN. You know how to handle a gun?

THE GIRL. I know how.

YOUNG MAN. Don't be a fool. (*Takes off his shoe, brings out some currency*) Don't be a fool, see? Here's some money. Eighty dollars. Take it and go to Frisco. Look around and find somebody. Find somebody alive and halfway human, see? Promise me—if I'm not here when you come back, just throw the gun away and get the hell to Frisco. Look around and find somebody.

THE GIRL. I don't *want* to find anybody.

YOUNG MAN (*swiftly, desperately*). Listen, if I'm not here when you come back, how do you know I haven't gotten away? Now, do what I tell you. I'll meet you in Frisco. I've got a couple of dollars in my other shoe. I'll see you in San Francisco.

THE GIRL (*with wonder*). San Francisco?

YOUNG MAN. That's right—San Francisco. That's where you and me belong.

THE GIRL. I've always wanted to go to *some* place like San Francisco—but how could I go alone?

YOUNG MAN. Well, you're not alone any more, see?

THE GIRL. Tell me a little what it's like.

YOUNG MAN (*very swiftly, almost impatiently at first, but gradually slower and with remembrance, smiling, and* THE GIRL *moving closer to him as he speaks*). Well, it's on the Pacific to begin with —ocean water all around. Cool fog and sea-gulls. Ships from all over the world. It's got seven hills. The little streets go up and down, around and all over. Every night the fog-horns bawl. But they won't be bawling for you and me.

THE GIRL. What else?

YOUNG MAN. That's about all, I guess.

THE GIRL. Are people different in San Francisco?

YOUNG MAN. People are the same everywhere. They're different only when they love somebody. That's the only thing that makes 'em different. More people in Fricso love somebody, that's all.

THE GIRL. Nobody anywhere loves anybody as much as I love you.

YOUNG MAN (*shouting, as if to the world*). You see? Hearing you say that, a man could die and still be ahead of the game. Now, hurry. And don't forget, if I'm not here when you come back, get the hell to San Francisco where you'll have a chance. Do you hear me?

(THE GIRL *stands a moment looking at him, then backs away, turns and runs. The* YOUNG MAN *stares after her, troubled and smiling. Then he turns away from the image of her and walks about like a lion in a cage. After a while he sits down suddenly and buries his head in his hands. From a distance the sound of several automobiles approaching is heard. He listens a moment, then ignores the implications of the sound, whatever they may be. Several automobile doors are slammed. He ignores this also. A wooden door is opened with a key and closed, and footsteps are heard in a hall. Walking easily, almost casually and yet arrogantly, a* MAN *comes in. The* YOUNG MAN *jumps up suddenly and shouts at the* MAN, *almost scaring him*) What the hell kind of a jail-keeper are you, anyway? Why don't you attend to your business? You get paid for it, don't you? Now, get me out of here.

THE MAN. But I'm not the jail-keeper.

YOUNG MAN. Yeah? Well, who are you, then?

THE MAN. I'm the husband.

YOUNG MAN. What husband you talking about?

THE MAN. You know what husband.

YOUNG MAN. Hey! (*Pause, looking at* THE MAN) Are you the guy that hit me over the head last night?

THE MAN. I am.

YOUNG MAN (*with righteous indignation*). What do you mean going around hitting people over the head?

THE MAN. Oh, I don't know. What do you *mean* going around—the way you do?

YOUNG MAN (*rubbing his head*). You hurt my head. You got no right to hit anybody over the head.

THE MAN (*suddenly angry, shouting*). Answer my question! What do you mean?

YOUNG MAN. Listen, you—don't be hollering at me just because I'm locked up.

THE MAN (*with contempt, slowly*). You're a dog!

YOUNG MAN. Yeah, Well, let me tell you something. You *think* you're the husband. You're the husband of nothing. (*Slowly*) What's more, your wife—if you want to call her that—is a tramp. Why don't you throw her out in the street where she belongs?

THE MAN (*draws a pistol*). Shut up!

YOUNG MAN. Yeah? Go ahead, shoot—(*Softly*) and spoil the fun. What'll your pals think? They'll be disappointed, won't they. What's the fun hanging a man who's already dead? (THE MAN *puts the gun away*) That's right, because now you can have some fun yourself, telling me what you're going to do. That's what you came here for, isn't it? Well, you don't need to tell me. I *know* what you're going to do. I've read the papers and I know. They have fun. A mob of 'em fall on one man and beat him, don't they? They tear off his clothes and kick him, don't they? And women and little children stand around watching, don't they? Well, before you go on *this* picnic, I'm going to tell you a few things. Not that that's going to send you home with your pals—the other heroes. No. You've been outraged. A stranger has come to town and violated your women. Your pure, innocent, virtuous women. You fellows have got to set this thing right.

You're men, not mice. You're home-makers, and you beat your children. (*Suddenly*) Listen, you—I didn't know she was your wife. I didn't know she was anybody's wife.

THE MAN. You're a liar!

YOUNG MAN. Sometimes—when it'll do somebody some good—but not this time. Do you want to hear about it? (THE MAN *doesn't answer*) All right, I'll tell you. I met her at a lunch counter. She came in and sat next to me. There was plenty of room, but she sat next to me. Somebody had put a nickel in the phonograph and a fellow was singing *New San Antonio Rose*. Well, she got to talking about the song. I thought she was talking to the waiter, but *he* didn't answer her, so after a while *I* answered her. That's how I met her. I didn't think anything of it. We left the place together and started walking. The first thing I knew she said, This is where I live.

THE MAN. You're a dirty liar!

YOUNG MAN. Do you want to hear it? Or not? (THE MAN *does not answer*) O.K. She asked me to come in. Maybe she had something in mind, maybe she didn't. Didn't make any difference to me, one way or the other. If she was lonely, all right. If not, all right.

THE MAN. You're telling a lot of dirty lies!

YOUNG MAN. I'm telling the truth. Maybe your wife's out there with your pals. Well, call her in. I got nothing against her, or you— or any of you. Call her in, and ask her a few questions. Are you in love with her? (THE MAN *doesn't answer*) Well, that's too bad.

THE MAN. What do you mean, too bad?

YOUNG MAN. I mean this may not be the first time something like this has happened.

THE MAN (*swiftly*). Shut up!

YOUNG MAN. Oh, you know it. You've always known it. You're afraid of your pals, that's all. She asked me for money. That's all she wanted. I wouldn't be here now if I had given her the money.

THE MAN (*slowly*). How much did she ask for?

YOUNG MAN. I didn't ask her how much. I told her I'd made a mistake. She said she would make trouble if I didn't give her money. Well, I don't like bargaining, and I don't like being threatened, either. I told her to get the hell away from me. The next thing I knew she'd run out of the house and was hollering. (*Pause*) Now, why don't you go out there and tell 'em they took me to another jail

—go home and pack up and leave her. You're a pretty good guy, you're just afraid of your pals. (THE MAN *draws his gun again. He is very frightened. He moves a step toward the* YOUNG MAN, *then fires three times. The* YOUNG MAN *falls to his knees.* THE MAN *turns and runs, horrified*) Hello—out there! (*He is bent forward.* THE GIRL *comes running in, and halts suddenly, looking at him.*)

THE GIRL. There were some people in the street, men and women and kids—so I came in through the back, through a window. I couldn't find the gun. I looked all over but I couldn't find it. What's the matter?

YOUNG MAN. Nothing—nothing. Everything's all right. Listen. Listen, kid. Get the hell out of here. Go out the same way you came in and run—run like hell—run all night. Get to another town and get on a train. Do you hear me?

THE GIRL. What's happened?

YOUNG MAN. Get away—just get away from here. Take any train that's going—you can get to Frisco later.

THE GIRL (*almost sobbing*). I don't want to go any place without you.

YOUNG MAN. I can't go. Something's happened. (*He looks at her*) But I'll be with you always— God damn it. Always! (*He falls forward.* THE GIRL *stands near him, then begins to sob softly, walking away. She stands over to one side, stops sobbing, and stares out. The excitement of the mob outside increases.* THE MAN, *with two of his pals, comes running in.* THE GIRL *watches, unseen.*)

THE MAN. Here's the son of a bitch!

ANOTHER MAN. O.K. Open the cell, Harry.

(*The* THIRD MAN *goes to the cell door, unlocks it, and swings it open.*)

(A WOMAN *comes running in.*)

THE WOMAN. Where is he? I want to see him. Is he dead? (*Looking down at him, as the* MEN *pick him up.*) There he is. (*Pause*) Yeah, that's him. (*Her husband looks at her with contempt, then at the dead man.*)

THE MAN (*trying to laugh*). All right—let's get it over with.

THIRD MAN. Right you are, George. Give me a hand, Harry. (*They lift the body.*)

THE GIRL (*suddenly, fiercely*). Put him down!

THE MAN. What's this?

SECOND MAN. What are you doing here? Why aren't you out in the street?

THE GIRL. Put him down and go away. (*She runs toward the* MEN. THE WOMAN *grabs her.*)

THE WOMAN. Here—where do you think *you're* going?

THE GIRL. Let me go. You've no right to take him away.

THE WOMAN. Well, listen to her, will you? (*She slaps* THE GIRL *and pushes her to the floor*) Listen to the little slut, will you? (*They all go, carrying the* YOUNG MAN's *body.* THE GIRL *gets up slowly, no longer sobbing. She looks around at everything, then looks straight out, and whispers.*)

THE GIRL. Hello—out—there! Hello—out there!

Except for certain explicit indications of attitude written into the stage directions, the script of *Hello Out There* depends for its effects upon the interchange of speech between characters. The stage directions here function precisely as narrative functions in prose fiction, except that they can be and are dispensed with *as audible speech* in the performance of the play. They are not, however, superfluous in the text. Without them, the actors of the play and the director of the play would miss, or risk missing, certain implications which Saroyan is anxious to underscore in the speeches. They are cues to interpretation of the play, cues to movement and gesture. They function as indications of tempo and tone function in the musical score; in this sense, reading the script of a play is like reading a musical score. Many people, lacking in ability to visualize and finding the strain on the imagination rather too heavy, dislike reading play scripts, though they may thoroughly enjoy the performed play. On the other hand, the challenge of the play script becomes absorbing for the imaginative reader who is able to make use of all the cues it contains, and who is fairly sophisticated in his acquaintance with the way in which literature functions.

The suggestion in the opening stage direction that the young man is trying to *communicate* with someone is central to the play's movement. It is underscored by what follows, but it is suggested at the very opening moment, before speech begins. The stage business is related to the implication in the title, which again suggests an appeal for response.

The story of the play is simple, and it begins near the climax of the action. The scene (involving a certain amount of summary which we call, in the play form, *exposition*) involves only the young man and the girl until the moment of the *crisis,* when the man enters. It is the entrance of the man which suggests to us that the play is not going to end with the young man's release, but probably with his death. This possibility has been pointed up carefully in the dialogue between the young man and the girl: the crime with which the young man has been charged is one often resulting in violent retribution, here spelled out in the girl's speeches:

. . . They were talking of taking you to another jail in another town.

. . . They're afraid these people from Wheeling will come over in the middle of the night and break in.

It is underscored in the speeches which follow between the girl and the young man. The crisis is not a trick, nor even a surprise; we have been carefully prepared for it, so that the action has some of the inevitability in its movement which we associate with all good serious drama.

In a sense, the play has a double climax: the first climax is the death of the young man; the second, the final speech by the girl. The second climax may properly be described as an epiphany, too. Why?

In another sense, the final speech by the girl is the *real* climax of the action. The play is not, after all, simply about a young man who dies for a crime which he did not commit; this is only the ostensible action which permits Saroyan to say something about the relationships between human beings in the course of living. The point is that through the young man, even though he dies, the girl, too, comes to a realization of the importance of finding "somebody alive and halfway human," and as the play ends she "looks around at everything" before she, too, calls, "Hello—out—there! Hello—out there!" Furthermore, because of the girl's love for him, the young man has been able to cry out, to the world,

"You see? Hearing you say that, a man could die and still be ahead of the game." The play is larger than the "story" it tells.

People who like Saroyan's play frequently comment on the "warmth" of the attitudes toward people expressed through the girl and the young man. People who do not particularly like Saroyan may be tempted to call this warmth by another name—sentimentality. Both responses recognize a poetic quality in the language of the play—a richly emotional attitude, a fondness for images, a tendency to use repetition:

Well, it's on the Pacific to begin with—ocean water all around. Cool fog and sea-gulls. Ships from all over the world. It's got seven hills. The little streets go up and down, around and all over. Every night the fog-horns bawl....

People are the same everywhere. They're different only when they love somebody. That's the only thing that makes 'em different. More people in Frisco love somebody, that's all.

Nobody anywhere loves anybody as much as I love you.

The play will not seem sentimental to you if the characters and their weight of emotion seem to you credible in terms of the play's meaning. (We are not now discussing the question of the sentimentality of the *play*. A playwright may successfully make use of a sentimental character in a play which is not at all sentimental.) It is true that the young man in the play may seem to you to have a kind of irresponsibility about him, and an ethical pattern which you personally may deplore. It is true, too, that the girl is severely limited in both education and judgment. But Saroyan is a master at making articulate people whom we would not expect to find articulate. Both the young man and the girl speak out of their limitations; Saroyan does not ignore the blind spots in them, but gives us those, too. It is for this reason that the characters (though given only type designations: girl, young man) seem to us three-dimensional. Since they are human beings, and find themselves in a situation where, as human beings, they suffer, we, as human beings, respond. It is the essential humanity of the two characters (not their morality, their level of taste, or their judgment) which makes the primary appeal. And in this humanity (mixed-up though it may be in such characters) there is an essential goodness: a desire to be in life, to share with others, to love, to find the kind of dignity which permits the individual to know himself as an individual. It's not quite a simple plea for "company." It's not just that the young man, for example, is lonesome. He says,

I been lonesome all my life—there's no cure for that—but you and me—we can have a lot of fun hanging around together.

... You got to have somebody staying with you all the time—through winters when it's cold, and springtime when it's pretty, and summertime when it's nice and hot and you can go swimming—through *all* the times—rain and snow and all the different kinds of weather a man's got to go through before he dies. You got to have somebody who's right. Somebody who knows you, from away back. You got to have somebody who even knows you're wrong but likes you just the same.

Because the characters are relatively simple as human beings (not, however, to be criticized on that score), Saroyan can let them look at life in large terms, simply, cutting through complications which more complex characters would have to face. Hence Saroyan can achieve a very moving "total" response to life, primitive in its simplicity but universal in its statement. Hence, also, his play has a strong emotionality, because his characters speak out of an emotional rather than an intellectual attachment to life. When the girl finally whispers, "Hello—out—there," she is probably not speaking out of any particular intellectual comprehension of the world and her place in it; but she certainly has a strong "feeling," now, that something meaningful has taken place. We would not expect her to be able to put it in words at this moment; we do not want her to try. The simple urgent whisper to the audience is all we ask. If we look at the characters and the play this way, it is difficult to call the play sentimental.

We have said almost nothing about the additional characters. The man (the husband) who appears at the crisis of the play is a particularly interesting character. He is in some ways the most complex character in the play. How? Why should Saroyan choose to make the murderer the most complex? What does this add to the statement being made by the play? How does *irony* function in the ending of the play?

Observe that the play is set in Matador, Texas. There is an irony here, too, in the use of the romantic name for so prosaic a town. Does the notion of bullfighting, inherent in the name *Matador,* enter at all into the action of the play? (Do you remember that the young man walks about "like a lion in a cage"?) It is clear that the dryness and the dustiness of Matador ("Nothing here but the lonesome wind all the time, lifting the dirt and blowing out to the prairie") contrast sharply with the sea and the gulls of San Francisco. The contrast is factual; the implications are symbolical.

How would you describe the relationship of the play to the audience in *Hello Out There?* (That is, in part, why does Saroyan begin and end the play with an address to "us"?)

Why is the girl seventeen? Why is she a cook at the jail? Why is her father on relief because "his side hurts"? Why do we know about the girl's parents but not about the young man's?

In a day like ours, when values seem constantly shifting and changing and when many people feel hopelessly entangled in the enormous complications of daily living, a play like *Hello Out There* has a very special appeal for most audiences, striking as it does through complexity to basic needs. All good literature relates in this fashion to the experience of living, though not all literature (it seems hardly necessary to say so) strips away so many of the complexities in imitating experience. It is not only possible but probable that the "solution" in *Hello Out There* would seem too simple as a settled view for many people who read the play; but this does not in any way negate the power of the solution as a solution for the young man and the girl through whom Saroyan speaks. As a work of literature, the play speaks for *itself*, not necessarily for *us*. What we ask of it is that it make sense on its own terms, to begin with. If it does, we doubtless value it as a work of art. Beyond that, without in any way denying the attributes of *Hello Out There* as a play, we may find that another play may speak to us more *fully* (or, to put it another way, may present us with an experience which seems fuller), and may prefer the second play.

There are always, for the reader as critic, two kinds of judgment involved: First of all, the judgment of the piece of literature as a work of art. *Is* it a work of art? Second, the judgment of the *value* of the work of art. How good is it of its kind? We must not make the error, in answering the second of these questions, of projecting our own feelings *into* the work, however. Remember that it is always possible for a reader to like "better" a work which is inferior or to "like" a work which he does not at the same time admire. The reader who cannot distinguish between these possibilities is never likely to become a good critic. The point at issue is the point which we have been discussing repeatedly through this whole volume: the nature of the relationship existing between the experience of the reader and the experience within the work of art itself.

PART 3

Literature and Expressive Action

12

Language and Literature:
Verbal Action

W̓HEN A PLAYWRIGHT succeeds in giving the *illusion* of common speech, we often admire him for his skill in being able to write as people talk. That it is an illusion does not interfere with our pleasure in listening. We may go further and recognize that Shakespeare's plays, written in blank verse, frequently did not even attempt the illusion of common speech, and yet his lines were intended to be spoken. The fact that a literary text is *written* does not mean that it cannot properly be *spoken,* though it may still be true that it does not correspond in any documentary sense to common speech.

The Values of Oral Reading

Indeed, we should argue that oral reading may lead the student to better understanding of literature. Alfred North Whitehead, writing in 1929 of the things that should be taught in schools,

said,[1] "Above all the art of reading aloud should be cultivated."
He was not thinking of the entertainment value for a listening
public; he was not recommending professional training for the
stage; apparently he was not even thinking of those forms of
literature for which there already exists an oral tradition, such as
drama and lyric poetry, for he goes on to say,[2] "The Roger de
Coverley essays of Addison are perfect examples of readable
prose."

What, then, are the reasons for Professor Whitehead's suggestion that students be taught to read aloud? They derive from
a deep-seated conviction that the antitheses of mind and body,
thought and action are disastrous. He says,[3] "I lay it down as an
educational axiom that in teaching you will come to grief as soon
as you forget that your pupils have bodies." The effect on the
body of reading literature has already been remarked; it has been
mentioned that thought is subvocal speech and that there is subliminal muscular activity in the vocal mechanism during silent
reading. Then, too, empathy and sympathy create physical tensions during the silent reading of exciting literature. But Professor Whitehead and others of his persuasion feel that students will
be brought to a more vivid sense of the reality of literary experience if they read aloud, for then their muted muscular or physical
responses will be brought to the level of full expression and there
will be a more complete "entering into" the experience of literature. Oral reading is especially valuable as a means of inte-
grating mind and body, for as Whitehead says,[4] "The connections
between intellectual activity and the body, though diffused in
every bodily feeling, are focused in the eyes, the ears, the voice,
and the hands."

In this chapter, the vocal aspects of language will be emphasized; but at almost every point it will be seen that verbal

[1] Alfred North Whitehead, *The Aims of Education and Other Essays,* The
Macmillan Company, New York, 1929, p. 91. Quoted by permission of the
publishers.

[2] *Ibid.,* p. 91.

[3] *Ibid.,* p. 78.

[4] *Ibid.,* p. 78.

language is conditioned by the physiological fact that it is muscular and neural action.

Spoken and Written Language

In the beginning, written and spoken language were unrelated, and in the evolution of language, talking came before reading and writing. But after a long history of transformations from picture writing to the association, as near as possible, of a single sign (a letter of the alphabet) with a single sound, there has come to be a very close relationship of written language with spoken language. It is very likely that literary men test their compositions "in the mouth" even as they write. Nevertheless, for expressiveness the spoken word continues to hold the edge over the written word.

Harold Whitehall points to the distinction when he writes,[5]

The basic form of English is the patterned code of rhythmed voice signals called speech. From this code, the English of writing is something of an abstraction, differing from speech in details of vocabulary, in details of grammatical pattern, in the absence of accompanying physical gesture, and in the absence of meaningful qualities of the speaker's voice. Written English is a somewhat abstract dialect of English ... [it] must be so managed that it can compensate, at least in part, for the absence of such accompanying features. It must be more carefully organized than speech in order to overcome its communicative deficiencies compared with speech.

Virginia Woolf, too, spoke of the difficulties of written expression in her essay on Montaigne:[6] "Face, voice, and accent eke out our words and impress their feebleness with character in

---

[5] Harold Whitehall, *Structural Essentials of English,* Indiana University, Bloomington, Ind., 1954, p. 1. This is a limited edition, intended for circulation in connection with the Indiana University Television Correspondence Course W101 and not for general distribution. However, the same material appears in somewhat revised form in his book of the same name published by Harcourt, Brace and Company, Inc., New York, 1956.

[6] Virginia Woolf, *The Common Reader: First and Second Series,* Harcourt, Brace and Company, Inc., New York, 1948, pp. 88–89.

speech. But the pen is a rigid instrument; it can say very little. ..."
As long ago as the early seventeenth century Ben Jonson [7] recom-
mended to those who would write well that they "observe the best
speakers." In the twentieth century Malcolm Cowley [8] says very
much the same thing: "...if many Southerners write well, that
is partly because Southerners as a type are good talkers."

It is probably true that writers are in love with both the spoken
and the written word. Certainly this was the case with C. E.
Montague, who wrote: [9]

You come, like other lovers, to feel an unreasoned sensuous thrill of
joy at a word because it is just what it is—the sound of it and the look
of it on a page.... [Your] mind will finger single words and caress
them, adoring the mellow fullness or granular hardness of their several
sounds, the balance, undulation or trailing fall of their syllables, or the
core of sun-like splendour in the broad, warm, central vowel of such
a word as "auroral." Each word's evocative value or virtue, its individual power of touching springs in the mind and of initiating visions,
becomes a treasure to revel in.

Montague's enthusiasm is expressed, at first, impartially for the
written and the sounded word, but when he begins to caress individual words, his adoration is for the associations and images
they stir in his mind and most particularly for their sound.

Inner Ear and Outer Ear

It is not the word on the page that delights Montague so much
as the word sounded, at least to his "inner ear." For the skilled
reader or writer, the inner ear will frequently seem to bring
enough delight. For the less experienced reader, the oral sounding of words will insure delight through the outer ear, which,
truth to tell, is more reliable than the inner. How often we have
tried to recapture a melody, and when we have thought that we

[7] *Timber, or Discoveries,* 1641.

[8] *Great Tales of the Deep South,* Lion.

[9] C. E. Montague, *A Writer's Notes on His Trade,* Doubleday & Company,
Inc., New York, 1930, p. 30. Quoted by permission of Mrs. C. E. Montague and
Chatto & Windus, publishers.

had it in our mind—that is, we thought we could hear it in our inner ear—we have been disappointed to find when we whistled or sang it aloud to the outer ear that it was not the right melody after all. The trick we play on ourselves in such cases is something like this: We shape our vocal mechanism for the few sounds that memory correctly supplies, and then because the movements are so slight and tentative we skip over the intervening sounds, which we do not remember, and get a vague impression of unity of melodic sounds when in truth there are only a few scattered sounds which are accurate—hence the sounds when uttered aloud do not in fact make up the correct melody.

Students have often reported that when they read poems to themselves silently, that is, subvocally, they recognize a more expressive interpretation than when they read the same poem aloud. This would seem to speak well for silent reading, but what it means, generally, is that the student is indulging himself in a certain subvocal freedom he would not allow himself in oral reading. It is very much like singing in the shower; there is little inhibition on the part of the singer and he deceives himself into thinking he is pretty good, but when he turns off the water and he hears himself plainly, his sober judgment will undeceive him.

Too often the reader will see the words of the text as a veil covering the harsh outlines of actuality, rather than as a revelation of the buried significance of reality. Such a reader will welcome the verbal "objectification" of experience by which he avoids the dramatic immediacy of feeling and action. It is true that all readers are somewhat removed from the actuality of the situations imaginatively described in the literature, but, perhaps, the oral reader can be brought closer to a sense of actuality through his outspoken manipulation of the language of the text. Whatever it is that language has become, written or spoken, it remains true that its roots are sensorimotor.

Behavioristic Interpretation of Speech and Language

This is not the place for an extended history of language and speech, nor for an exhaustive accounting of the theories of the origin of speech and language. But enough should be said to justify a view of speech that sees it as a physical act, a manner of behavior, to emphasize the biological intimacy of speech with active experience. It is necessary to counteract the tendency of the "intellectual" to substitute words for experience, in contempt of the rest of his personality. It is too often the case with us that we prefer to mediate with experience by interposing a screen of words between the environment and our own organism so that contact will be minimized. Too often, literature has been made to serve the reader's "escape" from contact with experience. It is easier to "escape" in silent reading, for the absurdity of our inappropriate responses does not show up as vividly as in oral reading; the poverty of poor literature is less apparent for the average reader in the dim light of his internalized reading than in the glare of externalized reading.

If we can accept speech as a form of behavior—sensory and motor—we can begin to see that speech and language are well integrated with experience itself. John Dewey can be quoted as the spokesman for a number of linguists, anthropologists, and social psychologists who accept a behavioristic interpretation of the origin of speech and language: [10]

Gestures and cries ... are modes of organic behavior as much as are locomotion, seizing and crunching. Language, signs and significance, come into existence not by intent and mind but by over-flow, by-products, in gestures and sound. The story of language is the story of the use made of these occurrences.

This social purposiveness of speech behavior is of prime importance in considering the transformation of organic gestures and cries into names—things with significance.

A number of theories try to account for this transformation.[11]

[10] John Dewey, *Experience and Nature,* The Open Court Publishing Company, La Salle, Ill., 1925, pp. 175-176.

[11] Grace DeLaguna in her *Speech, Its Function and Development,* Yale University Press, New Haven, Conn., 1927, advances the theory that language is a social phenomenon and that speech evolved from animal cries. A baby's gurglings are indulged in for the pleasure they represent, and then the sound

A recent theory developed by A. A. Roback is known as the "vocosensory" theory of the origin of language.[12] It is Roback's conclusion after experimenting with consonants that these sound units (phonemes) "have a symbolic value which is not subjective but bound up with the way the action of the various speech organs in different positions affects us." [13] This is not an "imitation" theory or an "onomatopoetic" theory, which explains the origin of speech as a codification of imitations of animal sounds or natural sounds. Roback insists that the various tensions and relaxations of the musculature in the production of sounds account for the appearance of these sounds in words that bear a meaning that corresponds in some degree to the tension or relaxation. For instance, he speaks of *k* as a hard sound because of the plosive quality in its articulation; hence its appearance in words of considerable tension such as *kick, cuff, cudgel, crabby, cranky,* etc. That the same sound is featured in such words as *calm, cool,* and *collected* does not seem to shake his confidence in the theory.

---

of his own voice and the kinaesthetic "feel" of it come to control his utterance. "When the play-activity of vocal utterance becomes adapted to and incorporated into the serious business of social living then we have speech" (p. 72).

Sir Richard Paget in his *Human Speech,* Harcourt, Brace and Company, Inc., New York, 1930, speaks of language as an elaboration of a form of phonetic imitation. His theory of language-gesture views vowels and consonants as essentially pantomimic in their imitation of movement. His theory regards the articulation of the word *least* as an imitation of the superlative of *little,* or as an empathic response to a minute quantity. That is, in the articulation of the vowel in *least,* the tongue is arched to its highest degree, thus reducing the oral cavity to its smallest, which, in Paget's view, is a phonetic gesture in imitation of a minute quantity.

Charles W. Morris in his introduction to George H. Mead's *Mind, Self & Society: From the Standpoint of a Social Behaviorist,* University of Chicago Press, Chicago, 1934, says, "For Mead, the vocal gesture is the actual fountain-head of language proper and all derivative forms of symbolism; and so of mind" (p. xxii).

[12] A. A. Roback, *Destiny and Motivation in Language: Studies in Psycholinguistics and Glossodynamics,* Sci-Art Publishers, Cambridge, Mass., 1954, chap. 4. There is a very brief summary of the vocosensory theory of language in A. A. Roback (ed.), *Present-day Psychology,* Philosophical Library, Inc., New York, 1955, pp. 905–907.

[13] Roback (ed.), *op. cit.,* p. 905.

He analyzes various sound combinations (phonexes) which are common in the language (he has examined Semitic words principally, but he offers many instances in English) and finds that the phonex *st,* for example, "occurs in so many words connoting re*st* or *st*opping or *st*anding because of the 'feel' in bringing the consonant *s* to a halt through slightly withdrawing the tongue." [14] Again he is not dismayed by the long parallel list of *st* words that carry no connotation of rest or stopping or standing—*strife, struggle, stride, stampede, stagger, stumble,* etc.

The contradictory evidence is not introduced here to discredit the vocosensory theory—too many scholars and writers attest to something like the response to the sounds of language which Roback describes. Nevertheless, an awareness of parallel lists of words which seem to contradict the generalizations made in support of the vocosensory theory will warn against oversimplification and will ultimately lead to an important correction of Roback's theory. For now it will be enough to pursue the vocosensory theory a little further for what it can offer the reader of literature as a justification of oral reading.

Sound and Sense

The tradition that there is some close connection between the sound of words and their meaning is very old; Alexander Pope (1688–1744) gave the notion admirable expression in his "Essay on Criticism":

> The sound must seem an echo to the sense:
> Soft is the strain when Zephyr gently blows,
> And the smooth stream in smoother numbers flows;
> But when loud surges lash the sounding shore,
> The hoarse, rough verse should like the torrent roar.
> When Ajax strives some rock's vast weight to throw,
> The line too labours, and the words move slow:
> Not so when swift Camilla scours the plain,
> Flies o'er the unbending corn, and skims along the main.

[14] *Ibid.,* p. 905. The phonex *st* is not italicized in Roback's text.

Even as Pope states his position, his verses illustrate the relation of sound to sense. Roback's theory takes a primary interest in phonemes and phonexes, but when it comes to lines of verse, or phrases, or sentences, then other features such as accent and stress begin to produce an effect that is startling when orally expressed. Consider Milton's line from a description of the effortful passage of Satan through Chaos in *Paradise Lost:* "Rocks, caves, lakes, fens, bogs, dens, and shades of death."

The lengthening of the line (for it does in point of time take longer to speak this line than a line of regular blank verse) gives a sense of strain and tension through *ex*tension which is appropriate to Satan's action here. By contrast Milton can suggest delicacy with another line, also of ten syllables but taking much less time to speak: "Mosaic; underfoot the violet." [15]

From these instances—Pope and Milton—it should be clear that the sounds of phonemes, phonexes, words, and phrases need not be onomatopoetic in their imitation of natural sounds in order to echo the sense.

Motor Aspect of Articulation Related to Sense

The expressive quality of speech may be not in the auditory element but in the motor or muscular aspect of articulation. The lover who persuades his sweetheart to say "prunes" is not interested in the sound she makes, but rather in the pursing of her lips as she articulates the magic word, which he then takes as an invitation to the kiss.

Roback tried some experiments with consonants in which he asked a great number of adult subjects what their responses to certain consonants were. He asked them to respond in terms of (1) hardness or softness, (2) consistency or texture, (3) coldness or warmness, and (4) color. Since k was a sound for which there was found to be statistical significance beyond the expectations

---

[15] There is an interesting discussion of the relation of sound and sense in poetry in Donald A. Stauffer, *The Nature of Poetry*, W. W. Norton & Company, Inc., New York, 1946, chap. 1, "Poetry Is Exact."

of chance, let us consider Roback's conclusions with respect to k. There was significant agreement among the subjects that k was "cold" and "hard." It is not surprising that there was so much agreement on this sound; it is a plosive with a rather sharp release of a voiceless sound which is not the most pleasant or the most musical sound human beings make. The k sound seems appropriate to the word *cold,* itself, but notice what happens when the word *cool,* which is a cognate in sound and meaning, is used in the colloquial sense of "smooth," "chic," "in the groove"; when the implications of "cold" and "hard" would be inappropriate to express this new meaning, the speaker will minimize the plosive quality of the k sound of *cool* and elongate the vowel *oo* and the continuant *l.* The effect of the articulation of *cool* in this colloquial sense is to emphasize the "smooth" feeling rather than the hardness and coldness. The same thing is done by a speaker who uses the word *kind* to mean "generous" or "considerate." If he is sincere, he will minimize the plosive force of the k and elongate the more pleasant, soothing qualities of the vowel and the continuant *n;* if, on the other hand, the speaker is ironic and uses the word *kind* when he really means that the person is "sharp," "cunning," "cruel," and "hard," then he will combine the full force of the plosive k with the elongation of the other phonemes and achieve the ironic effect in his combination of the pleasant and unpleasant.

Perhaps it is wiser to say only this about the affective quality of individual sounds: *When the sounds can be so articulated as to emphasize symbolically certain qualities of the experience expressed by the word or words that contain them, we articulate them emphatically; if the articulation of the sounds contradicts the sensorimotor symbolism, then they are articulated minimally.* The words must contain sounds which provide the opportunity for creative interpretation on the part of the speaker; however, it is an oversimplification to believe as Roback does that certain sounds have specific responses which are related to the articulatory activity of the speaker. If the vocosensory responses were uniform, we would expect homonyms to produce identical responses, for they contain the same sounds. *Butter* and *butter* would have the same effect on the listener though the first referred to the golden dairy product and the second to a goat. It is not likely that this would be the case; nor would it necessarily be true of homophones like *blue* and *blew*. Variations within the articulatory patterns for phonemes and phonexes allow for differences in the responses of listeners. The listener's interpretation of a sound will depend on the variations in energy with which the sound is enunciated or the length of time for which the sound is held or the accompanying emphatic or minimal articulatory gestures.

It is interesting that when Edward Sapir experimented with this vocosensory theory, which he called "phonetic symbolism," he took arbitrary words like *mal* and *mil* and gave them the arbitrary meaning of "table" and then asked observers to state whether these words symbolized for them a large or small table. *Mal* was more often associated with the large table and *mil* with the small. Sapir concludes [16] from these experiments "that we are really dealing with a measurably independent psychological factor that for want of a better term may be called 'phonetic symbolism.' " Further experiments were made by S. S. Newman,[17] M. Bentley and E. J. Varon,[18] and J. Wittmann.[19] Roback [20] sums up the

[16] Edward Sapir, "Phonetic Symbolism," *Journal of Experimental Psychology,* vol. 12, p. 233, 1929.

[17] S. S. Newman, "Further Experiments in Phonetic Symbolism," *American Journal of Psychology,* vol. 45, pp. 53–75, 1933. Newman confirmed Sapir's earlier work and concluded that "the basis of phonetic symbolism is objective."

[18] M. Bentley and E. J. Varon, "An Accessory Study of 'Phonetic Symbolism,' " *American Journal of Psychology,* vol. 45, pp. 76–86, 1933. These men concluded that there is such a thing as phonetic symbolism but that the explanation of its operation depends not on sound differences alone but (1) on the observation of articulation (open mouth, pursed lips) and (2) on the kinaesthetic experience of the physical production of the sounds themselves (the feel of the tongue, lips, etc.). It was found that the responses of the subjects to sounds were fairly uniform because the "feel" of phonation for specific sounds is generally uniform.

[19] Roback, *op. cit.,* p. 124. Roback reports the work of J. Wittmann at Kiel, where he has been studying the relation between sound and sense for years. Wittmann says, "The word is not an arbitrary and fortuitous symbol of an object, but rather the representation of a certain structurally perceived object in conformity with a sound structure and sound scheme. Sound structure of the word and object structure of the object as intended by the meaning of the word are in accord with one another."

[20] *Ibid.*

findings of these experiments briefly and, for our purposes, satisfactorily: "We may just take it that the objects and their phonetic
sign show agreement in a particular way."

It is possible to place too much emphasis on the objectivity of
phonetic symbolism. To an extent, the possibilities for plosion,
elongation, lip movement, and tongue placement, etc., are inherent in the word and its sounds, but equally important or, perhaps, more important is the creative sensibility of the speaker,
who may lengthen or shorten a vowel at his own discretion, or
emphasize or minimize the plosive force of a consonant. The
speaker may take advantage of phonetic structure and the articulatory movements to exaggerate the intonation of his speech or
to make a face.

Then, too, there is the possibility of an overriding vocal quality
that infects whole sentences and even paragraphs. The phonetic
symbolism of individual sounds is then made subordinate to a
unifying impression of a comprehensive tone or attitude which is
physical and at the same time symbolic. Darwin pointed to the
primitive practice of children who expressed their dislike of someone or something by sticking out their tongues and making a
sound something like a bleating sheep. Sticking out the tongue
was for Darwin a reinstatement of the primitive reflex of vomiting or rejecting something distasteful; so, too, was the sound,
which got its peculiar vocal quality from the extremely open
throat through which it came. The open throat was, of course, a
feature of the regurgitation, or vomiting, reflex. It is interesting
that the civilized adult will show his contempt or distaste in much
the same fashion, though much repressed. We are all familiar
with the tone of voice that we recognize as "superior" or "contemptuous" because it has that "open-throat" quality. (These illus-
trations from Darwin appear in a somewhat different context
in Chapter 3, pages 32 to 33.)

We have little difficulty in agreeing with Pope that the sound
and the sense of words are and must be in the best poetry congru-
ent. What we find more difficult to accept is that the sounds *alone*
in a poem are capable of inducing a mood appropriate to the sense

of the poem. Robert C. Givler [21] made experiments with selected verses of Byron, Keats, Tennyson, and Arnold, using transmogrified passages (that is, scrambled nonsense words that contained all the sounds of the original poem but made no lexical sense) which were read aloud. He found that *sound patterns alone* were capable of producing in the oral readers mood responses that were appropriate to the original tone of the poem. Henry Lanz [22] is somewhat more general in his conclusions about the affective power of sounds. He regards the emotions derived from musical or sound stimuli as of a nonspecific order—joyful, solemn, soothing, or stirring. He does agree, however, with Givler's notion that often the sound patterns of poetry are congruous with the mood appropriate to the meaning of the poem.

Literature and Development of Language

Whatever view we take of language, its origin and development, we recognize the indissoluble union of its content and sensuous expression. The mimetic movements that characterize language in its early stages are a part of the dynamism of emotion and expression, process and change. The fixation of such processes and changes by linguistic symbols, the transition from the dynamic to the static is part of the development of the "spiritual" out of the "physical." The natural economy of human ingenuity formalizes the mimetic expressions until they become simply indicative or suggestive of the full gesture or imitation. This second step in the development of language is analogical, as the first was mimetic. The grasping hand of early mimesis becomes in the second stage the grasping mind as the hand no longer literally seeks to grasp but only to indicate or suggest. The sounds of speech that once imitated objects and relations, as indeed they

[21] Robert C. Givler, "The Psycho-physiological Effect of the Elements of Speech in Relation to Poetry," *Psychological Review Monographs,* vol. 19, pp. 1–132, April, 1915.

[22] Henry Lanz, *The Physical Basis of Rime: An Essay on the Aesthetics of Sound,* Stanford University Press, Stanford, Calif., 1931, pp. 280–292, 296.

still do, become sufficiently fixed so that they can be arranged in related orders of words and phrases. As the content of speech becomes formalized, it operates by analogy. Language reaches its third stage of development when it achieves symbolic expression through its grammatical and syntactical organization—language is now capable of suggesting such basic intuitions as force, space and time. Language as we use it today contains evidence of all three stages of its development.[23]

The student of literature is apt to take a greater interest in the third stage of language development, and as long as he remains a *silent* reader, he may be content with a concentration of interest in the symbolic language of the literary text. If he should make a conscientious effort to become an oral reader of literature, he will be forced to realize the extent of the impact of the early stage of mimesis on the later analogical and symbolic levels of language evolution.

Literature is aesthetic experience and as such seeks a condition of stasis, but must never become static. Life is direct experience, vital and dynamic, but for the reasonable man it must never become chaotic. Language is the great medium of literature *and* life; its sensuous quality keeps literature from becoming completely abstract, ideal, or spiritual; its symbolic character provides a consciousness of life's form, content, and significance. The silent reader and the oral reader, alike, may be conscious of the symbolic function of language as it articulates an ideal experience, but it is more likely that the *oral* reader (through his intonation, vocal emphasis, emotional quality, and gesture) will reinstate the mimetic function of language and so provide the fullest interpretation of the text. The interrelation of the sensuous and the intellectual in language is attested to on the final page of Cassirer's study of language: [24]

Even though sensuous and spiritual elements seem to have been inextricably intertwined in the origin of language, this *correlation*, pre-

---

[23] Ernst Cassirer, *The Philosophy of Symbolic Forms,* vol. I, *Language,* Yale University Press, New Haven, Conn., 1953, pp. 186–197.

[24] *Ibid.,* p. 319. Quoted by permission of the publishers.

cisely because it is a correlation, does not argue a relation of *one-sided* dependency between the two. For intellectual expression could not have developed through and out of sensuous expression if it had not originally been contained in it; if, as Herder said, sensuous designation did not already embrace a basic act of "reflection." ... the characteristic meaning of language is not contained in the opposition between the two extremes of the sensuous and the intellectual, because in all of its achievements and in every particular phase of its progress, language shows itself to be *at once* a sensuous and an intellectual form of expression.

Breathing and Speech

Whatever in the life of the speaker affects his breathing will, of course, affect his speech because speech depends for its phonation and articulation on the expulsion of breath. Normal breathing has two to three times as many inhalation-exhalation cycles as breathing for speech. Vocal expression, therefore, requires considerable control of one of our most fundamental biological necessities—breathing. The psychological value of combining the satisfaction of a physical need and the expression of intellectual and spiritual thoughts and feelings in the same physiological process is immense. Respiration refers to the whole process of breathing, which includes *inspiration* (breathing in) and *expiration* (breathing out). The psychological background of these terms is hinted at in the metaphorical extension of *inspiration* when it is defined as "the inbreathing of an idea, emotion, or mental or spiritual influence," while *expiration* means "termination," "end," and *to expire* is "to die."

Whenever a healthy reader is excited by the events or conditions of a story or poem, he will find that the rate and the amplitude of his breathing will increase. He must have more oxygen to meet the increased metabolic demands. The degree of his excitement will depend, of course, on the strength of his contact and his concern with the environment of the text. The inhibited reader, on the other hand, will repress his excitement by controlling his breathing. He will reduce the amplitude of his breathing by constricting his chest; he is "unmoved," he is "self-controlled." Such a reader may not realize that he is suffering from anxiety, but "the experience of breathing difficulty during any blocked excitement ... the experience of trying to get more air into lungs immobilized by muscular constriction of the thoracic cage" [25] is nothing less than anxiety. If the reader will read the text aloud, he will demonstrate to himself whether his breathing is adequate to the high level of excitement of the scene he is reading or whether there is a frustration of the breathing mechanism. To discover one's adequacies or inadequacies in responding to a literary scene is valuable as self-revelation, for it helps the reader to place himself as a more or less qualified reader. We cannot evaluate literature properly unless we know our own limitations and virtues as human beings. Reading aloud brings into prominence one feature, breathing, which has sufficient objectivity to be judged with some accuracy. It is even possible to get some relief from anxieties met in reading literature by deliberately deepening one's breathing, thereby releasing the blocked excitements. Literature is not to be regarded as therapy, of course; neither is it to be condemned if, in its indirect way, it affects an easement of the reader's personal deficiencies.

Of course, it is possible that a reader's anxiety is aesthetically functional. To understand the anxieties of a character in a literary text it may be necessary for the reader to accept the character's symptoms. Anxiety so induced in the reader must always be understood as expressive of the *character's* condition, not the *reader's*. There can be no anxiety on the part of the reader about his acceptance of the character's anxiety. In other words, when we assume the qualities of another person in the interest of understanding the condition of that person, we recognize the qualities as expressive of the other and not of ourselves. There is always the risk of confusing the aesthetic experience with the actual or

[25] Frederick S. Perls, Ralph H. Hefferline, and Paul Goodman, *Gestalt Therapy: Excitement and Growth in the Human Personality,* The Julian Press, Inc., New York, 1951, p. 128.

real, but the qualified reader must learn to take the risk without losing his ability to discriminate what is expressive of another and what is expressive of himself.

Summary

Though the language of written literature may differ from that of common speech, it must not be inferred that it is therefore improper for written literature to be spoken. Shakespeare's plays are not written in common speech, but he intended that they be spoken. It is not unlikely that all creative writers test their written work on their tongues even as they write, and what seems to them awkward in the mouth will very likely seem awkward in print.

Speech as an activity of the body is closely related to the activity of the mind, and where body and mind can be intimately associated, there is likelihood of spiritual health. The sensorimotor origin of speech has left its mark on language; though we generally regard speech as symbolic in effect, there is considerable mimesis in its expression. The relation of sound to sense in language can be demonstrated especially in terms of the motor aspects of articulation.

Wherever the features of oral speech, such as emphasis, inflection, pitch, volume, or voice quality, can be added to the features of written language for the better understanding of the text, there would seem to be some advantage in the oral expression of literature. The case is clear for drama and some forms of poetry, but even the prose forms of fiction and, indeed, biography and essays may profit from oral reading.

Subvocal reading for the benefit of the inner ear is better than sight reading, but oral reading for the outer ear will give greater assurance of understanding because the inner ear may deceive us.

To say so much for the ear (inner or outer) as an instrument of literary appreciation is not to say that the eye is without importance; on the contrary, the eye is indispensable. For example, for many people there is no distinction in sound between *mourn-*

ing and *morning,* and hence without the *visual* distinction the final line of one of George Barker's sonnets, "That she will move from mourning into morning," [26] will be meaningless.

It is not too much to ask of the serious reader who would become a "qualified" reader that he read with both sets of eyes and both sets of ears, the inner and the outer. Except in the theater the outer ear is most seriously neglected as an instrument of literary appreciation, and so our plea for a recognition of the oral appeal that language makes has been strong. It is important to *listen* to literature, whether we read it aloud to ourselves or listen to others:

Attentive listening suspends that "irritable reaching after fact and reason" which Keats rightly deplored in the poet; it sustains a state of uncertainties, mysteries, doubts, a posture of total awareness and delicate response; it secures a personal integrity which is yet outward-turning, and that virginity of consciousness which is as priceless a gift to the reader as to the poet.[27]

Exercises

1. What are the differences between a written text and a spoken text? Consider the spatial relationships versus the temporal relationships, vocal inflections versus printed words (italics, punctuation perhaps). What precisely is it in the printed text that inspires the nonverbal action of the spoken text? What is it in the printed text that suggests or determines the volume level of your oral utterance? How are pauses in the oral expression related to the printed text?

2. Literature may be regarded as verbalization of what is essentially nonverbal—objects, processes, conditions, etc. When we talk about literature, that is, when we talk about talk, we may be engaged in a useful activity, or we may be indulging in a tendency to substitute the life of words for more direct contact with actuality. How closely related is your speech to your inner life, your thought? Is there a gap

[26] George Barker, *Selected Poems,* The Macmillan Company, New York, 1941, p. 143.
[27] George Whalley, *Poetic Process,* Routledge and Kegan Paul, Ltd., London, 1953, pp. 156–157.

between your public expression and your private or internal expression? Try this experiment: (*a*) Listen to yourself as you talk in company, or better still have a recording made of your social conversation. Notice how difficult it is to accept the voice as your own. Your actual personality is probably different from your own view of yourself. (*b*) Next listen to yourself recite a poem aloud. Don't try to *do* anything about your recitation, that is, don't increase your volume, or sharpen your diction, or alter your expressive range. Just practice listening to yourself speak. (*c*) Now recite the poem internally, subvocally, and listen to yourself. How does the silent reading differ from the reading aloud? Do you use a wider range of inflections in one or the other? Does your inner voice have any prevailing quality: is it an angry tone, a childish tone, a pedantic tone, or what?

If you practice this exercise sufficiently, you will find that you will be able to speak and listen at the same time. You will be able to hear yourself talk. If you read literature aloud, you will soon be able to judge your own oral expression for its congruence or incongruence with the literature.

3. When you read literature aloud, especially before the class, there will be some anxiety on your part about how well you are going to perform, what the others will think of you, etc.

Anxiety shows itself in the constriction of the breathing process, whereas the full excitement of significant contact with the literature and the audience releases the breathing mechanism and encourages a fuller amplitude of breathing. How is your breathing affected under various conditions of excitement? Try this exercise: (*a*) Begin by noticing the breathing of others—the rate, the amplitude, the irregularities, the stoppages. Notice whether they sigh, sniff, gasp, cough, choke, wheeze, vocalize their pauses. Notice, too, the circumstances under which they exhibit these breathing symptoms. (*b*) Notice your own breathing. Can you feel the air enter your nose or mouth? Can you feel it pass down your throat and neck into the bronchi? Are you aware of the expansion and relaxation of your rib muscles during breathing? Is the expansion and relaxation forced or effortless? Is the breathing cycle in any way different when you are lying down and when you are standing? (*c*) Try to relieve tensions in the breathing process by stretching and yawning. Draw in the breath as though you were filling your whole body, not just your lungs. At the peak of the yawn or stretch let the breath out quickly and with a full collapse.

4. Test the italicized statement on page 284 about the affective quality of sounds in literature. Examine, for instance, Stephen Spender's "The Express," a poem that describes an experience of an express train. You will find that the words used in the description also provide opportunities for the reader to emphasize certain qualities of the experience by his emphasis on certain sounds.

5. Look for instances of the three stages of linguistic development—mimetic, analogical, and symbolic—in your daily use of language and also in literature.

13

Language and Literature:
Nonverbal Action

IT IS EASY to say that literature is made with words: words that stand for things, words that express ideas, words that stimulate images. But literature, like the life that it so artfully imitates, is more than words. The skillful writer transcends the limitations of words when he manages to get his reader to experience imaginatively something that has not been explicitly expressed in the verbal text.

Implied Nonverbal Action

The writer may take advantage of a cultural tradition where a traditional phrase is accompanied by a traditional nonverbal act and simply state the verbal part and leave the reader to supply the nonverbal. For instance, the story may read, "He didn't give _that_ for her opinion." The inevitable gesture that accompanies such a statement is a snap of the fingers, and indeed the writer could have been explicit and said, "He didn't give a snap of his fingers for her opinion," but the use of *that* sharpens the effect of immediacy and vividness.

You may recall the same sense of immediacy through implied action in the passage from *Hubert's Arthur* (Chapter 7) when King Richard says, "...take his ribs and arms between your thighs and knees, riding him close clutched so." The rather gratuitous addition of the word *so* indicates that Richard demonstrated the position at that moment. As readers we have a flash of direct perception (illusory, of course, but vivid nonetheless) in which we see Richard bend his knees slightly and tense the muscles of his legs to show the proper position. Shakespeare, knowing that actors will be providing the nonverbal as well as the verbal action of his plays, can afford the same sort of ellipsis when he allows Hamlet to say in his famous advice to the players, "Nor do not saw the air too much with your hand, thus, but use all gently." The actor who plays Hamlet must, of course, employ a nonverbal gesture when he says *thus,* to illustrate a bad actor's behavior. We expect players to "fill out" the lines of a play with action.

Though a novelist cannot rely on actors to make the gestures in his text explicit, he can rely on the qualified reader to be something of an actor or, rather, an acter, who will at the very least make subliminal movements. Melville, in *Moby Dick,* could not bring himself to rely on the reader's interpretation of "There she blows" as anything more than a verbal indication that the whale was spouting; so he had to describe the way in which Ahab spoke the fateful words. In chapter CXXXIII Captain Ahab sights Moby Dick:

"There she blows! there she blows!—there she blows! There again!— there again!" he cried, in long-drawn, lingering, methodic tones, attuned to the gradual prolongings of the whale's visible jets.

Melville wants the reader to hear Ahab and to see the whale; if he can make the reader see the whale *through* Ahab, he will impress the reader with the kinship, the deep identity of Ahab and Moby Dick. So Ahab sings out, "There she blows!" in rhythm with the whale's spouting. Ahab's speech, therefore, is not merely an expression of the whale's proximity, but is itself a gesture in kinaesthetic imitation of Moby Dick.

When the words are themselves gestures the vitality of the symbolic nature of literature is guaranteed. Eugene O'Neill was very skillful in giving his characters speeches that were gestures expressive of their personalities even while they functioned as exposition or description. In the opening scene of *The Hairy Ape,* Paddy Driscoll, "an old, wizened Irishman . . . cries out in a voice full of old sorrow" that the days of the sailing vessel are gone. He speaks longingly of the gentle swelling of the sails, the fair breeze, the trailing wake, the tall masts stretching aloft, and finally he asks, wistfully, "That a great wave wid sun in the heart of it may sweep me over the side sometime I'd be dreaming of the days that's gone." This great long phrase spoken without pause is not just a collocation of words stating a melancholy wish but it is itself a sigh. The actor must take a deep breath and in an Irish dialect (by its nature very breathy speech) say this long phrase with the obvious effect of a sigh. Yank, who is a young man in the full strength of his youth, has no direct knowledge of the sailing ships and indeed prefers the herculean labors of stoking the furnaces of a transatlantic liner to what Driscoll has been describing. He interrupts Driscoll and delivers himself of a long speech, part of which says,[1]

I belong and he don't. He's dead but I'm livin'. Listen to me! Sure I'm part of de engines! Why de hell not! Dey move, don't dey? Dey're speed, aint dey? Dey smash trou, don't dey? Twenty-five knots a hour! Dat's goin' some! Dat's new stuff! Dat belongs! But him, he's too old. He gets dizzy. Say listen.

This speech, unlike Driscoll's, has short, iterative phrases with numerous initial plosive sounds that are gestures imitating the short, iterative movements of shoveling, of the pounding pistons

---

[1] Eugene O'Neill, *Desire under the Elms, The Hairy Ape, Welded,* Horace Liveright, New York, 1925, p. 119.

and rods, the banging of boiler doors, etc. O'Neill's words by their meaning express the differences in experience and philosophy between Driscoll and Yank. But more than that, the words are gestures which imitate symbolically, first Driscoll's sigh of longing and the slow, graceful movement of the sailing vessel, then the powerful, short driving thrusts of the coal heavers, the engine rods and steam pistons which constitute Yank's world. The words not only *tell* us what these two worlds are like, but they act them out for us so that we can see and hear and feel for ourselves their special qualities.

It is clear from the foregoing examples that speech is more than sound; it is at once verbal and nonverbal. Speech may be viewed as primarily expressive movement, "gestured meaning," or in the most limited sense, mouth gesture. It is important to relate the verbal action of language to nonverbal action so that we will not rely entirely on sound (in the simple phonetic sense) as the carrier of meaning. When speech is expressing ideas, we are content to accept it as symbolic, but when speech is understood as an expression of the *whole* personality, we must recognize the importance of the mimetic features that are essentially nonverbal.

Exclamations and Interjections as Gestures

So far we have considered principally the gestural value of sounds that are found in words with lexical meanings, or with sounds like the snapping of fingers that are not in themselves speech sounds. However, there are a great many sounds made with the articulatory mechanism that are purely gestural and emotional and have no lexical meaning. There is the vocalized pause, indicated by some writers as *er—er,* and the click of the tongue which is sometimes represented by writers as *tsk—tsk,* or the hiss as a mark of disapproval. The vocabulary of such exclamations and interjections is large and varied. Writers tend to be sparing in their specifications for definite sounds because the written equivalent is inadequate to suggest accurately the emotional qualities. A writer must depend on the sensitive reader to supply such exclamatory sounds as may seem appropriate.

Some exclamations appear in the dictionary with their definitions because they are compounded of simple emotional sounds and words with lexical meanings. Such a word is *alas,* which is a combination of the emotional sound *ah* and part of the Latin word *lassus* (weary). Interjections, like *gee* (a "minced oath" derived from *Jesus*), also appear in the dictionary. But whether their lexical meanings are as definite as that of *alas* or as indefinite as that of *gee,* their expressive function and emotional value are mimetic.

In the beginning man's impressions of and responses to ideas and feelings called out certain articulatory movements *as part of his natural kinaesthesis, and the eventuating sounds became associated with those ideas and feelings.* In other words, the mouth is an instrument of gesticulation first and an organ of sound-speech second.

Speech and Implicit Gesture

We have considered rather briefly in this chapter how speech itself may be regarded as gesture. The association through mimesis of nonverbal action with speech action is often so close that the two kinds of action seem inseparable and only analysis can distinguish them. But there is a looser association of gesture with speech that is nevertheless functional in ordinary communication and in the interpretation of literature.

There is a vast difference between the direct perception of an actual event in the real world and a verbal report of that event. One important difference is that any detailed verbal accounting must be expressed in a temporal sequence, while the actual event expresses its elements simultaneously. A verbal report of the actual event of swinging a golf club would be forced to say that "he shifted his weight to the right foot *as* he swung the club back over his right shoulder." The word *as* is employed to remind the reader that the two actions reported took place *simul-*

taneously, but the report cannot avoid the *sequential* effect of bringing to mind *first* the shifting of weight and *then* the swinging of the club. A further difference between the verbal report of the action and the action itself is that it takes longer to describe the action than to swing the club.

In literature there is a minimum of verbal distortion when the action reported is itself verbal action, as in dialogue, but when the reported action is nonverbal, then the discrepancy between the verbal report and the action itself make for difficulties. In social situations when one is recounting an event for the benefit of one's friends who were not present at the event itself, we interpose some kind of analogic gestures to mediate the differences between the verbal report and the original observation. We recognize, of course, that discursive language is, within its limits, reliable because of the precision of its linguistic meanings, and surely analogic gestures are often a poor imitation of the actual event. The thesis offered here is that we may have a more precise impression of the event and therefore a richer understanding of it if we encourage the use of analogical language as a mediation between actual behavior and discursive language.[2]

Gesture begins in the primitive necessity for adaptive adjustment to the environment, and so gesture originally served the needs of the individual. When the gesture ceases to be solely adaptive and becomes instead a statement to those who may perceive it or becomes simply expressive rather than adaptive, then it functions analogically as a kind of action language. Gestures achieve their highest degree of analogical value in emotional expression, but they also continue to serve as simple indicators in traffic, in games, and in love. Gestures have a communicative range from the universal down to the idiosyncratic; they may substitute for words or accompany words.

In social intercourse the words of conversation serve as statements, and the gestural accompaniment of inflections—interjec-

---

[2] See Jurgen Ruesch and Weldon Kees, *Nonverbal Communication: Notes on the Visual Perception of Human Relations,* University of California Press, Berkeley, Calif., 1956, p. 10.

tions, hand motions, bodily tensions, facial expressions, etc.—
provides the interpretation of the statements. In reading literature
we are often faced with the necessity of interpreting the author's
verbal descriptions of the nonverbal interpretations of the verbal
behavior. Inasmuch as literature is verbal, much of the normal
nonverbal behavior of social intercourse is omitted. To be explicit
in a literary text about all the nonverbal behavior that characterizes actual human behavior would be to encumber the text.
An author is selective in what he chooses to report, but he is also
hopeful that the reader will fill out the image he presents with
those features of human behavior that will give the event or the
character described a semblance of life.

If the reader is a sensitive, complex, sympathetic, intelligent
human being, he will provide the analogical gestures in a minimal
form that will serve him aesthetically and not exhaust him
physically. But the student who would learn what his own capacities for understanding are might do well for a time to be more
explicit and expressive of the analogical language of gesture which
provides the interpretation of the verbal statements in the text.
This *expression* of the student's understanding will give the
teacher and the other students an opportunity to evaluate his
understanding in a more objective and critical light.

Value of Gestures as Expressive Action

"Gestures are expressive movements of the whole body, of every
degree of intensity." [3] This broad and loose definition of gesture
suits the needs of the interpreter of literature because it does not
distinguish between self-expressive movements and consciously
communicative movements. In literature all the actions of the text
are selected for their expressive value, their capacity for making
statements about the reported experience. Even the autistic movements, which are directed toward the body and are not conceived
by the one who performs the actions as conscious communications

[3] Charlotte Wolff, *A Psychology of Gesture,* 2d ed., Methuen & Co., Ltd., London, 1948, p. 13.

of a state of mind or emotional state, are nevertheless capable of being interpreted by the qualified reader. Those self-expressive, unconscious movements which would ordinarily be excluded from a stricter definition of gesture *become* gesture when they appear in literature, because then they form part of a conscious pattern of expressive behavior which is communicated to the reader for his appreciation.

Some gestures will illustrate or imitate, others will point or indicate, still others will emphasize; always they are to be regarded as intimately related to verbal speech. It is important to realize at this point that not all the gestures in a literary text which are brought to our attention by the author are necessarily the overt gestures apparent in real interpersonal communication.

Gestures in literature range from the nervous behavior of some character in a story to the more highly symbolic gesticulation of the mouth in sounding a line of poetry. Properly, our interest has been in the question of how these gestures in the literature affect the behavior of the reader. The hope is that the reader's imitation of the gestures expressed in the text will lead him to an understanding of those whose gestures he successfully imitates. A gesture transmits subconsciously a quality of thought or feeling which can be satisfactorily appreciated only if the observer imitates the gesture. This does not mean that a full overt expression of anguish on the part of a character in a novel must be *duplicated* by the reader if he is to understand the anguish fully. It is perfectly possible to imitate certain tensions characteristic of the original gesture and still inhibit the cry of anguish which was part of the original gesture. The proper selection of characteristic tensions is both the responsibility of the author in his description and the responsibility of the reader in his imitation.

Wilhelm Reich, in speaking of the psychiatrist's relation to his patient, says,[4] "Only when we have *felt* the facial *expression* of the patient are we also in a position to understand it." Reich is warning that a verbal description of the patient's behavior does not in itself constitute understanding. On the other hand, he does

---

[4] Wilhelm Reich, *Character Analysis,* Orgone Institute Press, New York, 1949, p. 363.

not insist on a full correspondence or duplication of the patient's expressions. What he means by *felt* is some realization of the facial gestures through imitation. It is possible to be conscious of an imitation *because* one inhibits its full expression—it is the inhibition that brings the inhibited behavior to our conscious attention. Reich says,[5] "The emotional expression of the patient produces in our organism an involuntary *imitation*. Imitating, we feel and understand the expression in ourselves and with that in the patient." Because of its involuntary nature and because it is an expression *within* ourselves, it does not have to be *complete* or fully *overt*. Any inhibition we exercise in such imitative behavior may obscure the expression for others who observe us, but not for ourselves. In fact, it is the inhibition that brings the imitation to our consciousness and makes us aware of what might, by its involuntary nature, escape our awareness.

Socially we are not always free to express our imitative understanding. Frequently we must suppress it. In a *conscious* suppression or control there is little danger of our losing the *capacity* for understanding through imitation. The real danger lies in the *persistent* suppression of active social engagement, in the possibility that suppression will eventuate in *repression*. When the native disposition to imitate is so thoroughly discouraged (for whatever reason) that it becomes repressed, then we lose consciousness of some of the richer aspects of our humanity and we sacrifice a certain vitality in our contact with our environment. If we would be qualified readers, we must first be sure that we have a substantial capacity for identification before we trust ourselves to inhibit our imitation selectively.

The modern tendency to *over*suppression of the imitative, or mimetic, aspect of language is seen in the interpretation of language as primarily abstract, conceptual, and symbolic. This tendency has led to what Kenneth Burke calls "the purely ocular style."

But whatever may be the value of such styles, for bookkeeping purposes, they have wandered far afield from the gesturing of heard poetic

[5] *Ibid.*, p. 364.

speech. Paradoxically, their greatest accuracy, from the standpoint of mimesis, is in their *very absence* of such, for by this absence they conform with our sedentary trend from the bodily to the abstract (our secular variant of the spiritual). It is the style of men and women whose occupations have become dissociated from the bodily level, and whose expression does not arise from a physical act.[6]

Dissatisfaction with the "ocular style" in literature is not to be interpreted as a plea for an incantatory style which overwhelms the reader's critical disposition and renders him defenseless in the face of emotional suasion. A devotion to logic on the one hand or to sports on the other will not make the whole man. "The natural growth of the kinaesthetic imagination and ideo-motor expressions contribute to the self-assurance and integration of an individual as well as to his happiness and to the originality of all his expressions."[7]

The social self that has become institutionalized exercises restraint on the impulsive "I." The abstractive style in writing becomes associated with the conventional behavior of men, and the novelty of the less inhibited self is submerged. Good literature avoids the abstractive style because it expresses the tensions between the social self, the "me," and the more impulsive "I." Good literature reveals the submerged character of our motivations and behaviors while it relates the hitherto inhibited expressions of the self, the "I," to its socially controlled expressions in the "me." Literature, for the writer, is a parable of life itself in that there is a comparable tension between the creative freedom of the artist's intuition and the restrictive conventions of his art. It is the restrictive conventions of his art, however, that give expressive shape and form to his individuality and originality.

When we read literature, we assume the behavioral postures and attitudes of the text and we respond to our own assumed postures and attitudes even as we did originally to those in the text. In other words, we are *im*pressed by what we ourselves *ex*press.

[6] Kenneth Burke, *The Philosophy of Literary Form: Studies in Symbolic Action,* Vintage Books, Inc., New York, 1957, p. 15.

[7] Wolff, *op. cit.,* p. 62. Quoted by permission of the publishers.

When we read, we experience the novelty of relcased impulses through imitation. But the involuntary imitation is not fully released; it is formalized by the literary conventions and then revealed to consciousness through selective inhibition.

Summary

It is not inappropriate to conclude a critical introduction to the study of literature with a plea for the study of gesture, or nonverbal behavior. Even in dramatic literature, where the action of men is often significantly nonverbal, the approved method of study has too often ignored the gestural pattern of the action. The final emphasis in this text is on action language because the authors feel impelled to offer a corrective to the traditional method of literary study. Ruesch and Kees state the case for a changing view: [8]

As our society is ordered, verbal language is indispensable. Without numbers and words, the cumulative body of knowledge of mankind could not have been codified. Consequently the practice in higher educational procedure has been to spend some ten to twenty years indoctrinating the young in specific ways of reading, writing, speaking, and calculating. Unhappily, however, our verbal-digital education is not paralleled by a corresponding regard for training along nonverbal, analogic lines. Thus we continue to produce—as though completely to reverse the views of the Renaissance—more and more narrowly oriented human beings as well as increasing numbers of quasi schizophrenics, capable of grappling with the most complicated mathematical and technological problems but with no real understanding of the actions of human beings, their emotional expression, or even of gesture—all of which are necessary for the understanding of speech.

Exercises

1. What evidence of "implied nonverbal action" do you find in "Shower of Gold," "A Clean, Well-Lighted Place," or any of the other works reprinted in the text?

[8] Ruesch and Kees, *op. cit.*, p. 76. Quoted by permission of the publishers.

2. Devise explanatory gestures that will clarify statements found in the literature reprinted in the text.

3. Make a list of sounds which are used in expressive speech but which do not appear in the dictionary with lexical meanings. Try to use the sounds in an oral interpretation of a literary text. Do you find that they intensify your appreciation of the meaning of the literature?

4. Perform an action described by an author, and note the difference between the performed and the described action. The author must select certain features of the action since he cannot afford aesthetically to describe every feature of the action. Can you appraise the success of the author in making the best selection of features of the action?

5. Observe the behavior of your friends in normal social situations. Can you distinguish between self-expressive movements and those movements which are consciously communicative? In what respects are the self-expressive movements idiosyncratic, or "local," that is, "in the mode"? How primitive are the self-expressive movements? How universal are the communicative gestures?

Bibliography

The list of titles is of necessity highly selective. The arrangement is by topics rather than by chapters.

Generally speaking, the bibliography includes only full-length books, and in only a few instances are textbooks included.

No attempt has been made to include in the bibliography all titles which appear in documentation within the chapters of *Literature as Experience,* nor to repeat all titles which embrace more than one of the topics listed.

PART 1

Physiology

Carlson, Anton J., and Victor Johnson: *The Machinery of the Body,* 2d ed., University of Chicago Press, Chicago, 1941.

Langley, L. L., and E. Cheraskin: *The Physiology of Man,* 2d ed., McGraw-Hill Book Company, Inc., New York, 1958.

Psychology and Literature

Basler, Roy P.: *Sex, Symbolism, and Psychology in Literature,* Rutgers University Press, New Brunswick, N.J., 1948.

✓ Bergler, Edmund: *The Writer and Psychoanalysis,* Doubleday & Company, Inc., New York, 1950.

Edel, Leon: *The Psychological Novel, 1900–1950,* J. B. Lippincott Company, Philadelphia, 1955.

Friedman, Melvin J.: *Stream of Consciousness: A Study in Literary Method,* Yale University Press, New Haven, Conn., 1955.

Hoffman, Frederick J.: *Freudianism and the Literary Mind,* Louisiana State University Press, Baton Rouge, La., 1945.

Jung, Carl Gustav: "Psychology and Literature," *Modern Man in Search of a Soul,* Harcourt, Brace and Company, Inc., New York, 1933 (Harvest Books ed., n.d.).

Lesser, Simon O.: *Fiction and the Unconscious,* The Beacon Press, Boston, 1957.

Lucas, F. L.: *Literature and Psychology,* Cassell & Co., Ltd., London, 1951 (Ann Arbor Paperback ed., 1957).

Phillips, William (ed.): *Art and Psychoanalysis,* Criterion Books, New York, 1957.

Richards, I. A.: *Principles of Literary Criticism,* 5th ed., Harcourt, Brace and Company, Inc., New York, 1934.

Roback, A. A.: *Present-day Psychology,* Philosophical Library, Inc., New York, 1955.

Sachs, Hanns: *The Creative Unconscious,* 2d ed., Sci-Art Publishers, Cambridge, Mass., 1951.

Trilling, Lionel: "Freud and Literature," *The Liberal Imagination,* The Viking Press, Inc., New York, 1950 (Doubleday Anchor Books ed., 1953).

————: *Freud and the Crisis of Our Culture,* The Beacon Press, Boston, 1955.

Perception

Allport, Floyd H.: *Theories of Perception and the Concept of Structure,* John Wiley & Sons, Inc., New York, 1955.

Blake, R. R., and G. V. Ramsey (eds.): *Perception: An Approach to Personality,* The Ronald Press Company, New York, 1951.

Ittelson, William H., and Hadley Cantril: *Perception: A Transactional Approach,* Doubleday & Company, Inc., New York, 1954.

Sappenfield, Bert R.: *Personality Dynamics,* Alfred A. Knopf, Inc., New York, 1954.

Emotions

Alexander, Franz: *Psychosomatic Medicine: Its Principles and Applications,* W. W. Norton & Company, Inc., New York, 1950.

Boring, E. G., H. S. Langfeld, and H. P. Weld: *Foundations of Psychology,* John Wiley & Sons, Inc., New York, 1948.

Darwin, Charles: *Expression of the Emotions in Man and Animals,* Philosophical

Library, Inc., New York, 1955. (This work was first published in 1872. The present edition has an introduction by Margaret Mead.)

Dunbar, Helen Flanders: *Emotions and Bodily Changes*, 4th ed., Columbia University Press, New York, 1954.

————: *Mind and Body: Psychosomatic Medicine*, Random House, Inc., New York, 1947 (new enlarged ed., 1955).

Frank, Lawrence K.: *Feelings and Emotions*, Doubleday & Company, Inc., New York, 1954.

Morgan, C. T., et al.: *Introduction to Psychology*, McGraw-Hill Book Company, Inc., New York, 1956.

Munn, Norman L.: *Psychology: The Fundamentals of Human Adjustment*, 2d ed., Houghton Mifflin Company, Boston, 1951.

Rapaport, David: *Emotions and Memory*, The Williams & Wilkins Company, Baltimore, 1942 (International Universities Press, New York, 1950).

Reymert, Martin L. (ed.): *Feelings and Emotions*, Mooseheart Symposium, McGraw-Hill Book Company, Inc., New York, 1950.

Roback, A. A.: *Present-day Psychology*, Philosophical Library, Inc., New York, 1955.

Sartre, Jean-Paul: *The Emotions: Outline of a Theory*, Philosophical Library, Inc., New York, 1948.

Young, Paul T.: *Emotion in Man and Animal*, John Wiley & Sons, Inc., New York, 1943.

Social Behavior: In Relation to the Self

Fromm, Erich: *Man for Himself*, Rinehart & Company, Inc., New York, 1947.

Mead, George H.: *Mind, Self, and Society*, University of Chicago Press, Chicago, 1934.

Niebuhr, Reinhold: *The Self and the Dramas of History*, Charles Scribner's Sons, New York, 1955.

Perls, Frederick S., Ralph F. Hefferline, and Paul Goodman: *Gestalt Therapy: Excitement and Growth in the Human Personality*, The Julian Press, Inc., New York, 1951.

Reik, Theodor: *The Secret Self; Psychoanalytic Experiences, in Life and Literature*, Farrar, Straus and Cudahy, Inc., New York, 1952.

Schilder, Paul: *The Image and Appearance of the Human Body*, Routledge and Kegan Paul, Ltd., London, 1935 (International Universities Press, New York, 1950).

Symonds, Percival: *The Ego and the Self*, Appleton-Century-Crofts, New York, 1951.

Personality

Adams, Donald K.: *The Anatomy of Personality*, Doubleday & Company, Inc., New York, 1954.

Allers, Rudolph: *The Psychology of Character,* The Macmillan Company, New
York, 1931 (Sheed & Ward, Inc., New York, 1943).
Cameron, Norman: *The Psychology of Behavior Disorders: A Biosocial Inter-
pretation,* Houghton Mifflin Company, Boston, 1947.
Kluckhohn, Clyde, and Henry A. Murray: *Personality in Nature, Society, and
Culture,* Alfred A. Knopf, Inc., New York, 1949.
Montagu, Ashley: *The Biosocial Nature of Man,* Grove Press, New York, 1956.
Murphy, Gardner: *Personality: A Biosocial Approach to Origins and Structure,*
Harper & Brothers, New York, 1947.
Sappenfield, Bert R.: *Personality Dynamics,* Alfred A. Knopf, Inc., New York,
1954.
Wolff, Werner: *The Expression of Personality,* Harper & Brothers, New York,
1943.
————: *Diagrams of the Unconscious: Handwriting and Personality in Measure-
ment, Experiment, and Analysis,* Grune & Stratton, Inc., New York, 1948.

PART 2

Glossaries and Handbooks

Abrams, M. H.: *A Glossary of Literary Terms,* Rinehart & Company, Inc., New
York, 1957. (A revision of the work by Dan S. Norton and Peters Rushton,
1941.)
Deutsch, Babette: *Poetry Handbook: A Dictionary of Terms,* Funk & Wagnalls
Company, New York, 1957.
Shipley, Joseph T. (ed.): *Dictionary of World Literature: Criticism—Forms—
Techniques,* 2d ed., Philosophical Library, Inc., New York, 1954.

Literary Criticism

I. TEXTS AND HISTORY

Abrams, M. H.: *The Mirror and the Lamp,* Oxford University Press, New York,
1953.
Bate, Walter J. (ed.): *Criticism: The Major Texts,* Harcourt, Brace and Com-
pany, Inc., New York, 1948.
Daiches, David: *Critical Approaches to Literature,* Prentice-Hall, Inc., Engle-
wood Cliffs, N.J., 1956.
Smith, James Harry, and Edd Winfield Parks (eds.): *The Great Critics: An
Anthology of Literary Criticism,* W. W. Norton & Company, Inc., New York,
1951.
Wellek, René: *A History of Modern Criticism, 1750–1950,* 4 vols., vols. I and II,
Yale University Press, New Haven, Conn., 1955.

Wimsatt, W. K., Jr., and Cleanth Brooks: *Literary Criticism: A Short History,* Alfred A. Knopf, Inc., New York, 1957.

2. GENERAL CRITICAL DISCUSSION

Burke, Kenneth: *The Philosophy of Literary Form: Studies in Symbolic Action,* rev. and abridged, Vintage Books ed., New York, 1957.

Crane, R. S.: *The Languages of Criticism and the Structure of Poetry,* Alexander Lectures, University of Toronto Press, Toronto, 1953.

Daiches, David: *A Study of Literature,* Cornell University Press, Ithaca, New York, 1948.

Eliot, T. S.: *Selected Essays, 1917–1932,* Harcourt, Brace and Company, Inc., New York, 1932 (new ed., enlarged, 1950).

———: *The Use of Poetry and the Use of Criticism,* Harvard University Press, Cambridge, Mass., 1933.

Hyman, Stanley Edgar: *The Armed Vision: A Study in the Methods of Modern Literary Criticism,* Alfred A. Knopf, Inc., New York, 1948 (Vintage ed., abridged, 1955).

———: *The Critical Performance: An Anthology of American and British Literary Criticism of Our Century,* Vintage Books, New York, 1956.

Ransom, John Crowe: *The New Criticism,* New Directions, Brooklyn, 1941.

Richards, I. A.: *Practical Criticism: A Study of Literary Judgment,* 2d ed., Harcourt, Brace and Company, Inc., New York, 1930 (paperback ed. in Harvest Books).

———: *Principles of Literary Criticism,* 5th ed., Harcourt, Brace and Company, Inc., New York, 1934.

Stallman, Robert Wooster: *Critiques and Essays in Criticism, 1920–1948,* The Ronald Press Company, New York, 1949. (Excellent bibliographies.)

Trilling, Lionel: *The Liberal Imagination,* The Viking Press, Inc., New York, 1950 (Doubleday Anchor Books ed., 1953).

Vivas, Eliseo: *Creation and Discovery,* The Noonday Press, New York, 1955.

Wellek, René, and Austin Warren: *Theory of Literature,* Harcourt, Brace and Company, Inc., New York, 1946 (Harvest Book ed., 1956). (Excellent bibliographies.)

Wimsatt, W. K., Jr.: *The Verbal Icon: Studies in the Meaning of Poetry,* University of Kentucky Press, Lexington, Ky., 1954 (Noonday Press ed., 1958).

3. GENERAL AESTHETICS

Dewey, John: *Art as Experience,* Minton, Balch & Co., New York, 1934.

Gilbert, Katharine E., and Helmut Kuhn: *A History of Aesthetics,* 2d ed., Indiana University Press, Bloomington, Ind., 1953.

Hospers, John: *Meaning and Truth in the Arts,* University of North Carolina Press, Chapel Hill, N.C., 1946.

Langer, Susanne K.: *Feeling and Form,* Charles Scribner's Sons, New York, 1953.

———: *Problems of Art,* Charles Scribner's Sons, New York, 1957.

Pepper, Stephen: *The Work of Art,* Indiana University Press, Bloomington, Ind., 1955.

Rader, Melvin: *A Modern Book of Aesthetics,* Henry Holt and Company, Inc., New York, 1935.

Vivas, Eliseo, and Murray Krieger: *The Problems of Aesthetics,* Rinehart & Company, Inc., New York, 1953.

4. PSYCHOLOGY AND THE CREATIVE PROCESS

Arnheim, Rudolf, et al.: *Poets at Work,* Harcourt, Brace and Company, Inc., New York, 1948.

Bodkin, Maud: *Archetypal Patterns in Poetry,* Oxford University Press, New York, 1934.

Cowley, Malcolm (ed.): *Writers at Work: The Paris Review Interviews,* The Viking Press, Inc., New York, 1958.

Ghiselin, Brewster (ed.): *The Creative Process: A Symposium,* University of California Press, Berkeley, Calif., 1952 (Mentor Books ed., 1955).

Lucas, F. L.: *Literature and Psychology,* Cassell & Co., Ltd., London, 1951 (Ann Arbor Paperback ed., 1957).

Maritain, Jacques: *Creative Intuition in Art and Poetry,* Pantheon Books, Inc., New York, 1953 (Meridian Books ed., 1955).

Poetry

I. GENERAL CRITICAL DISCUSSION

Blackmur, R. P.: *Form and Value in Modern Poetry,* Doubleday Anchor Books, New York, 1957. (Cf. R. P. Blackmur, *Language as Gesture,* Harcourt, Brace and Company, Inc., New York, 1952, from which these essays were selected.)

Brooks, Cleanth: *Modern Poetry and the Tradition,* University of North Carolina Press, Chapel Hill, N.C., 1939.

———: *The Well Wrought Urn,* Reynal & Hitchcock, Inc., New York, 1947 (paperback ed. in Harvest Books).

——— and Robert Penn Warren: *Understanding Poetry,* Henry Holt and Company, Inc., New York, 1938.

Davie, Donald: *Articulate Energy: An Enquiry into the Syntax of English Poetry,* American ed., Harcourt, Brace and Company, Inc., New York, 1958.

Empson, William: *Seven Types of Ambiguity,* 2d ed., rev., Chatto & Windus, London, 1947 (Meridian Books ed., 1955).

O'Connor, William V.: *Sense and Sensibility in Modern Poetry,* University of Chicago Press, Chicago, 1948.

Pottle, Frederick: *The Idiom of Poetry,* rev. ed., Cornell University Press, Ithaca, N.Y., 1946.

Sewell, Elizabeth: *The Structure of Poetry,* Routledge and Kegan Paul, Ltd., London, 1951.

Tate, Allen (ed.): *The Language of Poetry*, Princeton University Press, Princeton, N.J., 1942.

2. PROSODY

Frye, Northrop (ed.): *Sound and Poetry*, Columbia University Press, New York, 1957.
Fussell, Paul, Jr.: *Theory of Prosody in Eighteenth-century England*, Connecticut College Monograph, no. 5, 1954.
Omond, T. S.: *English Metrists*, Oxford University Press, New York, 1921.
Saintsbury, George: *Historical Manual of English Prosody*, The Macmillan Company, New York, 1930.
Schramm, Wilbur Lang: *Approaches to a Science of Verse*, University of Iowa Studies, Iowa City, Iowa, 1935.
Stewart, George R., Jr.: *The Technique of English Verse*, Henry Holt and Company, Inc., New York, 1930.
Symposium on prosody, "English Verse and What It Sounds Like," *Kenyon Review*, Summer, 1956.

3. IMAGERY

Day-Lewis, Cecil: *The Poetic Image*, Oxford University Press, New York, 1948.
Murry, J. Middleton: "Metaphor," *Countries of the Mind*, Oxford University Press, New York, 1937. (Essay first appeared in 1931.)
Spurgeon, Caroline: *Shakespeare's Imagery and What It Tells Us*, Cambridge University Press, New York, 1935. (Beacon Paperback ed., 1958).
Tuve, Rosemond: *Elizabethan and Metaphysical Imagery*, University of Chicago Press, Chicago, 1947.
Wells, Henry W.: *Poetic Imagery*, Columbia University Press, New York, 1924.

Prose Fiction

Aldridge, John W.: *Critiques and Essays on Modern Fiction*, The Ronald Press Company, New York, 1952. (Excellent bibliographies.)
Bentley, Phyllis: *Some Observations on the Art of Narrative*, The Macmillan Company, New York, 1947.
Forster, E. M.: *Aspects of the Novel*, Harcourt, Brace and Company, Inc., New York, 1947. (First published in 1927.)
James, Henry: *The Art of Fiction*, Oxford University Press, New York, 1948.
———: *The Art of the Novel: Critical Prefaces*, Charles Scribner's Sons, New York, 1934, 1950.
Lubbock, Percy: *The Craft of Fiction*, Jonathan Cape, Ltd., London, 1926 (paperback ed., The Viking Press, Inc., New York, 1957). (The pioneer volume in the criticism of prose fiction.)
O'Connor, William V. (ed.): *Forms of Modern Fiction*, University of Minnesota Press, Minneapolis, 1948.

Schorer, Mark: *The Story: A Critical Anthology*, Prentice-Hall, Inc., Englewood Cliffs, N.J., 1950.

Drama

(Aristotle): *Aristotle's Theory of Poetry and Fine Art*, trans. and notes by S. H. Butcher, introd. by John Gassner, Dover Publications, New York, 1951. (Text of the 4th ed., of Butcher, as reprinted in 1911.)

Arnheim, Rudolf: *Film as Art*, University of California Press, Berkeley, Calif., 1957.

Bentley, Eric: *The Playwright as Thinker*, Reynal & Hitchcock, Inc., New York, 1946.

Clark, Barrett: *European Theories of the Drama*, rev. ed., Crown Publishers, Inc., New York, 1947.

Drew, Elizabeth: *Discovering Drama*, W. W. Norton, New York, 1937.

Eliot, T. S.: *Poetry and Drama*, Harvard University Press, Cambridge, Mass., 1951.

Fergusson, Francis: *The Idea of a Theatre*, Princeton University Press, Princeton, N.J., 1949 (Anchor Books ed., 1953).

———: *The Human Image in Dramatic Literature*, Doubleday Anchor Books, New York, 1957.

Gassner, John: *Form and Idea in Modern Theatre*, The Dryden Press, Inc., New York, 1956.

Granville-Barker, Harley: *On Dramatic Method*, Sidgwick & Jackson, Ltd., London, 1931.

———: *The Study of Drama*, Cambridge University Press, New York, 1934.

———: *The Use of the Drama*, Princeton University Press, Princeton, N.J., 1945.

James, Henry: *The Scenic Art*, Rutgers University Press, New Brunswick, N.J., 1948.

Krutch, Joseph Wood: *The Modern Temper* (with a chapter on tragedy), Harcourt, Brace and Company, Inc., New York, 1929. (Harvest Books prints a paperback edition.)

Peacock, Ronald: *The Poet in the Theater*, Harcourt, Brace and Company, Inc., New York, 1946.

Prior, Moody E.: *The Language of Tragedy*, Columbia University Press, New York, 1947.

Selden, Samuel: *Man in His Theatre*, University of North Carolina Press, Chapel Hill, N.C., 1957.

PART 3

Verbal Behavior

Burke, Kenneth: *A Grammar of Motives*, Prentice-Hall, Inc., Englewood Cliffs, N.J., 1945.

————: *The Philosophy of Literary Form: Studies in Symbolic Action,* rev. and abridged, Vintage Books ed., New York, 1957.

Cassirer, Ernst: *Language and Myth,* Harper & Brothers, New York, 1946.

————: *The Philosophy of Symbolic Forms,* vol. I, *Language,* Yale University Press, New Haven, Conn., 1953.

Cherry, Colin: *On Human Communication: A Review, a Survey, and a Criticism,* John Wiley & Sons, Inc., New York, 1957.

DeLaguna, Grace: *Speech, Its Function and Development,* Yale University Press, New Haven, Conn., 1927.

Duncan, Hugh Dalziel: *Language and Literature in Society,* University of Chicago Press, Chicago, 1953.

Gardiner, Alan H.: *The Theory of Speech and Language,* Oxford University Press, New York, 1932.

Hockett, Charles F.: *A Course in Modern Linguistics,* The Macmillan Company, New York, 1958.

Jespersen, Otto: *Growth and Structure of the English Language,* 6th ed., Teubner, Verlagsgesellschaft, Leipzig, 1930. (Doubleday Anchor Books reprints the ninth edition by arrangement with Macmillan, 1955.)

Lanz, Henry: *The Physical Basis of Rime: An Essay on the Aesthetics of Sound,* Stanford University Press, Stanford, Calif., 1931.

Meader, Clarence L., and John H. Muyskens: *Handbook of Biolinguistics,* H. C. Weller, Toledo, Ohio, 1950.

Pei, Mario: *The Story of Language,* J. B. Lippincott Company, Philadelphia, 1949.

————: *The Story of English,* J. B. Lippincott Company, Philadelphia, 1952.

Pike, Kenneth L.: *The Intonation of American English,* University of Michigan Press, Ann Arbor, Mich., 1947.

Rank, Otto: *Art and Artist,* Tudor, New York, 1932.

Roback, A. A.: *Destiny and Motivation in Language,* Sci-Art Publishers, Cambridge, Mass., 1954.

Sapir, Edward: *Language,* Harcourt, Brace and Company, Inc., New York, 1921 (paperback edition in Harvest Books).

Whitehall, Harold: *Structural Essentials of English,* Harcourt, Brace and Company, Inc., New York, 1954.

Nonverbal Behavior

Allport, Gordon W., and Philip E. Vernon: *Studies in Expressive Movement,* The Macmillan Company, New York, 1933.

Birdwhistell, Ray L.: *Introduction to Kinesics: An Annotation System for Analysis of Body Motion and Gesture,* University of Louisville, Louisville, Ky., n.d.

Efron, David: *Gesture and Environment,* King's Crown Press, New York, 1941.

Krout, Maurice H.: *Autistic Gestures: An Experimental Study in Symbolic Movement,* Psychological Review Co., Princeton, N.J., 1935.

Ruesch, Jurgen, and Weldon Kees: *Nonverbal Communication,* University of California Press, Berkeley, Calif., 1956.
Wolff, Charlotte: *A Psychology of Gesture,* 2d ed., Methuen & Co., Ltd., London, 1948.

Oral Interpretation

Dolman, John: *The Art of Reading Aloud,* Harper & Brothers, New York, 1956.
Lee, Charlotte I.: *Oral Interpretation,* rev. ed., Houghton Mifflin Company, Boston, 1959.
Lowrey, Sara, and Gertrude E. Johnson: *Interpretative Reading,* rev. ed., Appleton-Century-Crofts, Inc., New York, 1953.
Parrish, Wayland M.: *Reading Aloud,* 3d ed., The Ronald Press Company, New York, 1953.
Woolbert, Charles Henry, and Severina Nelson: *The Art of Interpretative Speech,* 4th ed., Appleton-Century-Crofts, Inc., New York, 1956.

Index

317

0